Mark Twain's Humor

Mark Twain's Humor

The Image of a World

Pascal Covici, Jr.

SOUTHERN METHODIST UNIVERSITY PRESS
DALLAS, TEXAS

LIBRARY OF CONGRESS CATALOG CARD NUMBER: 62-13274

PRINTED IN THE UNITED STATES OF AMERICA AT DALLAS, TEXAS

For Henry

Mark Twain would have liked him

When vigorous writers have reached maturity we are at liberty to look in their works for some expression of a total view of the world that they have been so actively observing.

HENRY JAMES

Preface

HUMOR IS man's most precious defense, whether against the encroachments of a fearsome world, or against the inner horrors of guilt and despair. Most people, even whole nations, pride themselves on their "sense of humor," and a veritable sixth sense it well may be. As a guide through the labyrinth, this sense may fail to keep one from going astray, but it does offer brave protection against the crushing feeling of calamity brought on by an awareness of the false steps. It enables one to pierce the gloom of popular scorn, to attain fresh perspectives on unfortunate experience. It is the sense that shows man how small he is beneath the stars, and yet enables him to smile forgivingly at his own littleness.

Critics have long been taught to take humor seriously, so Mark Twain's position at the forefront of America's literary consciousness is a logical one. Modern Americans still laugh at what tickles them, and are still susceptible to the tantalizing quill of America's greatest humorist. Moreover, they know that laughter, like all behavior, is meaningful, and they are, in this age of Freud, impatient in their need to understand themselves, their neighbors, their world, and their universe. To Mark Twain, humor—originally, perhaps, an end in itself—became a tool, a technique, for the artist; it became a means to a variety of ends which have in common

the clarification of a reader's vision of himself and of the
nature of the society, and of the cosmos, around him.

To see all that Twain does with his humor, a reader must
slough off two contradictory preconceptions. If one assumes
that the humor, delicious though it be, is somehow a
cheapening of Twain the Serious Artist, one wastes time
lamenting the habits of mind that make for the seriousness
of Twain's art in the first place. Not many people are likely
do this any more, at least not consciously, but we have seen
humor degraded into funniness so persistently by radio,
television, and even literary comics that we tend intuitively
to distrust it.

The more serious difficulty in the way of seeing clearly
what Twain is up to lies in the assumption that Twain is a
"Divine Amateur" and by no means an accomplished and
conscious artist. This theory, first articulated by Arnold
Bennett, has been slain by a series of commentators, but the
ghost refuses to be laid. All who have insisted upon Twain's
artistry in one breath have in the next diminished almost to
the vanishing point any sense of Twain as a deliberate
artificer. The physical facts of his life, or the reading he did,
or the nightmares of his psyche, have all been seen as possessing a one-to-one relationship to his work. Each of these
emphases has been made with the express purpose of showing
that Twain was not simply a backwoods yokel or a frontier
humorist, but a literate, sensitive artist with a sharp eye
for the telling detail: so far so good. But to make of Twain's
works a case history of the author's life—whether biographical, intellectual, or psychiatric—is to read means as ends
and to ignore the autonomy of art. The relationship between
the facts of Twain's existence and the books he wrote is
certainly important, but it does not in any simple way
"account for" what the literature is saying. Worse, to read
the ending of *Huckleberry Finn* as the work of a clumsy

"realist" and *The Mysterious Stranger* as the expression of a disillusioned old man's disgust for life is to blind oneself to what is most essential in the work of a major artist. Tom Sawyer's ridiculous high jinks in the pretended rescue of Nigger Jim communicate more than boyhood's fascination with burlesque, just as the Mysterious Stranger's condemnation of humanity is not the final word with which Mark Twain leaves us.

My concern is primarily with the use of humor in what Twain wrote. My intention has been to suggest several points of view that have not hitherto received adequate critical attention, so of necessity there will be places where a completely balanced judgment is noticeably lacking. That Twain's attempts to perform a multiple function through his humor did not always succeed will be obvious to the reader: "One can deliver a satire with telling force through the insidious medium of a travesty," Twain warned, "if he is careful not to overwhelm the satire with the extraneous interest of the travesty." Twain's attacks on the spirit of his times are often obscured by his delight in "travesty," but the precise nature of these attacks is worth determining. The reader's own sensibility will protect him from mistaking what I take to be Twain's intention for totally satisfying accomplishment. Still, by seeing what Mark Twain does with some of the humorous tales and comic devices popularized by his frontier and southwestern predecessors, and by examining some of the literary developments and philosophical attitudes crystallized by the humor itself, I hope to show what Twain was attempting, to suggest its importance, and to re-examine a few of his works in the light of the artistry organized and given meaning by the humor. If the subject is regarded seriously, let us remember that humor is not always a laughing matter.

Acknowledgments

MY INTELLECTUAL DEBTS to Walter Blair and Kenneth Lynn
are apparent, although in many cases unmentioned in the
footnotes. Many others of my predecessors in the area of
Mark Twain criticism and scholarship have influenced me
in one direction or another, but to trace the precise nature
of their effect upon my present offering would not be possible. Perry Miller ought to be held responsible for this work
in its entirety, for it was he who beguiled me into the
seductions of academic scholarship.

My colleagues in the Southern Methodist University
English Department provided a free and encouraging atmosphere in which to work, substantially aided by the generosity
of Lois Bailey and Robert M. Trent of Fondren Library in
furnishing from afar whatever books I asked for. The good
offices of Laurence Perrine and Marshall Terry, Jr. in commenting on the first chapter, and of Joan Covici in brutally
demolishing most of the first draft with her demands for
clarity, have saved me from many more stylistic blunders
than now appear. Various grants from Southern Methodist
University, most recently through the Graduate Council of
the Humanities, have afforded me the time to complete this
study. The patient kindness and knowledgeable counsel of
Allen Maxwell and Margaret Hartley of the Southern Metho-

dist University Press have made this venture educational as well as possible. To both, my deepest appreciation.

My good neighbors the Thomas Dills and the James L. Mitchells furnished occasional retreats in which to write, and Lassie Jo Mitchell's typing assistance proved invaluable. To my mother, who first suggested Mark Twain as a subject for my critical inquiry, and my father, who patiently allowed me the luxury of unharassed exploration, I owe more than I can say.

My feeling for one who has made his impression on almost every page of this book is expressed in the dedication.

PASCAL COVICI, JR.

Dallas, Texas
April 24, 1962

Contents

I

The Material of Humor

1

From the Old Southwest

MARK TWAIN's relationship to the humor of his region is probably less direct than it is usually thought to be. That the humor of the old Southwest is indeed part of his heritage can be, and has been, demonstrated; the proposition is by now axiomatic. Mark Twain transcends this tradition. Faced with the literary problem of presenting many of the themes and moods that in various ways attracted such diverse minds as Poe, Hawthorne, Melville, Henry James, and Henry Adams, Twain, to be sure, found solutions different from theirs. But this difference is not to be measured solely by the scale of Twain's adherence to the models of his southwestern predecessors.

Nevertheless, to understand Mark Twain's use of humor is, at least partly, to put oneself in tune with the early frontier and western humor of America. Many scholars, among them Franklin Meine, Mody C. Boatright, Bernard DeVoto, and, most recently, Kenneth S. Lynn, have shown in a multitude of ways how oral humor became more than mere pastime for hunters and keelboatmen confronting violence and loneliness, and for any raw westerner confronting the snickering East. Such personal uses of humor only gradually became literary, however, for the literate tellers of tales in the pre-Civil War Southwest almost without exception were newcomers to the regions in which their stories were set. As a result, they were moved by compulsions different from those of the "natives." Lawyers, judges, and doctors, educated on the Atlantic seaboard and suddenly thrust into the continent, they looked with wonder at the "manners, customs, amusements, wit, dialect" so different from what they had left behind.

The stories that flowed from this wonderment were largely organized around two impulses: a need to belittle and a desire to report. The gentlemen from the East looked upon their presence in the West—Alabama, Georgia, Mississippi— as a blessing to the barbarous natives from whom the Gentleman must always be careful to distinguish himself, at least in print. The lawyer might slap backs all he chose, but his duty was to make sure that the barbarian knew his place, that the political and economic fortunes of the new country were safeguarded by his own kind from public ravishment. An illuminating and just emphasis is Kenneth Lynn's on the political bias revealed through the framework of countless yarns in which a "Self-controlled Gentleman"[1] presents the actions of an uncouth lout. Lout and gentleman are separated by dialect as well as by action; there is no chance that a reader might confuse the two.

This need of gentlemanly authors to establish a moral and cultural distance between themselves and the places where they earned their living was at one with, and perhaps even helped to develop, the second impulse behind the humorous tales of the Southwest, that of realistic description. A writer who views his environment from a distance is less likely to take that environment for granted than is one wrapped up in the mores of the people he is observing. The living habits of the folk—how they talk, the pranks they play, what interests them—will seem worth reporting in proportion to their variation from the "normal" life left behind. One can see now that the striving for objectivity implicit in the aim of setting

down the oddities of a new sort of civilization—or lack of one
—clashed with the feeling of superiority so meticulously cultivated by the writers. Brutality and coarseness were blown up
out of all proportion in order to solidify the position of the
detached witness; most of the events narrated could never
have been enacted by mere human beings: the half-horse,
half-alligator men of the Mississippi, in fact, a whole
menagerie of frontier titans, were used to accommodate the
Gentleman's need for low behavior from which to disassociate
himself.

But beneath the violence and exaggeration of mid-
nineteenth-century southwestern humor there lies an impulse
toward realism, toward a faithful presentation of the life
of the region. Repeatedly, the stories about Simon Suggs, Sut
Lovingood, Major Jones, and their picaresque brethren are
introduced as offering intimate knowledge of a particular
locality and its particular citizens. William Tappan Thompson, as he says in his preface to *Major Jones's Chronicles of
Pineville* (1843), "endeavored, in a small way, to catch [the
Georgia "cracker's"] 'manners living as they rise' . . . I claim
no higher character for my stories" than that they present
"a glance at characters not often found in books, or anywhere
else, indeed, except in just such places as 'Pineville,' Georgia."
The vividness with which the frontier and the backwoods
live for Americans today is at least partial testimony to the
realistic bent of Thompson and his fellows. Although they
dealt in exaggeration, tall tales, impossible violence, satire,
and other distortions of reality, their intention to be faithful
to the felt quality of life in their region cannot be mistaken.

The realism in the stories of George Washington Harris,
W. T. Thompson, Augustus Longstreet, Johnson J. Hooper,
et al. implies more than close observation and a nice ear for
the spoken word. The expressed intention "to supply . . .
the manners, customs, amusements, wit, dialect, as they

appear in all grades of society to an ear and eye witness of them"[2] yielded time and again to the more subtle, less often articulated, pressure to crack the local yokels, or the damn-yankees, on their presumptuous and ill-bred snouts. The content of these satiric thrusts was apt to be anything but realism, narrowly considered, yet the distance, or disengagement, from local life that provided the perspective for satire also fostered the careful reporting of minute detail. But no sense of a transcendental oversoul, infusing both squatter and sophisticate, pervades the realism of the Southwest. Although the writers described the commonplace, they did not, with Emerson, embrace it. The effect of their stories upon a reader is to insulate him from any emotional involvement or identification with events, characters, or region.

These pre-Howells realists present the externals of action and dialogue. Had they explored through their fiction interior states of being, or even acknowledged through analysis the existence of human feelings in their characters, we could not laugh at the predicaments set before us. A concern limited to the realistic surface of behavior is made almost obligatory in the case of the southwestern humorists by the nature of the humor which the "school" employed. If a reader is asked to respond to victimized protagonists, or to protagonists' victims, as though they were of the same flesh and spirit as himself, he is not going to laugh as he watches their cruel and exaggerated suffering. When Sut Lovingood leaves half of his skin stuck to his shirt by some newfangled, gluelike starch, one can laugh only if Sut is nothing more than the "nat'ral born durn'd fool" he represents himself to be. The quality of Sut's humanity is so removed from ours that the distance between the two is never bridged, nor was it meant to be. On the other hand, were Huck Finn to be comparably flayed, the reader would wince, not smile; no one laughs when Nigger Jim is bitten by a snake, or when

Huck hides out from the Shepherdsons by climbing a tree.

The realism of the southwestern humorists consists, then, of content—a report on what life looks like in the sticks—and of an aesthetic distance, or psychological detachment, from the object of scrutiny. The juxtaposition of educated gentry and boorish locale goes far toward accounting for the content and the attitude that shaped so much of the writing which poured out of the region. But the seeds of this village realism in a still more important way came from outside, just as did the writers themselves. Behind the attitude of objective disdain lies an assumption right out of the rationalistic eighteenth century: that a man of common sense can distinguish truth from falsehood, reality from appearance, can know what is right, can see with clarity and dispassion the world around him. The unambiguous treatment of material reinforces the epistemology of realism: direct sense-impressions are to be trusted; what seems to be, is.

For the reader who aligns himself with the rational author, the world is no mystery. Sut Lovingood shatters the slumber of an unwelcome intruder by tying a nine-foot length of intestines to the man's shirttail: the terrified "snake-bit Irishman" lights out for home, convinced that " 'a big copperheaded black rattil-snake is crawlin up [his] britches,' "[3] but the reader never for a moment needs to doubt the reliability of his own senses. The boorish victims, on the other hand, repeatedly suffer from an inability to distinguish between the real and the pretended, for the discrepancy between what seems to be and what actually exists forms the crux of numerous pranks perpetrated by southwestern scalawags. It is not only Simon Suggs among them whose "whole ethical system lies snugly in his favorite aphorism— 'IT IS GOOD TO BE SHIFTY IN A NEW COUNTRY.' "[4] Repeatedly, characters are victimized because they fail to recognize that "reality" has been altered for their special benefit. William Tappan Thompson's "How to Kill Two Birds with One Stone"[5] ironically applauds young lawyer Jenkins' wisdom in persuading two men that each has stolen from the other when the lawyer himself has hidden Si Perkins' wagon in Absalom Harley's cellar, in turn loading Si's wagon with Harley's bacon and other articles, in order to foment a double lawsuit and pocket double fees. The ruse works perfectly, and the reader appreciates with a Whig's awareness the "democratic" acuteness of Thomas Jefferson Jenkins while condemning with a laugh the litigious pretensions of his victims. The characters are fooled; the reader is not.

The refined reader is encouraged to trust his sense of ethics as well as his sense of what is real. The behavior of the fictional characters is held up against an implicit standard accessible to all men of reason. Again, simply the surface of what happens, the mere action, speech, and setting as they impinge upon the senses of the realist, is adequate to the purpose of the writers. What really counts is "manners"; the way in which the characters act is of more import than what they do or why they do it. When Sut Lovingood works himself into that fancily-starched shirt which subsequently rips the hide off him, he isn't being unethical, but, rather, pretentious. His pretensions to city grandeur do not mesh with his backwoods ignorance, and one laughs because Sut is ridiculous.

If there is any one pattern basic to the humor of the Southwest it is precisely this: a character is pushed by the author into a situation in which he either exposes the pretensions of others or himself emerges as ridiculous because of his pretentious behavior. The eighteenth-century concept of decorum comes to mind in this connection; what is being criticized more often than not is a failure to adhere to the standards of a cultivated civilization, a failure—so annoyingly common in raw, frontier democracy—to recognize and to accept one's inferior position in society. By considering himself to be as good as the next man, the country democrat becomes pretentious, at least in the eyes of the transplanted easterners whose aloof standards shaped the Southwest humor of the nineteenth century.

The satire embedded in this humor is a satire of the ridiculous, which means that when we talk about the humor of the American Southwest we are really talking about the kind of humor described by Henry Fielding in his preface to *Joseph Andrews,* the humor of eighteenth-century England. The tales so often and so delightfully anthologized that Americans think of as so particularly their own are American in content but English in theory and in organization. Through affectation, "the only source of the true ridiculous," according to Fielding, characters are made into figures of fun. Sometimes the affectation is motivated by vanity, "which puts us on affecting false characters, in order to purchase applause," sometimes by hypocrisy, which "sets us on an endeavor to avoid censure by concealing our vices under an appearance of their opposite virtues." Hypocrisy and vanity—under which headings outsiders could lump almost all attempts to transcend the unmannerly boorishness of a frontier community—lead to affected behavior, and "from the discovery of this affectation arises the Ridiculous—which always strikes the reader with surprise and pleasure." Fielding had no need to add that the reader's pleasure depends on his identifying with the objective viewer rather than with the vain or hypocritical character, for the very attribution of vanity or hypocrisy automatically establishes the proper aesthetic distance between author and reader on the one hand, ridiculous character on the other.

A careful reading of southwestern "American" humor will give substance to the suggestion that this particularly

American tradition is in fact derived explicitly from English
theory and practice of the eighteenth century. Hooper,
Harris, Thompson, and others show a keen sense of the
ridiculous as Fielding defines it. Repeatedly, their humor
embodies Fielding's contention that "from affectation only,
the misfortunes and calamities of life, or the imperfections
of nature, may become the objects of ridicule." The victims
of Simon Suggs's camp meeting, for example, endure considerable misfortune and calamity when the worthy Captain
rides off with the dollars they have donated toward his
pretended efforts to establish a church. One might expect to
find a reader's sympathies aroused for the swindled congregation, but, instead, one finds oneself chuckling along with
wicked old Simon as he canters off at the end of the story.
Simon's victims are ridiculous, not because of what they are,
necessarily, but rather because the reader has been made to
observe them from the point of view of a refined and
rational being.

As Hooper leads his reader into the camp meeting, he
first describes realistically and objectively the various kinds
of religious hysteria manifested by the throng. Then he
kills off any incipient identification with the masses that may
have sprung up in the reader's open mind: "The great object
of all seemed to be, to see who could make the greatest noise—

'And each—for madness ruled the hour—
Would try his own expressive power.' "[6]

One of the ministers, under the guise of religious zeal, is
"lavishing caresses" upon the prettier among the young
women. The Negro woman who is most profoundly moved by
religious emotion is "huge" and "greasy," adjectives which
cast doubt on the delicacy of her spiritual awakening. The
minister to whom Simon attributes his spectacular—though

bogus—conversion is a presumptuous ass; the whole crew get what's coming to them.

'I—I—I can bring 'em!' cried the preacher . . . in a tone of exultation—'Lord thou knows ef thy servant can't stir 'em, nobody else needn't try—but the glory aint mine! I'm a poor worrum of the dust,' he added, with ill-managed affectation.[7]

Affectation renders the people ridiculous and permits one to laugh at them. At the very moment when Simon is cajoling them into contributing money so that he can found a church "in his own neighborhood" and "make himself useful as soon as he could prepare himself for the ministry," his smooth talk is aimed not at their religious enthusiasm but at their desire to appear wealthy and generous before their neighbors: "Simon had excited the pride of purse of the congregation, and a very handsome sum was collected in a very short time."[8]

Nineteenth-century Americans not only ridiculed the affectations of louts, but also went still farther into eighteenth-century English practice when aiming at more specific targets. By pretending that the object of attack was simply affecting the qualities that made him dangerous—courage, intelligence, power, or whatever—Jonathan Swift, and many others, could cut their enemies down to size, denying in the process that the enemy was worth taking seriously in the first place. George Washington Harris, for one, borrows a page from Swift when he recounts Sut Lovingood's travels with "Old Abe Linkhorn"[9] in a way that "diminishes" Lincoln to the disappearing point. The leader of the antislavery faction so inimical to Harris is too stupid to be dangerous, too cowardly to be feared. Moreover, his ugliness is inhuman enough to suggest that he can be disposed of as easily as any other harmless amphibious reptile:

I ketched a ole bullfrog once [says Sut] and drove a nail through

his lips into a post, tied two rocks to his hind toes and stuck a
darnin needle into his tail to let out the moisture, and left him
there to dry. I seed him two weeks after'ards: and, when I seed old
Abe, I thought it were an awful retribution come onto me, and
that it were the same frog—... same shape same color same feel
(cold as ice), and I'm damned if it ain't the same smell.[10]

This technique of belittling the object of attack is by no
means limited to eighteenth-century England, but belongs
to a tradition of literary satire familiar to any classically educated American of the nineteenth century. Since *meiosis,* *
whether applied to northern Presidents or backwoods boobs,
was so frequently and deliberately and even characteristically
employed, it is fair to say that no matter how firmly anchored
to American experience their lives and writings might be,
the pre-Civil War humorists of the Southwest had at least
one eye on foreign literary sources.

II

The characteristics of southwestern humor, then, are
those of realism in content and in epistemology. Even the
satirical intentions behind the humor call upon the reader to
agree to the existence of clearly defined standards, identically
visible to all thinking men. Instead of the moral hesitancies
to be found on a frontier where old codes are daily called in
question by the exigencies of a new life, this humor reflects
the bland assurance of eighteenth-century men of reason that
the cultivated mind can measure all things.

*The "technique of rendering devils flabby is a common literary device
which was discussed in rhetorical handbooks under the Greek title, *meiosis*,
meaning, literally, 'belittling' or 'diminuation.' Diminuation may be described
briefly as the use of any 'ugly or homely images' which are intended to
diminish the dignity of an object. . . . diminuation is any kind of speech which
tends, either by the force of low or vulgar imagery, or by other suggestion, to
depress an object below its usually accepted status." (John M. Bullitt,
Jonathan Swift and the Anatomy of Satire: A Study of Satiric Technique
[Cambridge: Harvard University Press, 1953], p. 45.)

But to Mark Twain there was little, if any, validity in the realistic assumptions behind the humor of the frontier. When, in *Mark Twain at Work*,[11] Bernard DeVoto asserts that Twain's aim in writing *Huckleberry Finn* was to record life by the banks of the Mississippi, his comment is less applicable to the complex and ambiguous novel Twain wrote than to the literary tradition from which most of Twain's work emerges. Twain uses the materials of realism—the events and objects of the daily life of the region—but in a way that Americanizes American humor and puts it more closely in touch with the metaphysical facts of life in a new land and in our modern world: his effects do not, ultimately, depend on a detached objectivity that permits the reader to look upon scoundrels and boors as nonhuman beasts of no importance, or on a sense of the ridiculous as it arises from affectation, but, instead, on a knowledge—paid for by experience—that human reason is cruelly limited, too often unable to discriminate between what is and what seems; that the shibboleths of one generation are the jests of another; and that the powers of irrationality, rather than the deliberate exercise of will, make people appear to be other than what they are.

This is, to be sure, taking humor seriously. Yet even in the simplest episodes of Twain's narrative humor lies the basis for such a contrast between what Twain does and what his predecessors did with similar raw material. In Chapter XX of *Huckleberry Finn* (1885), the king attends a camp meeting at Pokeville much like the one to which Johnson J. Hooper had sent Simon Suggs forty years earlier. Both meetings are minutely described, and both congregations are subtly robbed. The essential difference is between the frailties that in each case lead the people to allow themselves to be cheated. Simon Suggs defrauds those who are guilty of affectation: the laity are purse-proud, and the clergy are

concerned either with taking up the collection or with
hugging the prettiest girls. Simon's benefactors give money
to create the impression of wealth; their show of pious
charity is transparently hypocritical and vain, and they are
made to seem ridiculous because of affectation. Mark Twain's
king exploits a very different sort of meeting: his victims,
not "ridiculous through affectation," neither hypocritical nor
vain, are victimized because they share humanity's penchant
for romantic excitement. The king, improbably representing
himself as a pirate, succeeds completely in taking in the
communicants because they want to believe that an Indian
Ocean pirate could brush against their own dull lives. In
exchange for this fatuous belief they are willing to pay their
money: "The king said . . . it warn't no use talking, heathens
don't amount to shucks alongside of pirates to work a camp-
meeting with" (XIII, 184-85).[12] This has nothing to do with
vanity or hypocrisy—and, therefore, has no connection with
affectation, either. The gulled ones are just as charitable and
religious as their actions suggest, but they are motivated less
by charity and zeal than by their desire to share in a sensation.
This, however, they do not know about themselves. In contrast to the earlier tradition, the people of Pokeville are not
trying to appear to be what they are not. Rather, they are by
their very nature other than they seem.

Mark Twain's fictional world is different from that of his
immediate regional predecessors because it is organized
around a real, and not a contrived, discrepancy between
reality and appearance. The orderly and comprehensible
universe presided over by the Self-controlled Gentleman is
one in which author and readers can all relax together, assured that only those who stand outside their circle can be
deceived by the contrived accidents that befall frontier
clowns. Sut Lovingood gladly swallows Sicily Burns's "love-
potion," with terrific results, but the civilized reader knew

all along that it was soda. Such assurance is foreign to the nineteenth-century American fiction most cherished today. Nathaniel Hawthorne's explorations of the effects of sin on the human heart force one to reorganize one's sense of what sin itself is, and Melville's presentation of the Mount of Titans in *Pierre*, and of Moby-Dick himself, compels one to question the seeming beneficence of smiling nature. More to our immediate purpose, Mark Twain, using the materials and surroundings of his southwestern literary progenitors, throws into doubt—as they never do—a reader's complacent evaluation of common sense as applied first to daily human behavior, and finally to man's role in the universe.

Twain's preoccupation with revealing a discrepancy between seeming and reality is central, not peripheral, to his work. A striking example, built from bits of Twain's frontier heritage, is Huck's trip to the circus to counterpoint through humor one of the most somber episodes in *The Adventures of Huckleberry Finn*. In Chapter XXI, Old Boggs, a harmless drunk, is shot down in cold blood by the ruthless but gentlemanly Colonel Sherburn. Huck Finn is the one sympathetic witness of the slaying. An orphan himself, Huck is especially touched by the pathos of Boggs's daughter as she weeps over the dying man. "She was about sixteen, and very sweet and gentle looking, but awful pale and scared." The other witnesses are totally detached. In fact, "the whole town" watches callously as Boggs breathes his last in a drugstore window, a weighty Bible laid upon his chest to ease his departing soul and increase his agony. They might be watching a show, to hear the people farther back from the window talk to those hogging the front row: " 'Say, now, you've looked enough, you fellows; 'tain't right and 'tain't fair for you to stay thar all the time, and never give nobody a chance; other folks has their rights as well as you' " (199).

Huck subsequently (Chapter XXII) watches another

drunk at a local circus whose life is endangered not by pistol-
fire but by his insistence that he be permitted to attempt
equestrian acrobatics. Finally the patient ringmaster ac-
quiesces; amid howls of laughter and derision, the drunk
mounts a horse, "his heels flying in the air every jump, and
the whole crowd of people standing up shouting and laughing till tears rolled down." The horse breaks loose from the
roustabouts, and the drunk seems headed for certain death,
to the vast delight of the audience. "It warn't funny to me,
though," says Huck; "I was all of a tremble to see his danger"
(206). The seeming "drunk" turns out to be a seasoned performer, a member of the circus-troupe who rides like an
angel, and the laugh is on naïve Huck Finn, so easily taken
in by a circus act. Huck has been sentimental, the reader may
feel, in separating himself from the crowd that first jeers,
then laughs at the performer. His delicacy of feeling is
worthless, for the crowd's callous merriment has injured no
feelings. The laughers, indeed, have added to the effect
of the circus routine. As for the heartlessness of their in-
stinctive response, well, their sympathies were as unsought
as they were unstirred.

But when the reader remembers the similar excitement
of this same toughened crowd when it witnessed the murder
of Boggs and the drama of his death, he sees that though
Huck is naïve, his simple compassion is preferable to the
"smart" sensation-seeking of the empty-headed mob. Not
only had the people clustered around the store window in
which Boggs lay dying, but they also had had the cold-
blooded detachment to enjoy a re-enactment of the slaying
after the event, even offering their flasks to the "long, lanky
man" who "done it perfect ... just exactly the way it all
happened" (200). In each case, Huck's reaction differs from
the crowd's. Moreover, Huck's sympathy for Boggs arises
from the same qualities of spirit that make Huck a gull at the

circus, just as the same shallow craving for excitement motivates the crowd in both instances. Thus, although Huck's attitude at the circus appears to stem from a foolish and valueless naïveté, its true source is his fineness of soul. The reader, therefore, is compelled to reinterpret the "reality" that has been set before him. What has seemed to be and what is are inexorably opposed.

We know that Twain's murder of Boggs is in itself "realistic," for it is "almost without a hairsbreadth of variation" a duplication of Judge John Clemens' account of the shooting of "Uncle Sam" Smarr by William Owsley in Hannibal, when Sam Clemens was just over nine years old.[13] Moreover, the circus incident itself was borrowed from an earlier southwestern writer. What is at issue here, though, is something more than a question of how photographic the writer's memory happens to be. The murder and the circus not only are events in themselves; they also reveal hidden duplicities in the world. The analogue of Twain's circus scene, however, concerns itself with no such opposition between what seems and what is; it never challenges the reader to revise his first impressions. William Tappan Thompson's circus in "The Great Attraction! or The Doctor Most Oudaciously Tuck In"[14] anticipates by some forty years the one Huck attends: in each case, a conventional equestrian act precedes the pseudo-drunken "head-liner"; a witty clown cracks jokes of surpassing cleverness; and then comes the rider who turns out to be sober after all and astonishes his beholders by rising to his feet on the horse's back, then stripping off assorted suits of clothes, "twenty or more" for Thompson's hero, a mere seventeen for Twain's.

The effect of Thompson's circus is considerably simpler than that of Twain's. It appears to be, and it is, a short satire on pretension. Doctor Jones, the unhappy protagonist of the piece, is insufferably impressed with his own sophistication.

Denizen of Pineville though he be, he has once visited
Augusta, "that Philadelphia of the South," and feels that he
is "—to use one of his own polished expressions—'bully of
the tan-yard.' "[15] Everything about Augusta is immeasurably
superior to whatever Pineville has to offer, and Jones, because
of his exposure to the metropolis, includes himself among its
wonders. He has seen everything, done everything; and he
knows everything, too. When he guides the untutored young
ladies of Pineville to their first circus, he assures them that
what they are seeing is "nothing to what he had seen in
Augusta."

Thompson's attitude toward Jones is one of ironic scorn,
as any reader quickly perceives. The Doctor is pretentious.
Vanity leads him to affect a sophistication, a *savoir-faire,* that
he doesn't really possess, and the circus proves to be his un-
doing. When the "drunk" tries to ride, thus interrupting the
performance, Doctor Jones rushes to the ring, intent on being
the hero of the hour. Despite explicit warning by two of the
townsfolk that "that chap belongs to the show," he tries
valiantly to prevent the ride, only to be rudely rebuked by
the clown and finally jostled into the colored section. The
Doctor has failed to understand the niceties of circus shenanigans, and so is made a laughingstock, "oudaciously tuck in."
Needless to say, the citizens of Pineville rejoice in his downfall. " 'Is that the way they does in Augusta?' . . . and a hundred other such jeers" bring both the story and the Doctor's
local glory to a close.

Thompson's story is excellently organized and accomplishes the effect that one can assume Thompson meant it to
have. Because his aim was not Twain's is no reason to criti-
cize Thompson, whose consciousness of theme is embodied
even in his language. Doctor Jones's refinement is called into
question by a report of his own coarse epithet for himself—
"bully of the tan-yard"—a bit of backwoods lingo echoed in

the description of big Bill Sweeney as the rough and tough "bully of the county." Mr. Sweeney, whose place in the story is quite subordinate, shares with Jones the fault of pretentiousness. His pretensions are not to sophistication, however, but to gentility. When he refuses to remove his hat so that others can see the show, the ensuing fracas reveals that he has no right to sit among gentlefolk, just as the main action of the story annuls the Doctor's claims to intellectual supremacy. Both men, each in his different way, have striven to "purchase applause," in Fielding's words, by "affecting false characters." There are no hidden subtleties in the story, no extraneous reverberations. Its satiric impact is obvious and direct. The motives of the characters appear clearly at the start, and one never needs to revise his estimate. This is not true of the king's camp meeting victims or of Huck Finn at his circus.

The two examples of the circus and the camp meeting suggest that although Mark Twain's writing draws upon the traditions and materials utilized by earlier southwestern humorists, its humor goes beyond an exposure of deliberate affectation. In psychological awareness, Twain is closely akin to Melville and Henry James, for he presents human beings as more disposed to misunderstand themselves, as do Pierre and the first-person protagonists of *The Turn of the Screw* and *The Sacred Fount*, than to mislead others deliberately. Consequently, his technique, his literary organization of material, is more concerned with laying bare the human heart than with presenting the rogue's world as it was at a given time and place. Anyone who reads carefully the introduction to the king's camp meeting cannot help but be impressed by the meticulous acuteness of the description, even down to the benches "made out of outside slabs of logs, with holes bored in the round side to drive sticks into for legs" (XIII, 181). To say that Twain is not concerned at all with the surface appearance of the life surrounding his characters is clearly to overstate the point. It is his particular use of appearances that sets him off from his humorous predecessors.

III

The most direct way to suggest the unique quality in Twain's use of surface, or reportorial, realism is to turn from specific analogues to a technique as general as the use of spoken language. That Twain cared about reproducing the exact inflections of dialect, and that he was proud of his abilities in this direction, the author's "Explanatory" to *Huckleberry Finn* makes clear. Seven distinct varieties of speech are mentioned, and, we are reminded, "The shadings have not been done in a haphazard fashion . . . but painstakingly, and with the trustworthy guidance and support of personal familiarity with these several forms of speech" (XIII, xxi). Repeatedly he tries to make his people talk as their environment and training might make them talk in real life, adopting the vocabulary and imagery that will most precisely evoke the varieties of backwoods experience.

His westerners, for example, repeatedly speak the language of the poker table, and in this respect they are not alone in nineteenth-century fiction. Poker talk was a common device of local-color characterization in the writings of the transplanted lawyers and judges who found rural Tennessee, Georgia, Alabama, and Mississippi strikingly different from the metropolitan East they had left behind. There were many stories about gamblers in the new country, and the vocabulary of gambling provided a quick metaphorical index to the habits and origins of the speaker. " 'No matter what sort of a hand you've got . . . take stock!' " exhorts Simon Suggs. " 'Here am *I*, the wickedest and blindest of sinners—has spent my whole life in the sarvice of the devil—has now come in

on *narry pair* and won a *pile!'* "[16] That Simon presents his
recent "conversion" in poker language serves to place him as
a backwoods con man; also, one notes the dramatic irony of
his words, for Simon's auditors interpret "narry pair" as a
reference to Simon's sinful life prior to the camp meeting,
his newly-won "pile" as a joyful allusion to God's free grace
which Simon appears to be experiencing, whereas the reader
is aware that Simon is planning to win a "pile" of money
on the strength of his pretended conversion, his bluff "hand"
with "narry pair" in it. When he urges unrepentant sinners
to join him on the mourners' bench, he reassures them that
" 'The bluff game aint played here! No runnin' of a body
off! Every body holds four aces, and when you bet, you
win!' "[17] Summing up his achievement at the end of the story,
Simon concludes that " 'Ef them fellers aint done to a
cracklin, . . . *I'll* never bet on two pair agin!' "[18] The principal
effect of this terminology is to present Simon as a card-
sharper, willing to gamble on the gullibility of the average
man. But this the reader knew from the opening pages of
the story. The poker talk has revealed nothing new about
the Captain; it is simply part of the author's impulse toward
realism, toward presenting the audible surface of the time
and place.

In a bit of Mark Twain's earlier writing the same limited
effect appears: poker vocabulary denotes the westerner but
tells nothing specific about him as a man. Describing a rising
river in 1859, Sergeant Fathom "would suggest to the
planters, as we say in an innocent little parlor game, com-
monly called 'draw,' that if they can only 'stand the raise'
this time, they may enjoy the comfortable assurance that the
old river's banks will never hold a 'full' again during their
natural lives."[19] This is an amateur's imitation of a technique:
the effort to westernize the speaker is unsupported by dialect,
and the humor is heavy-handed. Fathom is a stick figure who

never comes to life. But Twain was to discover the possibilities latent in simple speech: the preparations for Buck
Fanshaw's funeral in *Roughing It* not only amuse one but
present a fully-drawn character as well. Scotty Briggs and
the minister converse for seven pages of western slang and
eastern elegance where a single page of less characteristic
talk might have sufficed, but one finds that Scotty emerges
in the round because of the way he talks.

The first stage of the interview presents Scotty's effort
to tell the minister that Buck is dead and that the "boys"
would appreciate a few comforting words at the funeral:
" 'Are you the duck that runs the gospel-mill next door?' "
(IV, 45) asks Scotty. After the minister counters that he is,
rather, " 'the spiritual adviser of the little company of
believers whose sanctuary adjoins these premises,' " Scotty
"scratched his head, reflected a moment, and then said:
'You ruther hold over me, pard. I reckon I can't call that
hand. Ante and pass the buck.' "

Scotty's perplexities increase. The minister asks for
simpler language, but the request is too complexly worded.
" 'I'll have to pass, I judge.' " " 'How?' " " 'You've raised me
out, pard' " (46).

Eventually the two understand each other. But the minister wonders about Buck Fanshaw's religious affiliations in
language that leads Scotty to complain, " 'Why, you're most
too many for me, you know. . . . Every time you draw, you
fill; but I don't seem to have any luck. Let's have a new deal.' "
" 'How? Begin again?' " " 'That's it.' " " 'Very well. Was he a
good man, and—' " " 'There—I see that; don't put up another
chip till I look at my hand' " (50).

Apart from giving the western flavor that Twain explicitly
means to impart (42-43), poker terminology here accomplishes two ends. First, the metaphoric equation of chips
and cards with words ties the episode together by providing

a secondary story line. The inability of Scotty and the minister to communicate becomes as much the subject of the
brief scene as is the arranging of Buck Fanshaw's funeral.
The two confuse each other with their language, and a reader
wonders how long their differences of terminology will keep
each from "seeing" the other's point. The minister, slick
though sickly easterner that he is, keeps on talking, and
Scotty is "raised" out of several conversational "pots" by
his flow of words. Finally, however, Scotty can "call"—" 'I
see that' "—and the episode comes to a close with mutual
comprehension.

Secondly, Scotty's poker vocabulary displays his character. Never does he try to bluff. He admits the minister's
ability to "draw and fill"; he quickly acknowledges the
inadequacy of his own "hand"—his comprehension of language—and forthrightly "passes," having been "raised out."
When he understands the minister's words—the "bet"—he
will "see that," but he wants to "look at [his] hand" before
any more chips—words—fall. Scotty's discourse is scrupu-
lously honest and manly; his terms never suggest that he
thinks the minister's ignorance is pretended—a suspicion
that the reader cannot help entertaining—and he never tries
to run a bluff of his own. Scotty's self-revelation prepares the
reader for Twain's concluding presentation of him as a
sympathetic Sunday-school teacher whose rendition in slang
of Bible stories "was listened to by his little learners with a
consuming interest" (53). The contrast between East and
West is clearly presented, but the story differs from most
western stories of the time in that the contest and victory are
moral and are presented through language, not through violent action: the rough westerner, in the terms of his own
rough game, shows himself to be a more honest man than the
educated easterner. The language of poker ties Scotty's character and story together into a simple, kindly unit.

Scotty's simplicity of 1871 contrasts with the simple-minded duplicity of Saladin Foster in "The $30,000 Bequest" (1904). The anecdote of Scotty and the minister is more or less a "set piece," an exhibition of language for its own sake. The story of the Fosters, on the other hand, has a definite plot organized around a specific theme; its concern is not to demonstrate speech but to use it to reveal character. Saladin's use of poker metaphor establishes him as an unpretentious, rather commonplace man—which is important for the total effect of the story, since the reader is supposed to feel that what happens to Saladin might happen to anyone—and simultaneously reveals his understanding of himself. The effect of the device is double: it both vivifies him and foreshadows his actions.

Saladin exhibits more self-awareness than Scotty. When his wife expresses joy at the news that his rich uncle—from whom they expect to inherit $30,000—is still living, Saladin derides her for being "'immorally pious'" (XXIV, 12). Electra is tartly certain that "'there is no such thing as immoral piety,'" and Saladin is soon overwhelmed because he doesn't know when to stop talking. He multiplies his excuses, only to entangle himself still further. "Then, musingly, he apologized to himself. 'I certainly held threes—I *know* it—but I drew and didn't fill. That's where I'm so often weak in the game. If I had stood pat—but I didn't. I never do. I don't know enough'" (13).

Saladin, one sees, laments two things. Superficially, he bemoans his unavoidable failure to "fill"—and superficially the story is built upon the Fosters' expectations (doomed to disappointment) that the uncle will make the bequest that he promised. No one can control the run of the cards at poker; likewise, Saladin is not responsible for his uncle's malicious deceit. But Saladin does have a weakness and sees it clearly: he knows that he cannot bluff successfully, whether before or after the draw. Later, as the Fosters come to live more and more in their imaginations, daydreaming about their lives as millionaires once the bequest shall have been invested a few dozen times, Saladin sinks to degrading debaucheries. He gambles; he drinks; he fornicates. His transgressions are purely mental, but Electra detects the glazed eyes and the slack face as he sits lost in fantasy. He is unable to "bluff" her; he cannot deny what in imagination he has been up to, and the happiness of their marriage is blighted. The misery that results from his failure to "stand pat" is a direct outgrowth of the character revealed through the poker-talk monologue.

Finally, to choose an example near the chronological middle of Twain's career, when Hank Morgan presents himself in Arthur's dining hall near the beginning of *A Connecticut Yankee in King Arthur's Court* (1889), one finds an intensive use of American frontier, or "Yankee," poker talk not only to characterize the protagonist but also to anticipate theme and prepare for the satiric irony behind the story. Faced with the dismal fact that he is either in the sixth century or in a lunatic asylum, with no way to determine which until an eclipse occurs or fails to occur, Hank decides to dismiss the problem from his mind: "One thing at a time, is my motto—and just play that thing for all it is worth, even if it's only two pair and a jack" (XIV, 16). Ironically, Hank Morgan's career as "The Boss" will be an attempt to inculcate the masses of Great Britain with the habits of rationality and the attributes of reflective intelligence; his whole program will be one of education in the "Man-factory." But here, he shows that he is a man who will play a bluff with the best, and foreshadows his successful eclipse-bluff, his repeated "miracles," and his final saturnalia of destruction when his "bluff" is called. The conflict between reason and irrationality, between, one may say, the doctrines of the perfectibility of man and of innate human depravity, is played off against the background of Hank's poker-faced opportunism. In the great tournament between the "magic of fol-de-rol" and the "magic of science" (396), the magic of science triumphs, but "it was a 'bluff' you know. At such a time it is sound judgment to put on a bold face and play your hand for a hundred times what it is worth; forty-nine times out of fifty nobody dares to 'call,' and you rake in the chips" (395).

Such a passage is of the frontier tradition; it is the realistic speech of an uneducated man who, by speaking the way he does, convinces a reader of the existence of his environment. Yet it accomplishes a good deal more. Hank Morgan's use of poker terminology is more significant than that of Captain Simon Suggs at his camp meeting. Suggs's poker metaphors come at the end of his story, when the reader already knows all about the Captain, but Hank's "two pair and a jack" serves to introduce both his character and the essential conflicts to be presented in his story. Hooper's satire, moreover, has nothing to do with the characterization of Simon Suggs through poker talk. Simon is no outsider whose entrance into a previously stable society disrupts the status quo. He is immediately recognized as "the very 'chief of sinners' in all that region,"[20] his physiognomy as familiar as his reputation. His vocabulary adds little to the meaning of the story, because Simon's function—to victimize the affected—does not depend on his origin as signaled by his talk. Hank Morgan, however, is an unknown quantity. His very clothing seems miraculous, and his vocabulary repeatedly sets him off from his captors. His mere presence in Arthur's court will serve to contrast Yankee ingenuity and energy with Arthurian romance and sloth; the contrast between his American language and sixth-century, knightly habits of thought will be essential to the development of the book's theme.

IV

Even when Hank Morgan is roaming the streets of Old England, his Americanism is guaranteed by his poker talk. Of even broader usefulness in suggesting nationality is the poker face, more a way of saying something, or nothing, than a vocabulary. Because it embodies an attitude rather than a regional heritage, the frontiersman's poker face was more widely appropriated than his slang by writers presenting an American to the outside world; and from the very beginning, the outside world was inescapably present in the American consciousness. Distant though he was, the frontier settler was fair game for the polished easterner, the easterner himself open to wisecracks from abroad. The conflict embodied in such antitheses as country and city, West and East, became a theme common to writers as far removed from the conventional eighteenth- and nineteenth-century nature-civilization dichotomy as Twain, Henry James, and Sinclair Lewis. In many cases, what began as western humor was quickly pressed into service on behalf of the national honor.

One may think of the tall tale as a traditionally western way of cutting the pompous outsider down to size. The heaping up of exaggerations by a narrator who never cracks a smile, or in any other way indicates that he is joking, stretches to the breaking point the stranger's predisposition to assume the worst about the new region. The Texan who disdainfully put a braggart in his place by saying, " 'Only after my fourth killing, gentlemen, did I consider myself worthy of becoming a citizen of Texas,' "[21] is satirizing an unthinking acceptance of malicious anti-Texas gossip; the previous speaker, with but one corpse to his credit, plays the role of straight man.

This is folk humor hot off the range, but the technique

antedates the frontier. As a defense against slander, the tall tale and the poker face enabled no less a man than Benjamin Franklin to counteract falsehoods about America that were circulating in London in 1765. Rather than attack detractors in passionate rage, Franklin quietly admitted in a letter to a London newspaper that no story, however extravagant it seemed, could give a false picture of America, which was itself so grandiose. He went on to speak of the cod and whale fishing on the Great Lakes, concluding that

Ignorant People may object that the upper Lakes are fresh, and that Cod and Whale are Salt Water Fish: But let them know, Sir, that Cod, like other Fish when attack'd by their Enemies, fly into any Water where they can be safest; that Whales, when they have a mind to eat Cod, pursue them wherever they fly; and that the grand Leap of the Whale in the Chase up the Fall of Niagara is esteemed, by all who have seen it, as one of the finest Spectacles in Nature.[22]

In fiction, however, the development of a poker-faced manner was a sophisticated refinement that occurred only after more violent techniques of presenting western antipathy toward eastern elegance had been fully explored. The rough squatter of Hannibal, in Sam Clemens' "The Dandy Frightening the Squatter" (1852), wastes no words, forthrightly punching the overarmed but unmanned Dandy into "the turbid waters of the Mississippi."[23] Sut Lovingood frightens his intrusive Irishman right back across the ocean, to the land where there are no snakes. Thompson's Doctor Jones is led to the circus for the single purpose of being "oudaciously tuck in," for Augusta, "the Philadelphia of the South," has rendered him objectionable to his fellows at Pineville. Even in real life, the young men of Hannibal, incensed at the citified airs of one of their number who had returned from Yale in all the appurtenances of eastern fashion, turned to action, not talk: they "dressed up the warped negro bell ringer in a travesty of him—which made him descend to village fashions."[24]

The country resents the city, the West resents the East, and the theme of this hostility toward what is different—and therefore threatening—is expressed in countless stories, first by those who were intent on capturing the feelings of the folk around them, regardless of where their own sympathies lay, and, later, by men who identified themselves at least partially with their adopted, or even natal, home on the frontier. This same opposition found its way into serious fiction as a contrast between America and Europe, although as early as Revolutionary times Royall Tyler's comedy—titled, of course, *The Contrast*—was elevating the manly American above the effete Englishman. By the last third of the nineteenth century, though, the contrast had become considerably more complex. For many writers, to place an American in a European context was to provide the *donnée* for infinitely suggestive adventures. This confrontation carries with it a minor, but interesting, literary problem: how shall the author establish implicitly the particular qualities of his characters' nationality without writing an essay? Mark Twain, in *The Innocents Abroad* (1869), points the way to one sort of solution through characters whose use of a poker face stamps them as Americans from a frontier rawer than a genteel reader will approve yet worthy of respect for its clear-sighted resistance to humbug.

The immediate impulse of Twain's traveling Yankee is to disguise emotion, whether fear of Europe as it threatens an American's self-image or awe of Europe as it suggests unexplored possibilities of experience. Accomplished poker-players that they are, they deceive for gain on the byways of the Continent as expertly as they might at the card table. When Twain-the-character and his friends in *The Innocents*

plague a series of guides, all rechristened "Ferguson," the
iron-visaged idiocy displayed leads to one very specific
gain: "The guide was bewildered—nonplussed. He walked
his legs off, nearly, hunting up extraordinary things, and
exhausted all his ingenuity on us, but it was a failure; we
never showed any interest in anything" (I, 306). By criticizing "Christopher Colombo's" poor penmanship, by asking
if an Egyptian mummy is dead, the Doctor—who "asks the
questions, generally, because he can keep his countenance,
and look more like an inspired idiot, and throw more
imbecility into the tone of his voice than any man that
lives" (303)—forces the guide of the moment on to ever
greater exertions.

Like any clever poker-player, the Doctor is versatile.
When a guide persists in taking Twain, Dan, and the Doctor
to silk stores rather than to the Louvre, the masquerade of
boredom changes to one of simulated enthusiasm. As "Ferguson" foolishly persists in his commercial scheming, the
Doctor's mounting anger expresses itself as aesthetic pleasure: "'Ah, the palace of the Louvre; beautiful, beautiful
edifice! Does the Emperor Napoleon live here now, Ferguson?'" (115) And at the third silk store: "'At last! How
imposing the Louvre is, and yet how small! how exquisitely
fashioned! how charmingly situated! Venerable, venerable
pile—'" (116). This reaction is, strictly speaking, irony, but,
as an attitude adopted by the Doctor for slicing through a
foreigner's deceit, it also belongs to the species "poker face."

When the Doctor stonily asks, "'Is, ah—is he dead?'"
before every statue, he is clearly deceiving for gain. The
guide, intent on drawing a conventional show of enthusiasm
from the passive Doctor, works much harder than he is paid
to do in the hopes of shattering his employer's calm. But
there is another side to the coin. The Innocents are impressed
by what they see, for if they were not, they would find no

practical advantage in pretending to be bored. "We came very near expressing interest, sometimes—even admiration—it was very hard to keep from it" (306). But the pretense means more than just a desire to gain additional sights, as one sees when the group visits the vault beneath the Capuchin Convent. The walls are decorated by the dismembered skeletons of dead monks. The guide—in this case one of the monks who will some day add his mite to the communal fresco—has shown them everything, and now they stop to examine in particular one skeleton, robed and intact, whose skull has preserved "a weird laugh a full century old!" "It was the jolliest laugh, but yet the most dreadful, that one can imagine" (II, 5). Terror and humor coalesce: "At this moment I saw that the old instinct was strong upon the boys, and I said we had better hurry to St. Peter's. They were trying to keep from asking, 'Is—is he dead?' " (5)

In this instance, the poker face gains a very real but immaterial advantage for its user: it allows him to inject humor into a situation that frightens him. Certainly this is a common technique all through *The Innocents Abroad*. When Twain, the American narrator, is overwhelmed by Europe, he can find relief by laughing at it, or simply by laughing, a response similar to that of Melville's Ishmael who emerges from his first violent brush with a whale to conclude that life's vicissitudes, from "small difficulties" to "extreme tribulation" and "peril of life and limb," must be taken "for a vast practical joke" if sanity is to be retained.[25] That Twain's American laughs does not mean, always, that he is happily at ease in his world.

Twain's awareness of the impact of Europe on Americans abroad is hardly the central theme of his fiction. Still, he helped to develop the terms through which American writers were to confront the Old World with representatives of the New. The fears and insecurities that Twain revealed through

humor became the clichés of the future tourist class, whether
from Lewis' Zenith or from James's New York City. The
materials of the humorist became touchstones of allegiance
for the novelists.

Like other Americans in Europe, the Innocent Abroad
is troubled; the "dreadful" laugh that is "a full century old"—
older than the town of Samuel Clemens' birth, or of most
nineteenth-century Americans' birth—is different from anything Mark Twain has ever known. The very existence of the
skeleton suggests a way of looking at life that is foreign, for
the fashions of American interior decoration have never
emulated the Capuchin vaults. Twain's fascination with
that ancient, that noticeably "un-American," laugh suggests
Lewis' Sam Dodsworth, who is at first intrigued by and
attracted to the laughter of the Count von Obensdorf, his
wife's future lover: " 'Kind of like an American, this fellow—
this count,' said Sam. 'Got a sense of humor....' " But Sam
is wrong.

> "Oh no, it's a very different thing," Fran [Sam's wife] insisted.
> "He's completely European. Americans are humorous to cover up
> their worry about things. They think that what they do is imme-
> diately important and the world is waiting for it. The real Euro-
> pean has a sense of a thousand years... behind him."[26]

Dodsworth does "worry about things." He cannot keep
from himself "a deep and sturdy recognition of his own
ignorance,"[27] and on many occasions we are told, more or
less directly, that "he suddenly felt insecure."[28] When he
successfully orders French station-attendants around, "he
admitted that he was possibly being the brash Yankee of
Mark Twain."[29] But Sam Dodsworth eventually chooses a
European way of life, and Lewis pointedly foreshadows
Sam's un-Americanism by contrasting his unexpected appreciation of art with "the Mark Twain tradition," in which

"the American wife still marches her husband to galleries from which he tries to sneak away."[30] His appreciation is unexpected because Sam Dodsworth is first presented as being very much in the tradition: "He liked whiskey and poker,"[31] and his fondness for poker is referred to often enough and in the proper contexts to make it a metaphor of his desire to be with and like Americans.[32]

Now the American poker-player's approach to European art is established for all time by Mark Twain, and the establishment sanctioned by no less a pontiff than Henry James. Twain's Innocent tells us that he "could not help noticing how superior the copies were to the original.... Wherever you find a Raphael, a Rubens, a Michael Angelo, a Caracci, or a Da Vinci (and we see them every day) you find artists copying them, and the copies are always the handsomest" (I, 190). Henry James gives us, in his *The American* (1877), the transitional step between the completely westernized narrator of *The Innocents Abroad* and the potential renegade of *Dodsworth*. Christopher Newman is a synthesis of American types. He looks back upon the isolated spirit of Natty Bumppo as "he laughed the laugh in which he indulged when he was most amused—a noiseless laugh, with his lips closed."[33] He shows a more sociable sort of frontier experience, too, for—like Twain—"Newman had sat with Western humorists in knots, round cast-iron stoves, and seen 'tall' stories grow taller without toppling over, and his own imagination had learned the trick of piling up consistent wonders."[34] Finally, he is mythologized as an American titan in the "*légende*" of western wealth and power that the stout Duchess, Madame d'Outreville, invents for him,[35] a myth that will be echoed by Lewis in Dodsworth's determination, at the start of his travels,[36] to return to America and create such a city as is attributed to Newman.

In our first view of him, Newman is presented most simply

as the "specimen of an American," as "the American type," and although his visit to the Louvre fills him, "for the first time in his life, with a vague self-mistrust,"[37] his habitual front possesses "that typical vagueness which is not vacuity, that blankness which is not simplicity."[38] He is aware of his fears, but, good American that he is, he is poker-faced. Like Sam Dodsworth, he has gambled quite literally, in business and in sport, "glad enough to play poker in St. Louis."[39] Unlike Twain's *persona,* he has come to Europe—as so many of James's people do—to learn; but his European education does not begin until after his first stroll through the Louvre, when he is most pointedly still the American: Newman looks "not only at all the pictures, but at all the copies that were going forward around them, . . . and if the truth must be told, he had often admired the copy much more than the original."

Newman's poker-faced admiration of Mlle Nioche's copies soon gives way to an acknowledged emotional involvement with Claire de Cintré, and to Newman's efforts to register directly on his feelings a sense of Europe. Mark Twain, playing the game of the American in Europe, retains the poker face that Newman struggles to put off, that is torn from Dodsworth by fate. (Dodsworth is not trying to educate himself into an involvement with Europe; events conspire to educate and to involve him despite himself.) For Lewis and James as well as for Twain, the American approaching Europe is poker-faced, and his reactions to European culture and customs are similar, initially, for all three writers. As James's and Lewis' protagonists succumb in their respective ways to the lure of the Continent, they lose their poker-faced detachment that has served as a defense against involvement, but their point of departure is defined by Twain's Innocent.

The three authors are concerned with tracing three variations of their common theme. For James, the impact of

Europe as a civilizing force on the visiting American—
Christopher Newman, Isabelle Archer, Lambert Strether,
et al.—is the central concern, whether the force initiates a
progression that culminates in grandeur or in futility. Lewis'
Dodsworth, as one of the many novels in which Lewis
presents America as seen through the eyes of H. L. Mencken,
stresses the tawdry quality of American society, touching on
the world of George F. Babbitt and focusing on the insubstantial character of Fran Dodsworth's worship of all things
European. The actual impact of Europe on Sam Dodsworth
is great—he chooses to leave America and live in Italy—but
the weight of Europe itself is felt less throughout the book
than is the density of the America from which Sam turns.
The behavior of Mark Twain's Innocent merely suggests the
rejection of America, and even the suggestion is only occasional. Most of the time, he appears brashly complacent in
his Americanism. Indeed, his fear of Europe drives him
happily back to his native shores, although he captures
undertones that will become more significant in Twain's later
work.

Twain's protagonist is really the most subversive of the
three. Happy though the traveler returned may be, his first
official act is to summarize the pilgrimage for the New York
Herald, as Twain in fact did do, and his summary is not
flattering to his fellow-Americans. His sarcastic irony—"We
always took care to make it understood that we were Americans—Americans!" (II, 401)—evokes such samples of nation-
alism as the expedition's criminal archeological activities
among the pyramids and their bad manners among the
French. Boorishness and ignorance are the two most conspicuous qualities of these wandering representatives of
God's latter-day Chosen People, as their spokesman's news-
letter paints them. There clearly is more to Twain's treatment
of America than simpleminded adulation. His ambivalence

is as real as James's and Lewis', although one must see it in a more finished work to appreciate it.

Twain's use of the theme—Europe and America, East and West—and the central image for embodying this theme (the poker face) both arise from his immediate background in the humor of the Southwest, of the frontier. The same theme and the same image became equally part of the equipment of writers totally removed from both the frontier and the Southwest. Twain's use of this material differs from that of James and Lewis; the gap between Twain and his own tradition is equally significant. To be clear on this point one has only to remember Hank Morgan in Arthur's Court and Simon Suggs at his camp meeting: they are both slang-slinging adventurers, out for what they can get, but Hank's use of poker talk achieves effects that Simon's does not even suggest. Mark Twain's adaptation of the standard elements of frontier humor enlarged their usefulness for literary art. How radical some of his departures were we have yet to see.

II

The Narrator

2

Beginning of a Strategy

THE VOCABULARY of the poker table is essentially an element
of local color, or realism, when it appears in stories; a character talks as he talks to suggest a region or a background. The
poker face, on the other hand, is a pose adopted for the
purpose of twisting reality in one way or another; it is a
mask behind which a player may conceal emotion and intention, past, present, and future. When the person with the
poker face is simply a character in a story, his mask characterizes him as realistically as his talk, for the author can
always tell the reader what the mask conceals. Mark Twain
explains the Doctor's "inspired idiocy," just as Johnson J.
Hooper reveals Suggs's inveterate mendacity. The reader
can chuckle at the discomfiture of those who accept the
poker face at par because he himself is let in on the secret
from the beginning. In many of Twain's more complex
stories, however, the person who tells the tale is himself
poker-faced. The narrative point of view then becomes especially important, not only as a source of humor but also as
a key to the narrative's significance and effect. We need at
this point to consider Mark Twain's narrators and how they
function.

The first-person narrator of the Old Southwest came
increasingly to be a comic figure. The Self-controlled Gentle-

man—to borrow again Kenneth Lynn's apt phrase—began as
the central intelligence, a favorable and sober contrast to
the low life around him. Augustus B. Longstreet's *Georgia
Scenes* (1835) illustrates the principle perfectly: backwoods
speech is illustrative of backwoods manners, but never is the
backwoods speaker given leave to shape a story. Even
before the Civil War, however, the lowly native began to
capture the imagination of the very authors who looked
down upon him. At the same time that the boob was a
social threat and therefore the object of scornful literary
lampoon, his irresponsible adventurings seemed to express
the wistful envy of the educated literati. More and more,
the lout was allowed to talk for himself, partly because of
the sheer aesthetic delight in setting down his strange
language, and partly because his talk would by itself illus-
trate the uncouth ignorance of the frontier. Finally, as
Professor Lynn has shown, his name was Huckleberry Finn,
and it was he, rather than any socially distant Gentleman,
who pointed the way to moral salvation.

From Simon Suggs and Sut Lovingood to Huck Finn is
a large jump, and Mark Twain did not make it in one inspired
leap. Also, the high motives of sociology and the low ones of
escape were probably of less conscious importance to writers
than the human desire to amuse their friends and readers.
Men have always liked to laugh, and there was plenty of
humor to be tapped simply by presenting to an educated
audience the spelling, grammar, and dialect of the un-
schooled southwesterner. By recording the ignorant spelling
of Thomas Jefferson Snodgrass, Sam Clemens—in 1857 he
was not yet Mark Twain—created a humorous effect by
mechanical means alone: "It mought be that some people
think your umble sarvent has 'shuffled off this mortal quile'
and bid an eternal adoo to this subloonary atmosphere—
nary time. He ain't dead, but sleepeth."[1] This opening of the

third Snodgrass letter anticipates by one year Artemus Ward's similar denial that he has "'shoveled orf this mortal Koil,' and seazed two be no moore."[2] Both disclaimers are part of a tradition, as Walter Blair has pointed out, and both depend for their fun on the narrative device of allowing the protagonist to speak for himself, although few people any longer share the nineteenth-century American humorists' belief in the effectiveness of mere bad spelling and rough dialect.

The three Snodgrass letters of 1856 and 1857, however crude and obvious, are an important step toward *Huckleberry Finn,* away from the dead language and blurred focus of "The Dandy Frightening the Squatter" (1852). In Twain's earliest published piece,[3] the principal characters are but outlined, in the roughest of sketches, as "a tall, brawny woodsman," standing by the river, and "a spruce young dandy, with a killing moustache, &c., who seemed bent on making an impression upon the hearts of the young ladies on board" his steamboat. The Dandy, armed to the teeth, awkwardly announces: "'Ladies, if you wish to enjoy a good laugh, step out on the guards. I intend to frighten that gentleman into fits who stands on the bank.'" He accosts the squatter, who, in full view of the passengers, calmly knocks him into the river. The reader is in vain left to imagine how the would-be hero and his conqueror feel, for neither victor nor vanquished is ever realized as a character; they are both stick figures in an old drama which Twain is viewing from a conventional distance. Furthermore, a fatal contradiction exists between the "form" of the story and its "content." The attitude embodied in the language of the third-person narrator is analogous to that of the Self-controlled Gentleman of earlier tales: the squatter contemplates with no comprehension an "approaching object, which our reader would easily have discovered to be a steamboat."

Author and reader are cultivated and informed; the woodsman is rudely untutored. But the representative of culture
is the one who is worsted: the reader is supposed to acknowledge the innate superiority of the westerner over the dude,
although the inconsistent emphasis makes it impossible to
care one way or another about either of them. Thomas
Jefferson Snodgrass, however, comes clearly and outrageously
to life. One would not welcome him into a drawing room,
but one would know him anywhere.

Snodgrass, the traveling correspondent, presents himself
as a virtuous country boy, experiencing for the first time the
perversities of city civilization. With no overt guidance from
the author, one is left to discover for oneself the delightful
gap between what Snodgrass thinks he is and what he really
turns out to be. The simpleminded country lad is scarcely
an example of the "noble savage." Although "Cincinnami,"
the city he visits in the third letter, is evil enough—there is
mention of a poor Irish widow who "friz" to death because
administrative red tape, the product of civilization, kept her
from getting coal for her stove—Snodgrass himself is as
callous as any city official, for he tries to drown a baby, the
archetype of all innocence. Both yokel and metropolis are
morally inadequate and stand condemned, whereas in "The
Dandy" the affected city slicker was poles apart from the
straightforward, virile squatter.

Thomas Jefferson Snodgrass is vain and stupid. "A young
lady with a big basket birsted in on my revery. 'I say,
mister,' says she, 'is your name' —— 'Snodgrass,' says I,
wonderin' how on airth *she* knowed me."[4] His facile self-
deception is sufficient proof for the damsel that he is indeed
"'the very man'" she wants. When she tells him that she
has "'always hearn you was sich a good, kind feller,'" he
fairly glows and is quite happy to hold her basket for a
moment while she just runs into the grocery store to recover

her "portmoney." In her absence, Snodgrass dreams of the wealth and happiness that must inevitably lie ahead: the "gal" is of course "rich as a Jew"; Snodgrass will kill off any other suitors, and, as "she's already struck with my personal appearance," her father will "come and tell me how many banks and raleroads he owns, and ask me to marry his darter. And I'll *do* it!" But the girl has been gone an hour and a half. "Pooty soon there commenced the eternallest, confoundest, damnationist kickin in that basket . . . . I run to the gas lamp and jerked off the kiver, and thar was the nastiest, ugliest, oneriest he-baby I ever seed in all my life. 'Sold! by Jeminy! *Der-r-n* the baby!'" Taking the noisome infant home, Snodgrass proceeds to frighten it into ever worse howlings, "jest by way of revenge, you know," and when he tries to drown it he is thrown into jail until "I promised—No sir, I *swar* I won't tell what I promised them sharks. But betwixt you and me, somethin dark's agoin to happen. It 'pears to me that that baby'll larn to swim *yit* afore it's six weeks older,—(pervided it don't perish in the attempt.)"

Snodgrass thinks highly of himself, and it takes no subtle imagination to relish the gap between his own self-appraisal and Twain's characterization of him. The first-person narrative, while by no means as supple a technique as it will become, enables Twain to communicate an attitude more complex and interesting than that in "The Dandy." It also allows Twain at a still tender age to surpass the achievement of one of his southwestern predecessors, William Tappan Thompson. Thompson's Major Jones provides the raw material of Twain's Snodgrass letter, but the difference between the two writers is as striking as the likeness between their yarns. In *Major Jones's Travels*, the Pineville celebrity journeys, in the spring of 1845, to the "big cities of the northern states," "from Pineville to Quebeck, and back agin," and

writes "this little sketch of my perry grinations" in the form
of letters to Thompson, just as Snodgrass leaves Keokuk to
record, in equally scrambled orthography, his own impressions of travel and of city life. But Thompson's intention is
single, as Twain's is not. To Jones, and to Thompson, southern
slavery is a beloved institution, anything southern is good,
and the North, particularly the city of New York, is hopelessly corrupt. As he walks the streets of Gotham, Major
Jones is repeatedly shocked at the squalor and mendacity
which present themselves to view. Just as the kindhearted
Major resolves to pay no heed to any more phony hard-luck
stories, a poor woman, ill-nourished and harassed, approaches
him; the Major cannot ignore her pleas. Her husband is
sick, her children are hungry, and she is so weakened herself
that she can barely stand. Her representation of misfortune
convinces the Major that she is a fit object for charity, and
he gives her a dollar with which to buy medicine for her
husband. Eagerly, she rushes off to the corner drugstore,
leaving her bundle of "ironing" with the Major, lest it
wrinkle in the congestion of the store. When the woman fails
to return, Jones moves to a lamppost to examine the bundle,
"and Mr. Thompson, would you believe me, IT WAS A LIVE
BABY! . . . I started for the drugstore with the baby squallin
like rath, and the more I tried to hush it the harder it
squalled!" A crowd gathers; Jones is threatened with imprisonment; but then his testimony that he is just plain Major
Jones of Pineville, Georgia, and not a New Yorker at all,
mollifies the angry crowd, which, indeed, expresses admiration for its favorite author. The baby is sent to a foundling
home, and Jones spends a pleasant evening with fellow-
Georgians in the city. "P.S.—Don't for the world let Mary
Jane know anything about the baby . . . I never could explain it to her satisfaction."[5]

Jones's response to city corruption has been a sterling

example of country kindness and morality. Nor is the Major presented as being unintelligent: the woman's story holds together; Jones wants merely to aid a fellow-human, not to flatter himself. Also, he has no thought of material profit. Simply, he is victimized because he is nobler than the life around him. Major Jones's low evaluation of New York City is Thompson's; at least there is no suggestion to the contrary in the Major's letter. Author and character take the same attitude toward events, and the only gains to Thompson in telling his story in the first person through Jones's letters are the suggestion of immediacy and the humor in Jones's spelling and grammar. Snodgrass, however, is not morally acceptable to Twain. Callous and greedy, Snodgrass sees only the woman as guilty of unsavory behavior. Twain tells Snodgrass' misadventure in the first person not only for humor and immediacy, but also to underline character. If the characterization is weak—why should Snodgrass, so hardhearted when confronted with a helpless babe, show compassion early in the letter for the bureaucracy-ridden Irishwoman who freezes to death?—the attempt is at least being made, and in a way that illuminates a significant ambivalence toward country and city.

One must not claim too much for the Snodgrass letters; they are important as symptoms of a later development, but primarily they are of a piece with earlier western efforts. Even though Twain discards the framework typical of other southwestern tales, wherein a cultivated observer implicitly comments upon the roughneck by way of a contrast between the language of the two, his pleasure in ridiculing the sort of self-satisfied boorishness represented by Thomas Jefferson Snodgrass interferes with his sympathy for Snodgrass' untrammeled vulgarity. The delightful later tales concerning Mr. Mortimer McWilliams and his domestic problems, however, exemplify Twain's learned ability to subordinate the demands of social commentary to the artistry of characterization in order to achieve a central rather than a confused effect.

Mortimer McWilliams, who was to become one of Twain's favorite narrators, tells of "The Experience of the Mc-Williamses With the Membranous Croup" (1875), of "Mrs. McWilliams and the Lightning" (1880), and of "The Mc-Williamses and the Burglar Alarm" (1882). Mr. McWilliams is, to this reader, one of the most appealing henpecked husbands of all time: "Whenever I want a thing, and Mrs. McWilliams wants another thing, and we decide upon the thing that Mrs. McWilliams wants—as we always do—she calls that a compromise" (XXVII, 315). One finds Mr. Mc-Williams attractive because his spirit is unbroken, and the method Twain takes to show this wholeness of soul is to endow Mr. McWilliams with a self-awareness, a critical sense, and an ability to take with humor whatever miserable plight his wife gets him into, all of which break gently upon the reader's sensibility through the carefully deadpan tones of Mortimer himself.

If his story were told in the third person, one would see McWilliams as an ineffectual and rather foolish man, deserving either scorn or pity. One might patronize him, but one could never respect him. His utter failure to cope with his own burglar alarm, his ridiculous precautions during what his wife takes to be a thunderstorm (it is really a cannon salute on election eve), and his inability to control his wife's exaggerated response to a supposed illness are all intrinsically degrading. But Mr. McWilliams is just as aware as the reader is of the ludicrous figure he makes. He is telling his own story with resignation and humor and complete insight. When his wife blames the "thunderstorm" on his neglect of prayers, he tells her with gentle irony, " 'I don't think it's just fair for you to make so much out of it, anyway, seeing it happens so seldom; I haven't missed before since I

brought on that earthquake, four years ago' " (XV, 333).
When his wife suggests that pine is good for babies to chew
on, he is only too glad to " 'go and order two or three cords
of the best pine wood to-day' " (VII, 86).

Because one knows that it is Mortimer himself who is
reporting his words and actions, one can respect him as a
self-aware human being. His view of himself becomes as
important as what happens to him. The reader shares in his
intelligence, observes from his point of view. Because the
reader has been made to be at one with Mortimer through
the narrative method itself, Twain can "afford" to amuse
him through the incidents of the story by placing Mr. Mc-
Williams in the role of the much-abused male who cannot
cope with the troubles in which he finds himself. The
reader's dual reaction of both amused and sympathetic involvement indicates the stories' particular variety of humor:
we read into Mr. McWilliams' fate our own ineffectual
protests against life's irrationalities, and smile wryly at
ourselves as well as at Mortimer. The subtle artistry of the
McWilliams narratives is an immense improvement over the
sledgehammer technique in the Snodgrass letters.

II

Just as William Tappan Thompson's Major Jones was
created primarily to provide humor, so were narrators of
the Snodgrass and McWilliams variety. They are all part of
the western humorist's repertoire. The idiosyncratic narrator
provokes laughter through his personal connection with the
events presented, even when those events themselves are
intrinsically far from funny. Because he has been caught up
in events, he is moved to speak. Sometimes the events themselves claim attention; more often the reaction of the narrator
to what has befallen him stirs the reader's feelings. Either

way, the narrator speaks because he has acted. There is
another group of narrators in Twain's works whose narrative
point of view becomes important not because of any participation in events but solely because of an attitude toward
events witnessed. The narrator tells a story, and, as with the
Doctor and the tourists in *The Innocents Abroad*, his poker-
faced reaction, or lack of reaction, to his own words becomes
more important than the referents of the words themselves.
The focus is on attitude, not on event, nor on a character's
involvement in event, and the attitude suggested by the
poker face is an important facet of Twain's use of the comic
narrator.

Although Mark Twain never mentions the poker face by
name, he shows it in action again and again. "Riley—Newspaper Correspondent," in *Sketches New and Old* (1875),
is in miniature a digest of the poker face. Riley, the kind of
Yankee Twain had portrayed in *The Innocents Abroad*,
"has," the reader is told, "a ready wit, a quickness and aptness
at selecting and applying quotations, and a countenance that
is as solemn and as blank as the back side of a tombstone
when he is delivering a particularly exasperating joke"
(VII, 180). There follows a sample of Riley's humor, the relation of the mock-tragic roasting to death of a neighbor's
cook, and of the landlady's determination to erect a fitting
monument to her memory: " 'And Mr. Riley if you would
have the goodness to think up a little epitaph to put on it
which would sort of describe the awful way in which she
met her—' " " 'Put it, "*Well done*, good and faithful servant," '
said Riley, and never smiled."

Riley's performance is only an academic indication of
the poker face. To see it in action, carefully developed, one
can examine the technique of Simon Wheeler as he tells
the tale of Jim Smiley's frog. Like Riley, Simon can keep a
straight face. Twain tells us that

He never smiled, he never frowned, he never changed his voice from the gentle-flowing key to which he tuned his initial sentence, he never betrayed the slightest suspicion of enthusiasm; but all through the interminable narrative there ran a vein of impressive earnestness and sincerity, which showed me plainly that, so far from his imagining that there was anything ridiculous or funny about his story, he regarded it as a really important matter, and admired its two heroes as men of transcendent genius in *finesse.* (VII, 17)

Wheeler's way of telling a story is the development into a literary form of what is merely casual humor and characterization in the cases of Riley and the Doctor. Both the Doctor and Riley use humor to insulate themselves from unpleasantness; that this humor is poker-faced simply serves to characterize them as Americans of a relatively raw vintage. Wheeler's narrative method determines the organization of his story; it is precisely the "American" technique that Mark Twain was later to outline in his "How to Tell a Story" (1895):

The teller does his best to conceal the fact that he even dimly suspects that there is anything funny about it. . . . To string incongruities and absurdities together in a wandering and sometimes purposeless way, and seem innocently unaware that they are absurdities, is the basis of the American art, if my position is correct. Another feature is the slurring of the point. A third is the dropping of a studied remark apparently without knowing it, as if one were thinking aloud. The fourth and last is the pause. (XXIV, 264, 267)

All of these techniques are devices of indirection—and, as any player will immediately understand, techniques of betting at poker in order to disguise the true value of a "hand." As the narrator of the "Jumping Frog" story, Simon Wheeler is made to play his cards skilfully; "two pair an' a jack" is bet as though it were a full house, a straight flush appears to be a "bust" hand. Trivial incidents and crucial exchanges are presented with equal emphasis. Jim Smiley's rage as the stranger's trick is discovered is followed in casual sequence by the announcement that " 'thish-yer Smiley had a yaller one-eyed cow that didn't have no tail . . .' " (VII, 22). The frog story itself follows the account of Smiley's dog, Andrew Jackson, that " 'would have made a name for hisself if he'd lived, for the stuff was in him and he had genius—I know it, because he hadn't no opportunities to speak of, and it don't stand to reason that a dog could make such a fight as he could under them circumstances if he hadn't no talent.' "

Simon's "poker face" is communicated by the repetitive pattern of his harangue, and also by the attention to detail. Belief in a fact—or even in a tone of voice—is encouraged by circumstantial evidence. Thus Andrew Jackson's downfall is made more immediate—and more hilarious—by the evidence submitted: the dog he fought " 'didn't have no hind legs, because they'd been sawed off in a circular saw.' " When Andrew " 'come to make a snatch for his pet holt [on the opponent's hind leg], he see in a minute how he'd been imposed on.' " The opponent's biography and Andrew's disillusion contribute to the story's aura of outrageous plausibility, as Simon repeatedly attributes human thoughts and feelings, as well as human names, to Jim Smiley's betwinning animals.

Simon's apparent failure to discriminate between the real and the fabulous, or between the important and the trivial, is the chief source of humor in the story. Not what happens but the narrator's poker-faced attitude is what counts. The poker face is not, however, confined to Simon Wheeler. Twain opens and closes the story with a "frame," within which Wheeler's monologue takes place. A friend of Twain's, "from the East," has asked him to call on "good-natured, garrulous old Simon Wheeler" to find out about the "*Rev. Leonidas W. Smiley.*" Twain conjectures that his friend the easterner "never knew such a personage," but thought that "if I [Twain] asked old Wheeler about him, it would remind him of his infamous *Jim* Smiley, and he would go to work and bore me to death with some exasperating reminiscence of him as long and as tedious as it should be useless to me. If that was the design, it succeeded." Twain thus presents himself as the innocent victim of Simon Wheeler's poker-faced nonsense, and the situation described bears out the pretense. If one wants information about a minister of the gospel, then the account of the ups and downs of a compulsive gambler (Jim Smiley) will be an annoying waste of time.

Mark Twain, writing the story, offers up his innocent self as the Green Easterner imposed upon by the Old Westerner, thus perpetrating a double poker face. In the first place, the reader must detect Twain-the-writer's unspoken contempt for Twain-the-character's inability to appreciate Simon Wheeler's yarn for what it is. Secondly, Twain-the-character is setting forth, as the central focus for the story, his disappointment at Wheeler's inability to remember a *"Rev. Leonidas W. Smiley,"* while blandly repeating Wheeler's supposedly dreary and irrelevant account to the supposedly bored reader. Author and narrator both pretend that what is of no concern —the *Rev. Leonidas W.* Smiley; Jim Smiley's dog; the frog's disposition—is of great concern, and that what is of great concern—Simon Wheeler's delightful narrative method; the stranger's gulling of Smiley—deserves no special emphasis at all. A large part of the story's appeal lies in the reader's pleasure in discovering that he himself belongs to the poker-faced fraternity that sees through the characteristic pose of the western storyteller. He is immediately present around the campfire, sharing attitudes and speech-habits with the narrator. As a form—rather than as simply a technique of characterization or humor—the poker-faced narrative is essentially oral, for it implies the same immediate relationship between artist and audience as between the storyteller and his circle of listening friends.

III

Twain's ability to construct a narrative having the sense of immediacy associated with tales around a campfire depends first of all on his ability to distinguish between an "oral" narrative as it is written and as it is spoken. We all know, in a dim way, that a transcription of conversation usually sounds unrealistic. Twain most clearly indicates an artist's consciousness of the differences between a story as told and a story written as though it were being told in the tale of Jim Blaine's grandfather's old ram.

"Jim Blaine and His Grandfather's Ram" is a complete chapter in *Roughing It* (IV, 98-104). It begins with Twain-the-protagonist's presenting himself as an eager auditor of Blaine's tale and ends with his confession that "I perceived that I was 'sold,'" for "the mention of the ram in the first sentence was as far as any man had ever heard [Blaine] get, concerning it." This "frame" is of the same pattern as the frame for Simon Wheeler's Jumping Frog yarn, but here the resemblance ends. Within the frame, the reader is "sold" along with Twain, and the manner of the sell is never apparent until the end is reached. When Twain came to dictate his autobiography, a long passage—printed by Bernard DeVoto in *Mark Twain in Eruption*—deals with the version of the story that Twain used in his platform readings in 1884 with George Washington Cable, and during his later trip around the world.

I never knew how considerable the changes had been when I finished the season's work; I never knew until ten or eleven years later, when I took up . . . the platform form of the story . . . and I wish to recite it here, so that the reader may compare it with the story as told in *Roughing It,* if he pleases, and note how different the spoken version is from the written and printed version.[6]

There follows the version used for oral presentation, and then Twain concludes:

Upon comparing the above with the original in *Roughing It,* I find myself unable to clearly and definitely explain why the one can be effectively *recited* before an audience and the other can't; there is a reason but it is too subtle for adequate conveyance by the lumbering vehicle of words; I sense it but cannot express it; it is as elusive as an odor, pungent, pervasive, but defying analysis. I give it up. I merely know that the one version will recite, and the other won't.[7]

Mark Twain's intuition, here, is sound. Let the reader "recite" each version and he will see. If we look at the beginning and the end of Jim Blaine's story in the two versions, we may be able to understand how the "oral" narrative works when it is written.

Both versions begin *in medias res:*

BEGINNING OF WRITTEN VERSION, FROM *Roughing It*

I don't reckon them times will ever come again. There never was a more bullier old ram than what he was. Grandfather fetched him from Illinois—got him of a man by the name of Yates—Bill Yates—maybe you might have heard of him; his father was a deacon—Baptist—and he was a rustler, too; a man had to get up ruther early to get the start of old Thankful Yates; it was him that put the Greens up to j'ining teams with my grandfather when he moved west. Seth Green was prob'ly the pick of the flock; he married a Wilkerson—Sarah Wilkerson—good cretur, she was—one of the likeliest heifers that was ever raised in old Stoddard, everybody said that knowed her. . . .

BEGINNING OF ORAL VERSION, FROM *Mark Twain in Eruption*

Well, as I was a-sayin', he bought that old ram from a feller up in Siskiyou County and fetched him home and turned him

loose in the medder, and next morning he went down to have a
look at him, and accident'ly dropped a ten-cent piece in the grass
and stooped down—so—and was a-fumblin' around in the grass
to git it, and the ram he was a-standin' up the slope taking notice;
but my grandfather wasn't taking notice, because he had his
back to the ram and was int'rested about the dime. Well, there he
was, as I was a-sayin', down at the foot of the slope a-bendin' over
—so—fumblin' in the grass, and the ram he was up there at the
top of the slope, and Smith—Smith was a-standin' there—no, not
jest there, a little further away—fifteen foot perhaps—well, my
grandfather was a-stoopin' way down—so—and the ram was up
there observing, you know, and Smith he . . . (musing) . . . the
ram he bent his head down, so . . . Smith of Calaveras . . . no, no it
couldn't ben Smith of Calaveras—I remember now that he—
b'George it was Smith of Tulare County—course it was, I remember it now perfectly plain.

Well, Smith he stood just there, and my grandfather he stood
just here, you know, and he was a-bendin' down just so, fumblin'
in the grass, and when the old ram see him in that attitude he
took it fur an invitation—and here he come! down the slope thirty
mile an hour and his eye full of business. You see my grandfather's
back being to him, and him stooping down like that, of course he
—why sho! it *warn't* Smith of Tulare at all, it was Smith of Sacramento—my goodness, how did I ever come to get them Smiths
mixed like that—why, Smith of Tulare was jest a nobody, but
Smith of Sacramento—why, the Smiths of Sacramento come of the
best Southern blood in the United States; there warn't ever any
better blood south of the line than the Sacramento Smiths. Why
look here, one of them married a Whitaker! I reckon that gives
you an idea of the kind of society the Sacramento Smiths could
'sociate around in; there ain't no better blood than that Whitaker
blood; I reckon anybody'll tell you that. . . .

ENDING OF WRITTEN VERSION

Uncle Lem's dog—I wish you could 'a' seen that dog. He was a
reg'lar shepherd—or ruther he was part bull and part shepherd—
splendid animal; belonged to Parson Hagar before Uncle Lem
got him. Parson Hagar belonged to the Western Reserve Hagars;
prime family; his mother was a Watson; one of his sisters married

a Wheeler; they settled in Morgan County, and he got nipped by the machinery in a carpet factory and went through in less than a quarter of a minute; his widder bought the piece of carpet that had his remains wove in, and people come a hundred mile to 'tend the funeral. There was fourteen yards in the piece. She wouldn't let them roll him up, but planted him just so—full length. The church was middling small where they preached the funeral, and they had to let one end of the coffin stick out of the window. They didn't bury him—they planted one end, and let him stand up, same as a monument. And they nailed a sign on it and put— put on—put on it—sacred to—the m-e-m-o-r-y—of fourteen y-a-r-d-s —of three-ply—car - - - pet—containing all that was—m-o-r-t-a-l of—W-i-l-l-i-a-m—W-h-e—.

ENDING OF ORAL VERSION

. . . lemme see, what was that dog's name . . . (musing) . . . oh, yes, Jaspar—and a mighty good dog too; he wa'n't no common dog, he wa'n't no mongrel; he was a composite. A composite dog is a dog that's made up of all the valuable qualities that's in the dog breed —kind of a syndicate; and a mongrel is made up of the riffraff that's left over. That Jaspar was one of the most wonderful dogs you ever see. Uncle Lem got him from the Wheelers. I reckon you've heard of the Wheelers; ain't no better blood south of the line than the Wheelers.

Well, one day Wheeler was a-meditating and dreaming around the carpet factory and the machinery made a snatch at him and first you know he was a-meandering all over that factory, from the garret to the cellar, and everywhere, at such another gait as—why, you couldn't even see him; you could only hear him whiz when he went by. Well, you know a person can't go through an experience like that and arrive back home the way he was when he went. No, Wheeler got wove up into thirty-nine yards of best three-ply carpeting. The widder was sorry, she was uncommon sorry, and loved him and done the best she could fur him in the circumstances, which was unusual. She took the whole piece— thirty-nine yards—and she wanted to give him proper and honorable burial, but she couldn't bear to roll him up; she took and spread him out full length, and said she wouldn't have it any other way. She wanted to buy a tunnel for him but there wasn't

any tunnel for sale, so she boxed him in a beautiful box and stood
it on the hill on a pedestal twenty-one foot high, and so it was a
monument and grave together, and economical—sixty foot high—
you could see it from everywhere—and she painted on it "To the
loving memory of thirty-nine yards best three-ply carpeting containing the mortal remainders of Millington G. Wheeler go thou
and do likewise."

After which, in both oral and written versions, Jim Blaine
falls asleep.

Although both versions are approximately the same
length—1,500 words—the "written" narrative includes many
episodes and ideas that the "spoken" one omits. For the oral
presentation, Blaine's story must deal at length with a few
episodes, so that the audience can identify with—as well as
simply identify—Blaine's thought-pattern. The written version, however, can move more quickly, because the reader's
imagination supplies tone of voice, gesture, pause, expression.
Despite this difference in content, both versions embody the
quality of mind implicit in the form of frontier oral narration,
the "spoken" version most clearly: the narrator is interested
in each separate element of his tale, but fails—apparently—
to discriminate between the important and the trivial. In
his commitment to a faithful presentation of each and every
fact, he cannot—or so his pose indicates—distinguish the
relative importance of events. He works the audience up to a
pitch of interest regarding "what happened next," while
never appearing at all interested, or anxious, himself, about
the seat of his grandfather's pants. He is involved in recounting each incident as it comes along, and for its own sake;
one element is equated with another; incongruities arise,
seemingly without the narrator's awareness. In this sense,
the poker face of the narrator means not only a stony expression but, more importantly, a pretended failure to differ-
entiate between the values of experiences or of objects.

"Two pair and a jack" is played as though it were a full house.

The written presentation of the oral narrative makes use of the poker face by giving equal value to many episodes which differ in importance from each other. In a sense, the deception is in the grammar. Clause follows co-ordinate clause with the tacit assumption that no one particular fact is worth more than any other fact. The syntax itself communicates in a grammatical form the essence of the mental pattern. The transitions in the spoken version, on the other hand, are not handled syntactically. In moving from Uncle Lem's dog to Mr. Wheeler's sudden death, the platform lecture depends for its success upon a ruminative pause between the two paragraphs; the personality of the storyteller is the focal point. The audience must follow his facial gestures, uncritically empathizing with his habit of thought. By the time "Blaine" falls asleep, the audience has become completely at one with his mentality; the abrupt anticlimax is assured of a laugh.

The contrast most revealing of Twain's artistry is in the different ways audience and reader are led into the narrative "trap." Twain cajoles his hearers into an unguarded response to "Blaine" by the frame within which he presents the yarn; he tells his audience beforehand that

the idea of the tale is to exhibit certain bad effects of a good memory ... which ... retards the progress of a narrative, at the same time making a tangled, inextricable confusion of it and intolerably wearisome to the listener. The historian of "His Grandfather's Old Ram" had that kind of a memory. . . . he always got further and further from his grandfather's memorable adventure with the ram, and finally went to sleep before he got to the end of the story, and so did his comrades.[8]

After the story, Twain's closing words—a short paragraph—simply repeat what he has said about memory. The audience's

interest in the story, then, is the audience's responsibility.
It comes about through the *persona* of the narrator, and
despite Twain.

The written version in *Roughing It* goes about deluding
the reader in a different fashion. There is no abrupt with-
holding of an anticipated climax; there is no gradual entrap-
ment of the reader in the manner of narration. Rather, the
reader is made to respond to the tale as character Twain
himself once had done, and then to share Twain's chagrin
at being hoodwinked. The reader is told prior to the narrative
that Twain has long been anxious to find Blaine "satisfactorily
drunk," the boys having advised him that at just the right
stage of intoxication Blaine would at last tell to completion
"the stirring story of his grandfather's old ram" (IV, 98).
But at the end of Blaine's ramble through the byways of
memory, Twain notices that "the tears were running down
the boys' cheeks—they were suffocating with suppressed
laughter—and . . . I learned then that Jim Blaine's peculiarity
was that whenever he reached a certain stage of intoxication,"
he would start to tell of an adventure "he had once had with
his grandfather's old ram—and the mention of the ram in
the first sentence was as far as any man had ever heard him
get, concerning it" (IV, 104). On the platform, Twain's
problems are easily—or at least obviously—solvable, for the
narrator's personality can directly carry the weight of the
narrative. A skilful acting performance, rather than literary
ability, brings Blaine to life for an audience. In the written
form, Blaine and the reader cannot be so directly brought together. By calling attention to himself as author-narrator,
Twain provides the necessary link between them. The
creation of an intermediary character and the careful selection of framework "facts" are as much a part of Twain's
communication of oral humor as vernacular and western
"experience" themselves.

IV

Although Twain—at least by his own account—only late in his career became self-conscious about the process by which an oral flavor could be imparted to written narrative, his ability to solve the problem of selection was much earlier a part of his artist's equipment. His author-narrators have a knack for presenting just the right details, the relevant "facts," to take in the reader; and this judicious selectivity is the hallmark of the artist. When Twain introduced Jim Blaine's story to his lecture audience as an example of the "bad effects of a good memory," his jest was founded on a keen sense of when and when not to use unrelated details.

The humor involved in relating irrelevancies through the agency of an overly retentive and unselective memory appealed to Twain often enough. In his "A Petition to the Queen of England" (1887), he mentions to the Queen that he finds himself in trouble with one Mr. Bright, clerk of the Inland Revenue Office, and then goes on to elaborate:

I do not know Mr. Bright, and it is embarrassing to me to correspond with strangers; for I was raised in the country and have always lived there, the early part in Marion County, Missouri, before the war, and this part in Hartford County, Connecticut, near Bloomfield and about eight miles this side of Farmington, though some call it nine, which it is impossible to be, for I have walked it many and many a time in considerably under three hours, and General Hawley says he has done it in two and a quarter, which is not likely; so it has seemed best that I write your Majesty. (XXIII, 359)

The irrelevancy here serves to provide delicious humor; but in other contexts, the effect can be far different. In *Life on the Mississippi*, Twain tells us of a pilot, Mr. Brown, who

could *not* forget anything. . . . If he were talking about a trifling letter he had received seven years before, he was pretty sure to deliver you the entire screed from memory. And then, without observing that he was departing from the true line of his talk, he was more than likely to hurl in a long-drawn parenthetical biography of the writer of that letter. . . . Such a memory as that is a great misfortune. To it, all occurrences are of the same size. Its possessor cannot distinguish an interesting circumstance from an uninteresting one. As a talker, he is bound to clog his narrative with tiresome details and make himself an insufferable bore. . . . Mr. Brown would start out with the honest intention of telling you a vastly funny anecdote about a dog. . . . And the original first mention would be all you had learned about that dog, after all this waiting and hungering. (XII, 111-13)

Brown is elsewhere described, and at length, as a very objectionable person (164-76), but one feels that it is Brown's inability to narrate the important details and omit the rest that most condemns him in Mark Twain's eyes. Although "Jim Blaine" may seem to be unselective, every point in his yarn counts toward Twain's effect. In life, unselectivity is merely obnoxious; in art it is fatal.

Blaine on the lecture platform is amusing, as Brown could never be, and illustrates a point at the same time. In *Roughing It,* Blaine's story has two effects beyond amusement. In passing, it serves as one more of a series of events in which Twain-the-writer presents Twain-the-tenderfoot being taken in by the western brand of humor. The character has since been initiated into the fraternity of the accepted, but the "boys" once upon a time found him fair game. In its context, though, the main effect of the "Jim Blaine and His Grandfather's Ram" chapter in *Roughing It* is to provide local color against which to view economic and social facts of the mining community of Virginia City, Nevada. Twain, in many ways a writer of "realism," is, among other things, telling the reader how life in one part of the old West used to be. The chapter preceding Blaine's yarn deals in a dry, factual way with the amounts of bullion shipped and the methods of shipping it, and briefly indicates the extent of the mines themselves. The subsequent chapter presents the living conditions of the Chinese in Virginia City and in California, together with a defense of this minority against the violent prejudices exerted by "the scum of the population," by "their children," and by "the policemen and politicians, likewise, for these are the dust-licking pimps and slaves of the scum, there [in California] as well as elsewhere in America" (IV, 112). Both the mining statistics and the fact of racial tension acquire concrete meaning when placed next to the mentality of Jim Blaine and the "boys," for these are precisely the men who work the mines and stone the Chinese.

Although Mark Twain's use of the "ram" story is partially, even primarily, realistic, Twain's sense of the shortcomings of mere realism, of local color writing that presents the facts simply for their own sake, is clear enough in his comments on Brown. Brown is a boor as well as a bore, his personality as irritating as his memory; the whipping that young Sam Clemens administered to him still warms the heart of the author. An egocentric narrator who remains detached from experience and exploits his own personality to the exclusion of any moral involvement with the subjects of his story can be used to suggest the callousness at which the humorist and the satirist strike. Certainly one cannot help but see Jim Blaine and the "boys" as part of the racist "scum" that Twain castigates. Both Blaine and Brown are presented as being indifferent to anything beyond the facts, and both remember unselectively. Although Blaine's failing is itself made into harmless fun, while Brown's narrative habit is part of a moral indictment, both suggest Twain's concern for significant selection. If an author's intention is to present the look and "feel" of a place or an era, then a good memory and an abundance of detail are helpful. Yet the "local color"

writers of the nineteenth century—and there were enough of
them, surely—by and large bore today's readers, with exceptions, as much as Brown's narrative "technique" bored Twain.

When Twain goes beyond local color realism, he is himself considerably more interesting than when he remains
faithful to the facts as he once observed them. He uses facts,
of course, but in his best writing he transcends them in a way
that most of his contemporaries rarely, if ever, do. Twain is
aware that an aura of realism can be helpful in going beyond
the seeable and touchable. The attention that he gives to
small details is particular enough; yet the point of the detail's
use may be solely to give the impression of realism, of
vraisemblance. Miles Hendon, in *The Prince and the Pauper*,
threads a needle "as men have always done"; he "held the
needle still, and tried to thrust the thread through the eye,
which is the opposite of a woman's way" (XI, 93). The
reader is, at first, impressed by the precision of Twain's observation, but if one turns to a book that Twain was working
on simultaneously with *The Prince and the Pauper*, one
comes across Judith Loftus as she advises Huck Finn how
best to impersonate a girl in threading a needle: " 'Bless you,
child, when you set out to thread a needle don't hold the
thread still and fetch the needle up to it; hold the needle still
and poke the thread at it; that's the way a woman most
always does, but a man always does t'other way' " (XIII, 85).
What was the man's way in *The Prince and the Pauper* becomes the woman's way, and vice versa. One sees that Twain
cares not at all about the actual mechanics of the problem,
but, rather, that he wants to seem to care.

When in *Huckleberry Finn* the king visits the camp
meeting, there is the same attention to detail: "The benches
was made out of outside slabs of logs, with holes bored in
the round side to drive sticks into for legs. They didn't have
no backs" (XIII, 181). The clothing of the men, women, and

children is quickly but specifically described, and the variety of human activity is indicated by prefacing the hymn-singing and preaching with a mention of "knitting" and "courting on the sly." It is from this background, rich in specific detail and action, in "felt life," that the king proclaims his inspired decision to forsake piracy, return to the Indian Ocean, and lead his former fellows-in-sin "into the true path." Balanced against the homely realism of the Pokeville camp meeting, the king's sudden metamorphosis into a pirate captain whose "crew was thinned out considerable last spring in a fight" (183) forms the most striking of contrasts. The king, a raft-carried confidence man, is placed in direct opposition to the trusting villagers, not only by his actions but by the break in the authenticity of detail.

As has been noted, this episode is derived from what Bernard DeVoto has called a scene of "sharper realism"[9]— "Simon Suggs Attends a Camp Meeting"—for Johnson J. Hooper's realistic details exist for the purpose of presenting the scene and Simon Suggs as complementary components of a real environment, worth presenting for its own sake. Twain's purpose is to create a background against which the king-as-pirate can appear as absolutely foreign, out of place. This effect depends for its success upon the details presented and upon the attitude toward them that the reader is made to assume by the narrator, in this case Huck Finn. Neither the event alone nor the narrator's attitude alone will account for the impact of the scene. As the author behind the narrator, Twain controls in a very artful way the details that his narrator will present as well as the relationship between the narrator and what he is observing. Neither the detachment from events of a Jim Blaine and a Simon Wheeler nor the empty-headed, self-centered involvement of a T. J. Snodgrass is adequate to the telling of Twain's major stories. Huckleberry Finn and Hank Morgan occupy a middle ground among Twain's narrators, aware and involved at the same time. They are his solutions to the problems raised for the artist by the American comic narrator, and, as such, they require careful attention from a technical point of view. How are they placed? What are they like? What does a reader gain by considering them as narrators rather than simply as characters? Although these questions may be profitably asked of any of Twain's narrators, they will be especially helpful when applied to Huck and Hank.

3

The Strategy Developed

"YOU DON'T KNOW about me without you have read a book by
the name of *The Adventures of Tom Sawyer,*" says Huck
by way of introduction, and in these few words Huck not
only presents himself as an uneducated and therefore potentially comic boy, but also persuades us to take his existence
for granted. He arises fully created in the first sentence of
the book. The illusion that Huck is real is so intense that we
never ask ourselves where in the world of time Huck is
actually writing his story. He is immediately present as an
actor. Huck never has to establish his temporal relationship
to the events he narrates, in which respect he differs marked-
ly from his frontier predecessor Jim Blaine as well as from
his midwestern successor Nick Carraway. In presenting
The Great Gatsby, one of the more time-conscious narratives
in American literature, Nick is primarily the observer from
the West, even though he participates in the action of the
story to a larger degree than is at first apparent. He establishes his role as observer by putting himself outside the time
scheme of his story: "When I came back from the East last
Autumn" is his temporal base. Huck is at all times inside his
story, even at the very beginning and at the very end. He is
actor and observer at the same time, detached and involved.
Even when Nick Carraway acts, his actions are subsidiary to

his observations of the other characters; Huck, although he is one of the keenest observers to appear inside a book, hardly strikes us as anything else than an active member of the cast.

Unlike Nick's, Huck's role is at all times double. Even when he is the only actor on the stage, he manages to preserve his status as observer. His escape from Pap's cabin early in the book is as active an episode as Huck engineers:

> I took the ax and smashed in the door. I beat it and hacked it considerable a-doing it. I fetched the pig in, and took him back nearly to the table and hacked into his throat with the ax, and laid him down on the ground to bleed; I say ground because it *was* ground—hard packed, and no boards. Well, next I took an old sack and put a lot of big rocks in it—all I could drag—and I started it from the pig, and dragged it to the door and through the woods down to the river and dumped it in, and down it sunk, out of sight. You could easy see that something had been dragged over the ground. I did wish Tom Sawyer was there; I knowed he would take an interest in this kind of business, and throw in the fancy touches. Nobody could spread himself like Tom Sawyer in such a thing as that. (XIII, 46)

Huck's "smashing" and "beating" and "hacking" are actions as direct as anything in Ernest Hemingway. But by the time the pig is bleeding on the ground, Huck is beginning to watch as well as act: he notices the floor of the cabin and shows it to us. Dragging the sack of rocks is, once more, pure action, just as the appeal to the reader is a mark of the narrator's observation: Huck is looking at what he has done. Finally, in the last two sentences of the paragraph Huck is looking at the completed action from a point of view quite different from that of actor. He has become the observing artist, detached from his own work and commenting on its aesthetic relation to the "style" of another artist. The progression of Huck's narrative in this scene of direct, self-concerned action is away from his immediate performance itself and toward an observation of it from an enlarged perspective.

When Huck acts, he also watches. Similarly, when Huck experiences emotion, he manages to focus our attention, and his own, on events, actions, external to his own predicament. In *The Catcher in the Rye,* a different sort of young adolescent continually explains his feelings as he tells his story; perhaps the fact that he tells it from a psychiatric sanitarium is a sign of the times. Huck, however, never dwells on his own reactions. The climax of the Shepherdson-Grangerford feud touches off strong emotion in Huck, but his introduction to the episode sets the tone he will take as he recounts it: "I don't want to talk much about the next day. I reckon I'll cut it pretty short" (157). After Buck and his cousin have run to the river and Huck is left up in his tree, he hears and sees the feud going on around him: "I was mighty downhearted" is all that he tells us. When he finds the two bodies and covers their faces, "I cried a little when I was covering up Buck's face, for he was mighty good to me" (160). This is the only occasion in the whole book on which Huck weeps honest tears, although two times he "begun to cry" (101, 300) as a deceptive device. His feeling is clearly intense, yet the account of Huck's emotion never extends over any length of text. In contrast to what an Emmeline Grangerford would make of an occasion for bathos, he always swings back to the scene itself. Huck blames himself for the killing of the two boys because of his failure to tell Colonel Grangerford about Sophia's note from Harney Shepherdson, but the very mention of his sense of guilt takes the reader's attention away from Huck's present grief and back to the earlier incidents involving Huck and Sophia. When Huck rejoins Jim on the raft, his joy is great, but his own personal emotion is quickly generalized into a summation of the advantages of life on a

raft. The final sentence of the chapter is entirely a generaliza-
tion: "You feel mighty free and easy and comfortable on a
raft" (162).

In passages centering on action and on feeling, Twain
emphasizes through Huck's narrative stance Huck's role as
observer. In the description of Bricksville—a town in which
Huck, the duke, and the king stay for a long time, where
the murder of Boggs, the circus, and "The Royal Nonesuch"
are all performed—Huck's job is to observe, and then to record his observations. His three-page introduction to the
town is not, however, a "still life." Detached though Huck
be, his observation implies action.

> All the streets and lanes was just mud; they warn't nothing else
> *but* mud—mud as black as tar and nigh about a foot deep in
> some places, and two or three inches deep in *all* the places. The
> hogs loafed and grunted around everywheres. You'd see a muddy
> sow and a litter of pigs come lazying along the street and whollop
> herself right down in the way, where folks had to walk around her,
> and she'd stretch out and shut her eyes and wave her ears whilst
> the pigs was milking her, and look as happy as if she was on
> salary. And pretty soon you'd hear a loafer sing out, "Hi! *so* boy!
> sick him, Tige!" and away the sow would go, squealing most
> horrible, with a dog or two swinging to each ear, and three or four
> dozen more a-coming, and then you would see all the loafers get
> up and watch the thing out of sight, and laugh at the fun and look
> grateful for the noise. Then they'd settle back again till there was
> a dog-fight. There couldn't anything wake them up all over, and
> make them happy all over, like a dog-fight—unless it might be
> putting turpentine on a stray dog and setting fire to him, or tying
> a pan to his tail and see him run himself to death. (194-95)

This paragraph is purely descriptive. Huck does nothing;
none of the characters connected with the story do anything.
The impression it gives, however, is of furious activity. The
contrast between the sow's repose and her sudden squealing
eruption is partly responsible, but mainly it is Huck's habit of

describing scenes in terms of people and activity. The pedestrians have to *walk* around the sow. A cry is not passively heard, but rather a loafer would "sing out." The paragraph itself moves from a depiction of the streets of a town to the diversions of the loafers who line the streets, then to the feelings of those loafers, and finally to an implied judgment on the loafers, although the implication is not Huck's.

In the most idyllic passage in the book, the same technique is used. The description of life on the river is full of action. The current "breaks" on a snag and "makes that streak look that way." A woodyard across the river is "piled by them cheats so you can throw a dog through it." A raft slides by and there's "a galoot on it chopping" (164). In the midst of whatever action is described, the reader is put into the role of immediate observer by a casual "you'd see" or "you'd hear." The action becomes observation, the observation is expressed in terms of action. The duality of Huck's role is repeatedly emphasized, and it is this duality that constitutes the particular quality of his usefulness as narrator.

Huck is part of society, so far as his conscious moral commitments are concerned, but at the same time he is outside of any social group he comes into contact with. He is a boy and indulges in typically boyish pranks, such as his elaborate escape from Pap's cabin; but even though he invokes the spirit of the archetypal boy of all boys, Tom Sawyer, as he does so, his motivation for the deed is a grim, adult necessity. Repeatedly the reader is made to sense in Huck himself all the conflicts between rebellion and conformity that can threaten an individual or a society. Huck stands between; just as the river flows between slave and free states, so Huck's soul balances between an infinite series of opposites. His way of telling his story reinforces one's sense of his equivocal position and of its dynamic tension—dynamic because it is constantly changing, and because it drives Huck to his final commitment to "go to hell." A reader's interest in Snodgrass derives primarily from what happens to him; Jim Blaine and Simon Wheeler are remembered for their attitude toward their narratives. In Huck's case, the total effect is greater than the sum of its parts. Huck is both observer and actor; his method of narration pulls readers into the action and at the same time makes them stand back and watch.

Twain is able to achieve this double effect through his selection of the kinds of things that he has Huck notice, and through his fresh use of vernacular in the first person. In fact, to follow closely Twain's use of dialect is to find that the selectivity is governed by the kinds of words and expressions that the dialect allows the character to employ. Huck's description of a Mississippi sunrise, with its "galoot" and "them cheats," expresses none of the standard emotions that have been frozen into the set forms of genteel language. The dialect liberates Twain's imagination, exposing the reader directly to the thing itself, the particular sunrise seen at a specific time by an individual boy who carries with him not society's preconceptions but, rather, the hard-won experience of a knockabout existence.

The alternatives to Huck's uncontaminated vision are exemplified in Chapter IX of *Life on the Mississippi,* where Twain records in polite language two possible ways in which a civilized adult may view a sunset. For the romantic traveler, cut loose from responsibility and therefore free to respond aesthetically,

A broad expanse of the river was turned to blood; in the middle distance the red hue brightened into gold, through which a solitary log came floating, black and conspicuous; in one place a long, slanting mark lay sparkling upon the water; in another the surface was broken by boiling, tumbling rings, that were as many-tinted as an opal; where the ruddy flush was faintest, was a smooth spot that was covered with graceful circles and radiating lines, ever so delicately traced; the shore on our left was densely wooded, and the somber shadow that fell from this forest was broken in one place by a long, ruffled trail that shone like silver; and high above the forest wall a clean-stemmed dead tree waved a single leafy bough that glowed like a flame in the unobstructed splendor that was flowing from the sun. There were graceful curves, reflected images, woody heights, soft distances; and over the whole scene, far and near, the dissolving lights drifted steadily, enriching it every passing moment with new marvels of coloring. (XII, 78-79)

Language conditions attitude. Stock phrases communicate stale emotion, as the speaker echoes the sentimental moonshine about river splendors that decades of gentility have made commonplaces. Twain-the-passenger views the river with complete seriousness, and no satire. His fancy talk of "blood" and "opal" succeeds in obliterating from his description all specific and personal elements, which are buried beneath the sludge of sentiment. Is the viewer experiencing his own emotions or somebody else's? Is he "striking an attitude"? What in the world is he really looking at?

On the other hand, the professional pilot isolates the scene from all distractions to his work:

... those tumbling "boils" show a dissolving bar and a changing channel there; ... that silver streak in the shadow of the forest is the "break" from a new snag, and he has located himself in the very best place he could have found to fish for steamboats; that tall dead tree, with a single living branch, is not going to last long, and then how is a body ever going to get through this blind place at night without the friendly old landmark? (79-80)

The "boiling, tumbling rings, that were as many-tinted as an opal," become "those tumbling 'boils' [that] show a dissolving bar." The language and the attitude demonstrate the frag-

mented nature of the adult's existence.* Twain here anticipates Henry Adams' diagnosis that

> the typical American man had his hand on a lever and his eye on
> a curve in his road; his living depended on keeping up an average
> speed of forty miles an hour, tending always to become sixty,
> eighty, or a hundred, and he could not admit emotions or anxieties
> or subconscious distractions, more than he could admit whiskey
> or drugs, without breaking his neck.[1]

Mark Twain-as-pilot shows through his language that the
emotional distractions of sentimentality have no place in a
professional career, just as Twain-the-sentimental-traveler
likewise shows that the adult male is insulated from direct
emotion by the barrier of stock language. The language of
the educated adult sinks to the level of sentimental generali-
zation, or freezes into the nonhuman calculations of the
professional in his trade. The pilot is of necessity so closely
limited in what he sees that only the facets of reality that
directly affect his profession can claim his attention. The
passenger, on the other hand, is so detached from what exists
around him that he can't even see it directly. The distance
between him and the scene he encounters can be bridged
only by the clichés of generations of genteel viewers. Only
through the uneducated palaver of an adolescent could
Twain find expression for his unique point of view.

*In "The Pilot and the Passenger: Landscape Conventions and the Style
of *Huckleberry Finn*" (*American Literature*, XXVIII [May, 1956], 129-46),
Leo Marx demonstrates the aesthetic bias of the passenger, who views the
river as he would a painting, in contrast to the utilitarian commitment of the
pilot, who can have no eye for soft, surface beauties of shadow and shape
when these are the indications of the hard realities hidden beneath the water,
ready to snatch the life out of boat and man alike. Huck's description of a
sunrise recognizes both beauties and dangers—the "streak on the water" is
pleasing to Huck's eye, even though he knows "that there's a snag there in
a swift current which breaks on it and makes that streak look that way"
(XIII, 164). Mr. Marx says: "It does not occur to Huck to choose between
beauty and utility. His willingness to accept the world as he finds it, without
anxiously forcing meanings upon it, lends substance to the magical sense of
peace the passage conveys."

II

That a comic frontier narrator, speaking the rough dialect of his milieu, should present a point of view to be appreciated rather than ridiculed suggests a reversal of values from the formal narrative pattern of "Self-controlled Gentleman" and backwoods boor. This reversal was not simply a matter of Mark Twain's psychological warping as a westerner. The very language insisted on its own possibilities for rendering experience specifically and concretely, at least to one who could transcend the limitations of his training for the broader perspectives of art. The contrast between Huck's sunrise and the passenger's sunset is foreshadowed in George Washington Harris' Sut Lovingood story, "Eaves-Dropping a Lodge of Masons." Mark Twain was not the first to expand the limited outlook of the effete easterner or city-dweller by following the lead of language, nor was he exploring virgin territory when he used a traditionally comic sort of narrator to turn ridicule outward, against a sophisticated audience, rather than against the narrator's peers. Although Harris and Twain differ in their final effects, both were aware of the resources latent in language itself.

"Eaves-Dropping a Lodge of Masons" begins with a brief exchange between Sut and "George" that leads to a demand from "the crowd" that "George" tell of a misadventure to which Sut has apparently just alluded. "So I commenced," author Harris relates, "in my way to tell it somewhat thus."[2] Character "George's" own way is a delicate spoof of sentimental literature. "George" evokes the memory of stately ruins and of the stalwart men of bygone days; he sadly laments that "the quiet grave has long ago claimed the last of the band," and that "the march of improvement first, then the march and crash of armies, have nearly swept away those, to me, almost sacred places." "George" wanders on in this lachrymal fashion until his hearers can stand no more of it: "'Oh, komplicated durnashun! that haint hit,' said Sut. 'Yu's drunk, ur yure sham'd tu tell hit, an' so yu tries tu put us all asleep wif a mess ove durn'd nonsince. . . . I'll talk hit all off in English, an' yu jis' watch an' see ef I say, "echo," ur "grapes," ur "graveyard" onst.'"³ Then Sut begins to tell the tale.

"George's" way of telling the story has been to take the reader (auditor) by the hand and then to squeeze until tears come to the eyes of both narrator and listener. The halo around the past obscures all details of that past; the generalized emotion of the speaker is all that remains. Sut Lovingood, at one as he is with his community and its mores, sees nothing "picturesque" in the events of the characteristic tale that follows, and nothing to cry over, either. Brushing aside all sentimental generalities, he goes at once to the narrative kernel, the misfortunes that befell young George and his friend Lum when they once tried to overhear the secrets of Masonry from an insecure listening post under the eaves of the courthouse. "'I takes fur my tex, the fac' that eaves-drappin am a durn'd mean sorter way tu make a livin . . . an' hit has its retribushun, a orful wun, an' yu'd all (not scept George thar) say so when I'se dun.'" Sut is no preacher, but neither does he lead an existence so fragmented that he at any time fails to respond to the life around him.

The speech of the backwoods presupposes both a limited range of experience (Coleridge's comments in Chapter XVII of *Biographia Literaria* on the language of Wordsworth's rustics are to the point, here) and a preoccupation with the facts of that experience, no matter how metaphorically those facts may find their way into language. Both suppositions are confirmed in the second paragraph of Sut's narrative, a paragraph that fulfils the function that George's page and a half of sentimentality had not quite completed. Sut sets the scene of the action in the same courthouse that, to George, had been just one more excuse to snivel over the lost scenes of " 'happy, ragged, thoughtless boyhood' ": " 'The upstairs ove that Court-hous' wer one big rume, plastered over-head wif three quater plank, an' no floor ontu the jists in the loft abuv . . . .' " This is seeing the past with too great clarity to permit sentimentalization. From the perspective of an educated adult, "George" bemoans the loss of boyhood's happy thoughtlessness, but Sut recalls with gusto the mere events themselves; he has no need to force any special meaning into an episode that is so similar to Sut's own pranks as a "nat'ral born durn'd fool." Thirteen-year-old George and Lum, eavesdropping on the Masons, fall through the rickety courthouse ceiling, and the paddling that Lum's temptingly positioned posterior receives makes Sut squirm in his seat as he tells of it. "George's" encounter is itself the perfect comment on such sentimentalities as " 'the graveyard yu wer a-blatherin about jis' now,' " for in escaping from the courthouse, "George" had " 'run over the spot whar a fancy hous' 'bout five feet squar hed been upsot,' " and had gone home smelling like " 'yu wer the cholery a-cumin.' "[4]

The story, as Harris has Sut tell it, is something of a comment on sentimental language, for Sut's vernacular contrasts delightfully with "George's" vague moonings. Delight, indeed, is the principal effect achieved. Sut, backwoodsman that he is, uses poker-faced exaggeration and tall-tale techniques to expand a clever anecdote into a fully imagined incident. His function as narrator is neither to reform nor to instruct, but simply to amuse. In the process, he presents neither sentimental effusions nor dessicated sociology. Remembering Twain's Mississippi sunsets, one may say of "George's" evocation of the past that it is allied with the passenger's view of nature, while Sut's is equivalent to Huck's vision of the sunrise, at least in clarity if not in joy. To say

merely this, however, is to stop short of what specifically
Twain gains by his narrative strategy. Like Harris, he is
opposing the techniques of frontier humor to those of sentimental fiction; Twain himself could be just as resistant as
Harris' Sut to "the rot that deals in 'the happy days of yore,'
'the sweet yet melancholy past,' with its 'blighted hopes' and
its 'vanished dreams'—and all that sort of drivel."[5] Still, Sut
telling his tales and Huck describing the sunrise share a
common limitation as well as common advantages. They
both represent a point of view as general as the points of
view embodied by Twain-the-passenger, Twain-the-pilot,
and George-the-reminiscer. Huck's view of the sunrise no
more depends upon being uniquely Huck's than does Sut's
recounting of the "Eaves-Dropping" depend upon the particular personality of the teller. Both Twain and Harris here use
dialect and poker face to avoid fragmentation into sentimentality or professionalism, but as they do so their creations
become depersonalized, mere lenses through which the
reader is asked to look.

Huck, however, is more than a reflecting glass for author
Twain. There are scenes where Huck-as-narrator fulfils
quite another function through the quality of dramatic irony
in his point of view. A real difference, central to the meaning
of Twain's story, exists between the views of narrator Huck
and of author Twain, whereas author Harris and narrator
Sut share a common reaction to sentimental language.
(Narrator "George," as has been shown, is altogether a
different *persona*.) Morally, this is clear enough: Mark Twain
feels one way about slavery, Huck another, and the opposition between their attitudes is obvious and effective each
time Huck wrestles with his conscience. The irony of "All
right, then, I'll *go* to hell" derives not at all from Huck's
manner of narration, but completely from the separation
between author and narrator. When Huck watches the sun-

rise, author and narrator are one, but the narrator's dialect permits the author to show a reader precisely what is there, divorced from accreted meanings of either professionalism or sentimentality. Between these two narrative positions there is a middle ground which Twain explores most fruitfully.

III

Huck Finn is a dynamic character, not a stock representative of a point of view. Unlike Sut Lovingood and his frontier brethren, Huck changes, Huck grows. Sut's feelings about the Yankees, Irishmen, circuit-riders, and others who complicate his life never change; he offers a lens through which Harris can see reality and bring it into sharp focus for his readers. But because Huck's feelings change, his attitudes can only occasionally, and then fortuitously, be taken as the equivalent of Twain's. When Sut tells of his own adventures, his stance is similar to Harris' own: Sut looks objectively into the past; he is completely detached from what he sees and can comment on his own "durn'd foolishness" as dispassionately as any historian. But Huck is actor as well as observer, is both at once. The reader, therefore, is held in suspension between the objectivity of judgment and the immediacy of participation.

Since action and observation are so closely blended, one unhesitatingly ignores the fact that realistically it is impossible for Huck to be writing his own story: when would he have the time? More pertinent is the suggestive point that Huck begins his story with no hint that he is looking back on history. He looks back on another book, one "made by Mr. Mark Twain," but only at the end of his own story does he refer to his role as author:

If I 'a' knowed what a trouble it was to make a book I wouldn't 'a' tackled it, and ain't a-going to no more. But I reckon I got to light out for the territory ahead of the rest, because Aunt Sally she's going to adopt me and sivilize me, and I can't stand it. I been there before. (XIII, 405)

Huck has indeed "been there before," and because the dilemma of whether or not to "light out" is the same dilemma that Huck faced at the end of *Tom Sawyer*, and in summary at the beginning of his own book, it emphasizes the contrast between the narrative methods of the two stories. Tom's adventures, though closer to Twain's own autobiography than Huck's, are presented by an omniscient author. Why should Tom's story be told in the third person and Huck's in the first? Since Tom plays a large role in Huck's book, it may be helpful to distinguish between the two boys in order to see further into why Twain needed to tell *Huckleberry Finn* in the first person.

In *Mark Twain at Work*, Bernard DeVoto points out that *Tom Sawyer* was originally told in the first person. DeVoto considers the revision into the third person a "wise change," and sums up his position in a contrast between Tom's book and Huck's: Twain "found a perfect medium in Huck Finn's vernacular, whose rhythm and color are straight out of the Missouri earth. But lacking that idiom, Tom's memoirs would have been stilted and unreal. There is something essentially false in his referring to himself [in the original MS] as 'a poor, poverty-stricken boy.' "[6] No one will argue with this statement of the problem, so far as it goes, for to permit Tom to see himself through the clichés of sentimental language would be to destroy his vitality as a boyish character. But why didn't Twain use the frontier idiom for Tom's story? He had, after all, begun it in the first person, a useful narrative point of view for dialect stories, as the success of "The Celebrated Jumping Frog of Calaveras County" had shown. Since Twain was well able to utilize dialect by the time of

Tom Sawyer, there must have been something else in the story of Tom to account for the narrative point of view used to relate it.

Both Tom's story and Huck's are of growth, but the growth is of a different kind in each case. Tom's book begins with Tom's flight from Aunt Polly and from school, but it ends with his pronouncement to Huck that " 'we can't let you into the gang if you ain't respectable' " (VIII, 290). Huck consents to " 'stick to the widder till I rot, Tom; and if I git to be a reg'lar ripper of a robber, and everybody talking 'bout it, I reckon she'll be proud she snaked me in out of the wet' " (291). Tom needs the "gang" and society; his flight to Jackson's Island is for "effect" only: he leaves so that he may return; almost everything he does is calculated in terms of society's reaction. His growth is within the framework of village life and village institutions—school, Sunday school, jail, and courthouse. When Tom persuades Huck to become "respectable," he allies himself with society in general. His concern is not for Huck and Huck's happiness. His answer to Huck's complaint against the widow's infernal regularity is merely, " 'Well, everybody does that way, Huck' " (288).

Tom's life is a continual adjusting to ideas that originate outside himself. Even his self-pity comes from books, just as much so as does his stylized notion of what constitutes the legitimate composition of a robber-gang. The reader can see Tom in this light most easily through the satirical irony of the sentimental clichés in which Twain presents Tom's states of mind. Clearly, Tom cannot tell his own story in these terms, for then he would, *ipso facto,* be a different sort of character from what Twain wanted him to be. Tom, in his own book, is not an attitudinizing scoundrel, but simply a typical boy, sentimental and manly by turns, a representative of his time and place. Tom's story needs to be told from the outside, just as the implicit comment on Tom must be made in language not his own.

Tom grows socially; he comes to accept the responsibility of community life, with its compromises and public obligations. In the other three published stories in which he appears, this pattern is made even more explicit than in *The Adventures of Tom Sawyer,* as Tom finally becomes the direct agent of social justice in "Tom Sawyer, Detective." Tom is "typical," in the sense of being an archetype. Huck is individual. His growth is in a different direction from Tom's. Huck's book begins and ends with the same thematic element, the conflict between natural and civilized life. When at the end of the book Huck renounces civilization, his attitude toward the respectable life has not changed: he still admires those who can live it, such as the Widow Douglas, Colonel Grangerford, and Mary Jane Wilks, but it is not for him. His growth is in terms of his perceptions of other people, not in terms of any attitude toward society. He is from the start of his book involved in society without being a part of it, but his attitude toward specific individuals changes. His growth is neither the social growth of Tom, nor is it the expansion of moral perceptiveness which so many of Henry James's characters experience. Huck is not aware of his moral dilemma in terms that suggest an expanding consciousness, nor does he abandon boyish pranks for solid respectability. Rather, Huck becomes increasingly able to respond to people as individuals rather than as typical representatives of a cultural level. Huck's first response to the Widow Douglas is a response to a social status. When he leaves his sugar-hogshead to please Tom,

The widow she cried over me, and called me a poor lost lamb, and she called me a lot of other names, too, but she never meant no harm by it. She put me in them new clothes again, and I couldn't do nothing but sweat and sweat, and feel all cramped up.

Well, then, the old thing commenced again. The widow rung a
bell for supper, and you had to come to time. When you got to
the table you couldn't go right to eating, but you had to wait for
the widow to tuck down her head and grumble a little over the
victuals, though there warn't really anything the matter with them
—that is, nothing only everything was cooked by itself. In a barrel
of odds and ends it is different; things get mixed up, and the juice
kind of swaps around, and the things go better. (XIII, 2)

Nothing in the paragraph distinguishes Huck's feelings
about the widow from his feelings about any genteel female.
The contrast is between life in society and life outside it,
between the social regularity suggested by one style of cooking and the freedom of anarchy suggested by another. The
widow herself is simply representative. But near the end of
the book, Aunt Sally—who also wants to "sivilize" Huck—
asks Huck to stay in the house and not go looking for the
wounded Tom:

Laws know I *wanted* to go bad enough to see about Tom, and
was all intending to go; but after that I wouldn't 'a' went, not for
kingdoms.
But she was on my mind and Tom was on my mind, so I slept
very restless. And twice I went down the rod away in the night,
and slipped around front, and see her setting there by her candle
in the window with her eyes towards the road and the tears in
them; and I wished I could do something for her, but I couldn't,
only to swear that I wouldn't never do nothing to grieve her any
more. And the third time I waked up at dawn, and slid down, and
she was there yet, and her candle was most out, and her old gray
head was resting on her hand, and she was asleep. (391)

Her words had been gentle and Huck is moved. He is able
to distinguish between Aunt Sally's social role as a restrain-
ing influence—which he hates and will have none of—and
her personal feelings about himself, which he respects.
Huck's ability to make such a distinction improves as the

book progresses. Much earlier, his return to the Widow
Douglas' house after a muddy night out with Tom has led to
"a good going-over in the morning from old Miss Watson on
account of my clothes; but the widow she didn't scold, but
only cleaned off the grease and clay, and looked so sorry
that I thought I would behave awhile if I could" (15). The
difference between "thinking" and "swearing," between the
affirmative promise and the conditional hope, indicates the
intensity of Huck's change.

More spectacularly, Huck's view of Jim shifts from a
simple reflection of society's attitudes toward slaves to a free
response on the part of Huck the "natural man." Jim is a
slave, and, from beginning to end, slaves are property. Huck,
therefore, is sinful in helping a runaway "nigger" on his way,
as he himself clearly realizes. He accepts implicitly society's
judgment. Even the language in which he expresses the conventional promptings of social conscience is society's, not
Huck's own: "The plain hand of Providence," he feels, is
"slapping [him] in the face and letting [him] know [his]
wickedness was being watched all the time from up there in
heaven" (294-95). After he writes the note to Miss Watson,
he says that he "felt good and all washed clean of sin" (296).
Finally, he mentions a steamboat's blown cylinder-head to
Aunt Sally, who worriedly asks, " 'Good gracious! anybody
hurt?' " Huck's immediate response is, " 'No'm. Killed a
nigger' " (306). But Jim, a particular "nigger," is at last
viewed apart from his social rank. One-third of the way
through the book, just before Huck and Jim discover that
they have passed Cairo in the fog, Huck is horrified when
Jim talks of his plans to steal his children from captivity:

It most froze me to hear such talk. . . . Here was this nigger,
which I had as good as helped to run away, coming right out flat-
footed and saying he would steal his children—children that

belonged to a man I didn't even know; a man that hadn't done me no harm. (123-24)

Later in the book, however, Huck awakens on the raft to find Jim

with his head down betwixt his knees, moaning and mourning to himself. I didn't take notice nor let on. I knowed what it was about. He was thinking about his wife and his children, away up yonder, and he was low and homesick; because he hadn't ever been away from home before in his life; and I do believe he cared just as much for his people as white folks does for their'n. It don't sound natural, but I reckon it's so. (215)

If one thinks of how Pap "cared" for Huck, the irony becomes almost outrageous. The immediate point, though, is that Huck is making two contrasts here. Negroes and whites are different, and it isn't "natural" for Jim, a Negro, to have feelings for his children. At the same time, Jim is an individual, distinguishable from the group he represents, and as a person Jim has Huck's respect for his grief; Huck won't "notice nor let on."

Huck learns to make distinctions. Tom Sawyer never changes, never considers people as individuals. Huck's story is primarily of the conflict between the two kinds of perception that govern his thinking, a conflict that Tom never experiences. There is Huck the social being, involved to a degree in society and committed to society's values. There is Huck the "natural man," whose direct experience of life enables him to react to individuals without regard for society's artificial evaluation of them. As narrator and protagonist, he is both by turns. Somewhat apart from society, he approaches its various customs and institutions as a detached traveler whose naïve reactions to civilization can through irony illuminate his creator's judgments. In his "personal life," he gradually overcomes the crippling biases of the civilization he has known. If Huck's observations on the one hand and growth on the other are to be presented in a unified narrative, then Huck will have to tell his own story and at the same time be less aware of the meaning of what he sees and experiences than is Mark Twain.

IV

Huck's narrative point of view is required by the nature of his personal growth as a character in the story, and his way of telling the story is instrumental in giving an impression of his particular sort of growth. Huck Finn is unique in American literature, and it is his narrative technique that establishes his uniqueness. He is observer and actor, child and man; he knows with an adult's knowledge that all the subtleties of the poker table are needed to cope with life, and he never tries the same bluff twice. He is at the same time a "natural," for his reactions to most events are divorced from social clichés. When he accompanies the Grangerfords to the church they share with the Shepherdsons, he notices that all the men have their guns along,

and kept them between their knees or stood them handy against the wall. . . . It was pretty ornery preaching—all about brotherly love, and such-like tiresomeness; but everybody said it was a good sermon, and they all talked it over going home, and had such a powerful lot to say about faith and good works and free grace and preforeordestination, and I don't know what all, that it did seem to me to be one of the roughest Sundays I had run across yet. (152)

It is only through Huck that the satire is created, but to Huck himself there is no satire. The reader can smile at the boy's confusion and share the boy's pleasure in recounting his disparagement of a church service. Then the reader can take in the religious hypocrisy—as Twain is careful to keep Huck from doing—and extract a general maxim for himself based on abstract moral values. The third step in the reader's appreciation of the passage is to return to Huck's reaction and see his undercutting not only of the sermon and the hypocrisy but also of the reader's own moral abstraction, which is itself a part of "such-like tiresomeness." Always one is brought back to Huck's acceptance of the truth that this is how people are. Huck often seems naïve, but his is a very wise naïveté. "If you notice," says Huck, thinking of the cool puncheon floor of the church, "most folks don't go to church only when they've got to; but a hog is different" (153).

In Huck's apparent naïveté lies much of the humor in his narrative. He casually drops his bombshells with no indication that he has even considered causing any particular effect. Behind Huck, we may be aware of Twain's working the poker face for all it is worth, but as the story filters through Huck, no sense of manipulation lessens the shock of his observations. When Huck confronts a social institution, such as slavery, he knows only what he is used to and can never question the morality upon which slavery is based. The existence of any other point of view is unknown to him, and it is this complete submergence in one attitude that enables Huck to say the most damaging things of all about slavery, as when he is horrified at Jim's plan to steal his children. This is Huck as the innocent participant: he knows about slavery and shares the common attitudes toward it, naïvely ignorant that any respectable person could think otherwise.

At other times, Huck is the naïve observer, approaching a facet of society with mere common sense to fall back on. He doesn't know what a feud is until Buck Grangerford—who, the reader is told, is Huck's own age—explains it to him. Buck's scorn for Huck's ignorance places the feud in a context of understood and accepted convention: " 'Why, where was you raised? Don't you know what a feud is?' " (150) Buck goes on to expand his own immediate preconceptions into the code of the country when he casually mentions that after the original difficulty had been taken to court, " 'the suit went agin one of the men, and so he up and shot the man that won the suit—which he would naturally do, of course. Anybody would.' " Huck's naïve questions following this matter-of-fact overthrow of legality lead Buck on to an exposition of the feud, the moral naïveté of which makes one wince, and end by pointing up the uselessness of all violence as a means to settle any difference of opinion. Or rather it is Twain's manipulation of the Socratic method that accomplishes this. " 'What did he do to you?' " asks Huck, after Buck has tried to shoot Harney Shepherdson from ambush. " 'Him? He never done nothing to me.' " " 'Well, then, what did you want to kill him for?' " " 'Why, nothing—only it's on account of the feud.' " The conversation is brilliantly in character for the speakers, but the reiterated "nothing," grammatically equated with "feud," anticipates the "*nada*" of Hemingway's "A Clean, Well-Lighted Place" in its appearance of effortless artistry. Twain the writer carefully imposes nothing directly while choosing carefully the questions and answers that will make his didactic point clear without weakening a reader's belief in Huck.

Essentially, Twain's problem with Huck and the feud was to transform the facts of life into the form of art. Sherwood Anderson, himself an admirer of Twain's artistry, has said that " . . . art is art. It is not life. . . . The life of reality is confused, disorderly, almost always without apparent purpose, whereas in the artist's imaginative life there is purpose." This purpose is artistically presented, or made apparent, through a theme, and a story is given "form—to make it true and real to the theme, not to life."[7]

If Twain had deliberately set out to leave an example of how he worked his material into an art form, he could have done no better than in his Chapter XXVI of *Life on the Mississippi*. Of course, *Life on the Mississippi* is not "life," either; but the theme to which it is true is not the theme of *Huckleberry Finn*, just as its form is not the form of Huck's book. Among the narratives that Twain includes as sample of what he heard when he went back to the river just before expanding "Old Times on the Mississippi" into *Life*, is a nameless gentleman's account of feuding in general and the Darnell-Watson feud in particular. Twain allows the description to stand by itself; his comments at the end of the "quotation" are concerned solely with criticizing southerners for "*knowingly* and *purposely* debauching their grammar" (XII, 223) in the manner of the previous speaker. There is no way of knowing what Twain did to the story as he originally heard it, and recent researches suggest that he may well have heard no story at all.* Whether Twain deliberately recast his own version of the feud as told in *Huckleberry Finn*, or whether he altered something that he actually heard in order to emphasize the language of the teller, the account of the Darnell-Watson imbroglio differs so greatly from Huck's telling of the Grangerford-Shepherdson misunderstanding that it produces a totally different effect. The content—the facts of life—is similar and the first-person narrator is used, but two main differences make for a different story.

There is, to begin with, the narrator's distance from events. Huck is actually in the church about which the later narrator only talks:

*Walter Blair, in *Mark Twain & "Huck Finn"* (Berkeley: University of California Press, 1960), shows most convincingly that Twain wrote the feud-chapters of *Huckleberry Finn* before his return to the river in 1882. The story of the feud in *Life on the Mississippi* (1883), then, is either a reworking of the novel episode, or, just possibly, a report of still another retelling of the same story that had been lodged in Twain's mind since his pilot days.

The men and boys would lean their guns up against the wall, handy, and then all hands would join in with the prayer and praise; though they say the man next the aisle didn't kneel down, along with the rest of the family; kind of stood guard. I don't know; never was at that church in my life; but I remember that that's what used to be said. (XII, 221)

Equally obvious is the adult narrator's passing of judgment on the affair:

Some says it was about a horse or a cow—anyway, it was a little matter; the money in it wasn't of no consequence—none in the world—both families was rich. The thing could have been fixed up, easy enough; but no, that wouldn't do. Rough words had been passed; and so nothing but blood could fix it up after that. That horse or cow, whichever it was, cost sixty years of killing or crippling! (219·20)

Huck makes no judgments; he does not generalize. Never does he hold the feud off at arm's length. His questions to Buck form a pattern leading from general theory to particular humanity. Huck wants to know what a feud is, then how long "this one" has been going on, then what the trouble was that started it, then "who done the shooting," then if many had been killed, then if anybody had been killed "this year," and, finally, he suggests that the particular Shepherdson, old Baldy, who killed a twelve-year-old Grangerford, was a coward. After Buck refutes this misconception with a long harangue exalting the bravery of both families, Huck has nothing further to ask. His interest, as always, has led him away from the theoretical and toward the human side of the matter.

These qualities, personal involvement and human rather than moral interest, distinguish Huck's reaction to the feud from the approach of the nameless adult narrator in *Life*, and combine to make the reader recognize the feud and its participants as a part of humanity that must be acknowledged and lived with, whereas the effect of the story in *Life* is to make the reader laugh at the feuders as strange, warped characters from another world. Twain-as-author implies a satire as biting as that in *Life*, but Huck's way of telling, of transmuting life into art, leads one away from moral condemnation and toward aesthetic appreciation and sympathy.

Huck's willingness to accept life and people on their own terms is his most noteworthy quality. The duke and the Dauphin come aboard and want Huck and Jim to wait on them and call them "Your Grace" and "Your Majesty," and "that was all easy, so we done it" (XIII, 171). When Huck leaves three men to drown on the *Walter Scott*, he "begun to think how dreadful it was, even for murderers, to be in such a fix," because, says Huck, "I might come to be a murderer myself yet, and then how would I like it?" (100) He is the compassionate man—or boy—and accepts not only the enemies of society but society itself. He can see these very murderers as society sees them, and accepts society's view; for when his attempt to arrange their rescue seems about to succeed, Huck

was feeling ruther comfortable on accounts of taking all this trouble for that gang, for not many would 'a' done it. I wished the widow knowed about it. I judged she would be proud of me for helping these rapscallions, because rapscallions and dead-beats is the kind the widow and good people takes the most interest in. (104)

Huck says this with no rancor toward the widow; he has no sophisticated standard against which to measure the different codes of value he meets. The bitterness behind the passage is in Mark Twain's use of Huck's naïveté, the comic effect of which serves to establish the gap between author and narrator. Time and again Twain creates humor through

Huck's naïve acceptance of appearances, while simultaneously expressing his own indignation.

Huck, on the other hand, expects nothing, is surprised at nothing; although he is disgusted by the king's teary deception as dead Peter Wilks's brother, only after he becomes personally involved with the three Wilks sisters does he decide to "steal the king's plunder" (237). Huck is never outraged by deception in itself. His purpose is not to reform the world, or himself, either. Unlike Mark Twain, he quite simply takes humanity's failings for granted, and makes no effort to change them. If this is naïve, it is also wise, and even necessary if Huck is to survive among the river people.

The humor of naïveté is a tricky business to talk about, because, in Freud's terms, naïveté becomes wit the moment it is only pretended. When Huck is being naïve, Twain is being witty. Although both pretended and real naïveté can be funny, they are so in very different ways. Without going at all far into the psychology of the difference, one sees immediately that different effects might well be expected because of the difference in identification. Adults feel superior to a naïve child, and laugh. But what if one is forced to identify with naïveté? Surely we are all of us on that raft with Huck; surely we share his sense of relief when each danger is circumvented. Now the point of the book has very little to do with this easy kind of identification through which readers live vicariously. *Huckleberry Finn,* however good an action story it may be, is not a melodrama, does not present excitement for its own sake. But the reader is, in the simplest meaning of the word, made to identify with Huck, through whose eyes everything is seen. At the same time, the reader is assumed to possess, more or less, the knowledge and awareness of Mark Twain. The result of the interweaving of these two reactions to events is to make one see as something new the world that he has accepted without much consideration. This is as true morally as it is in every other way, according to Lionel Trilling's definitive statement that

no one who reads thoughtfully the dialectic of Huck's great moral crisis will ever again be wholly able to accept without some question and some irony the assumptions of the respectable morality by which he lives, nor will ever again be certain that what he considers the clear dictates of moral reason are not merely the engrained customary beliefs of his time and place.[8]

The division between Twain and Huck leads the reader to accept the human condition as Huck does, while lamenting abuses and perversions along with Twain. The balance is everything. Twain's art suspends the reader between outrage and sympathy. The clarity with which human frailty is presented is balanced by the compassion with which Huck views it, and only through Huck's narration could this particular balance be maintained.

V

Although the effect of the narrator's language is not to be underestimated, of first importance to Twain as he presents his major first-person narratives is the gap between the author and the narrator, in combination with a presentation of the narrator's development as a dynamic personality. The uneducated speaker is not simply a boor to be ridiculed; he is worth taking seriously, just as his clear vision—reflected through his language—is worth attention. In Huck, Twain presents an adolescent narrator from his own boyhood past with whom both author and reader are thrown into closest sympathy, despite the ambivalent evaluation of Huck's world, the devaluation of Huck's conscious moral precepts. In *A Connecticut Yankee in King Arthur's Court* (1889), the novel following *Huckleberry Finn*, Twain complicates his task by choosing to tell the story through a character whose actions and values are viewed ambivalently from the very beginning. Just how the reader is to respond to Hank is, indeed, the central critical problem in the book, for Hank Morgan is different from Huck Finn. He is proud of his ignorance, not ashamed of it; he is brash, not humble. Despite such differences—and many more exist—Twain approaches the writing of *A Connecticut Yankee* armed with the techniques of *Huckleberry Finn,* although his control is not as complete as in *Huckleberry Finn.* To read Hank's story with the possibility of a split between author and narrator in mind is, therefore, to see Twain's accomplishment more fully, and also to discover that *A Connecticut Yankee* is not the booster's pep-talk for nineteenth-century industrial materialism that it is often taken to be.

Hank's story lacks the clarity of focus that Huck's possesses, because the theme around which this re-creation of King Arthur's court is organized derives directly from Mark Twain's attitude toward his own era. And what Twain "really thought" about nineteenth-century industrial progress and its social and moral implications is an ambiguous question. Twain himself had difficulty defining his position, and the unevenness of his sympathies often mars his book. His feelings are as complex and as interesting as Thoreau's. (Within one book—*Walden*—Thoreau is "refreshed and expanded when the freight train rattles past," for the train is indicative of commerce, and "commerce is unexpectedly confident and serene, alert, adventurous, and unwearied," but also feels that "trade curses everything it handles," and sees the train as being thick with the filth of "State Street and the engine's soot.")

The same tension, vastly heightened, is evident in Twain's thinking. In "The Great Revolution in Pitcairn" (1879), a visiting American makes a tiny island into an empire. But his notion of progress is ridiculous, materialistic, and degrading. He tries to apply ideas in a context for which they are unsuited. Urging the confused islanders to " 'Look at Germany; look at Italy' " (XIX, 353), he brings chaos to the land and disgrace to himself. But although "The Great Revolution" has nothing good to say about modern civilization's aims and practices, it is certainly not Twain's final word. In a dictation on December 5, 1906, he says that in *A Connecticut Yankee* "I think I was purposing to contrast . . . the English life of the whole of the Middle Ages, with the life of modern Christendom and modern civilization— . . . the most advanced and most enlightened century of all the centuries the sun has looked upon."[9] There seems to be no intention of irony in his words, yet just the previous September he had written scathingly of an assembly which had applauded a noted soldier's pronouncement that " 'We are of the Anglo-Saxon race, and when the Anglo-Saxon wants a thing *he just takes it.*' " Twain "translates" this into "plain English" to read, " 'The English and the Americans are thieves, highwaymen, pirates, and we are proud to be of the combination.' " After several heated paragraphs, he concludes with an equally ironic summary of the great "lessons" that modern America has been teaching Europe:

. . . but for us her Insurance Trusts might never have found out the best way to work the widow and orphan for profit; but for us the long delayed resumption of Yellow Journalism in Europe might have been postponed for generations to come. Steadily, continuously, persistently, we are Americanizing Europe, and all in good time we shall get the job perfected.[10]

Twain loved the typesetting machine, and hated Paige, its inventor. Twain hailed the railroads, but loathed what they had done to the Mississippi river-boats. This tension in his feeling about the nineteenth century is given its fullest expression in *A Connecticut Yankee*. Hank Morgan, whose uncritical commitment to the nineteenth century leads to the destruction of his sixth-century world and of his own life, is not Mark Twain, although, as any reader of the book is but too aware, often the tone of Hank's narrative betrays an uncertainty of intention on the author's part rather than a clearly-defined expression of doubt belonging to the character.

But even Hank himself is not so simple a character as he may at first appear. He is not merely a static figure, although he is at first presented as one. He calls himself "A Yankee of the Yankees—and practical; yes, and nearly barren of sentiment, I suppose—or poetry, in other words" (XIV, 5). But this non-poet writes the book, and this man of no sentiment and great practicality later admits that he wrote long letters to his sixth-century wife simply "for love of it, and of her, though I couldn't do anything with the letters, of course, after I had written them" (428).

Twain communicates a sense of coming ambiguity before even launching into the action of the story, for Hank's lack of poetry provides a question mark to throw a reader off balance: why should a man who is by his own account not a literary artist (5) bother to turn a journal into a book (8) simply for the aesthetic pleasure it gives him to do so? A sense of doubleness is everywhere. As Hank's own writing begins, one wonders if this sixth-century chronicle can be the work of the nineteenth-century speaker just heard, although the language this early in the book is contemporary enough:

"Camelot—Camelot," said I to myself. "I don't seem to remember hearing of it before. Name of the asylum, likely."
It was a soft, reposeful summer landscape, as lovely as a dream, and as lonesome as Sunday. The air was full of the smell of flowers, and the buzzing of insects, and the twittering of birds,

and there were no people, no wagons, there was no stir of life, nothing going on. The road was mainly a winding path with hoof-prints in it, and now and then a faint trace of wheels on either side in the grass—wheels that apparently had a tire as broad as one's hand.

Presently a fair slip of a girl, about ten years old, with a cataract of golden hair streaming down over her shoulders, came along. Around her head she wore a hoop of flame-red poppies. It was as sweet an outfit as ever I saw, what there was of it. She walked indolently along, with a mind at rest, its peace reflected in her innocent face. The circus man paid no attention to her; didn't even seem to see her. And she—she was no more startled at his fantastic make-up than if she was used to his like every day of her life. She was going by as indifferently as she might have gone by a couple of cows; but when she happened to notice me, *then* there was a change! Up went her hands, and she was turned to stone; her mouth dropped open, her eyes stared wide and timorously, she was the picture of astonished curiosity touched with fear. And there she stood gazing, in a sort of stupefied fascination, till we turned a corner of the wood and were lost to view. That she should be startled at me instead of at the other man, was too many for me; I couldn't make head or tail of it. And that she should seem to consider me a spectacle, and totally overlook her own merits in that respect, was another puzzling thing, and a display of magnanimity, too, that was surprising in one so young. There was food for thought here. I moved along as one in a dream. (10-11)

The nineteenth-century factory-man has an eye miraculously open to nature, even while retaining a nineteenth-century factory-man's evaluation of it. There is an implied criticism in the words "no stir of life, nothing going on" which contrasts with the enjoyment implicit in the list of pastoral attractions. Similarly, "lovely as a dream" is played off against "lonesome as Sunday." The womb of time is ambiguously used. If there is peace, there is nothing stirring; if there is security, there is also imprisonment. Sir Kay, the first person encountered in this new world, is encased in armor which so dehumanizes him that Hank labels the knight "that apparition" (16). Armor is protective and makes a man as "snug as a candle in a candle-mold" (90), but it also makes one "feel so strange and stuffy and like somebody else— ... sort of numb" (91).

The young girl's reaction to Hank plays up another aspect of this theme: she is part of the primitive world and can remain indifferent to the knight (Hank's "apparition"), whom, in Hank's telling phrase, she treats as "a couple of cows." But Hank himself is recognized as something to be feared. He is not one of the animals. The girl is right, too, for Hank will do all he can to destroy the sheepfold of Mother Church. The reader can himself anticipate Hank's antipathy to the church from his equation of "Sunday" with loneliness.

The girl's "sweet outfit" suggests the sensual side of sixth-century life. King Arthur's court is primitive and even pagan. His men are "dressed in such various and splendid colors that it hurt one's eyes to look at them" (18). The knights and ladies use language that "would have made a Comanche blush" (31), and Queen Guenever throws "furtive glances at Sir Launcelot that would have got him shot in Arkansas, to a dead certainty" (24). The naked girl is an introduction to this side of sixth-century life, but sensual abandon is what Hank is least ready to accept. He retains the quality that Twain attributed to "that shrewd Connec-ticut Yankee, Heber C. Kimball," in *Roughing It*, who is a prominent Mormon, but above all else, and his dutiful polyg-amy notwithstanding, "a mighty man of commerce" (III, 96). Hank is much more concerned with "getting ahead in the world" than with having a good time, and the two seem to him to be mutually exclusive. Later on, Hank considers that he is much too busy getting Arthur's kingdom into smooth working order to take time off for knight-errantry, and his first reaction to the "interruption" of his work by Sandy is the complaint that, "if signs went for anything, she didn't know as much as a lady's watch," even though he sees that "she was a comely enough creature, and soft and modest" (XIV, 83). He is concerned with the productive mind, not with the responsive body, and even before he becomes in his own right a "mighty man of commerce," his whole nature rebels against sensuality—and sexuality. He relates that when on his arrival at the court his clothes were removed for fear of their magical powers, he "was the only embarrassed person there" (32).

In the opening pages of the book Hank appears as the one stable element in a strange world. He is the productive man of the nineteenth century who will change none of his values, no matter what he is faced with. He is, indeed, a Tom Sawyer grown up. He knows beyond all doubt what is "right" and holds to his conceptions, even when they are inadequate. Likewise, as with Tom in his *Adventures* and when Abroad, the conquest of space is important to him. Early in his reformation of the kingdom he begins to make an extensive survey of the country. This project must be carried out secretly, because the church is against it (81). The very idea of a map violates the whole irresponsible spirit of the sixth century: "Nobody could tell you how to find any place in the kingdom, for nobody ever went intentionally to any place, but only struck it by accident in his wanderings, and then generally left it without thinking to inquire what its name was" (80). Such lack of control over space arouses Hank's bitterest impatience when Sandy tries to explain how to get to the Ogre's castle. Then, when he asks her if she has " 'got such a thing as a map of that region,' " she wonders, " 'Is it peradventure that manner of thing which of late the unbelievers have brought from over the great seas, which, being boiled in oil, and an onion and salt added thereto, doth—' " (86-87). To Hank, this "kind of sizes up the whole party," an echo of Tom's scorn for Huck's, or Jim's, or Billy Rogers' ignorance.

Also like Tom's is Hank's irresponsible love of excitement (356), his indifference to the injuring of uninvolved bystanders (370, 381). His spectacular effects at the Valley of Holiness, when he resuscitates a dried-out well to an accompaniment of eerie jabber and electrifying pyrotechnics, leave Hank as pleased with himself as Tom Sawyer ever is after one of his more modest "effects." "It was a great night," says Hank. "There was reputation in it. I could hardly get to sleep for glorying over it" (218). Since both Tom and Hank are more interested in the "glory" of a thing than in who gets hurt, it is not surprising that they both tend to see people as objects to be manipulated, mere abstractions that respond in pleasing ways to the workings of genius. Finally, it is not a coincidence that early in his *Adventures* Tom is the general of a boy's make-believe army, and that at the end of his visit to King Arthur's land Hank Morgan is the leader of an army of "boys" (432).

But Hank does not remain a Tom Sawyer. Hank changes, Hank questions, as Tom never does. His growth is important, because only as the sixth-century pace affects him does the split in feeling between sixth-century man and nineteenth-century man come to the forefront of the book. Hank says of his proposed Republic: "Well, I may as well confess, though I do feel ashamed when I think of it: I was beginning to have a base hankering to be its first president myself. Yes, there was more or less human nature in me; I found that out" (400). Hank grows, and if the story were told in the third person it would be difficult to appreciate the tone of this retrospective shame. Although Hank can examine his own motives once his actions are well in the past, part of the point of Hank's character is that although he is a New England Presbyterian, he is not an introspective brooder. He is a doer, only slightly a self-examiner, and his final defeat would affect a reader differently if Twain had emphasized any deep sense of guilt in Hank. Twain makes this clear when he interprets Hank's final words: "He was getting up his last 'effect'; but he never finished it" (450). This is the last sentence in the book, and it underlines Hank's commitment to action, his tendency to avoid self-awareness.

More important than characterization communicated through Hank's self-revelation is the picture one receives of Hank's uncritical commitment to nineteenth-century materialistic values. Hank calls his educational institution the "Man-factory" (109), and while the expressed purpose of this significantly-named school is to teach habits of independent thought and of free citizenship, as well as reading and writing, the fruits of the "factory" as the reader sees them are all materialistic or mechanical. Fireworks, bombs, electrical engineers, "experts" of one technology or another, soldiers—all these are mentioned, but never is any humanistic endeavor associated with the place.

The man of the machine age, of the "productive" life of the nineteenth century, is simply not in harmony with the "receptive" life of the sixth century.[11] The idyll of Hank's first paragraph is continued, and elaborated on, in the introduction to Arthur's court, and Hank's own terms suggest how out of place he feels amid scenes of such joyous abandon. The knights of the court have fun; they "receive stimuli"; they don't make things. Eating, drinking, and joking constitute the main business at court, and Hank finds "very characteristic of the country" the enjoyment of "high animal spirits, innocent indecencies of language, and happy-hearted indifference to morals" (69). Over and over Hank refers to the knights and ladies as children, his principal conclusion being that "there did not seem to be brains enough in the entire nursery, so to speak, to bait a fish-hook with; but you didn't seem to mind that, after a little, because you soon saw that brains were not needed in a society like that, and indeed would have marred it, hindered it, spoiled its symmetry— perhaps rendered its existence impossible" (21-22).

Hank speaks of this primitive society as though it were a work of art, a painting whose "symmetry" could be "spoiled" by the addition of a clashing color, and he quickly shows us that he is not an art-lover. He notices the palace tapestries and remarks that "as for proportions, even Raphael himself couldn't have botched them more formidably, after all his practice on those nightmares they call his 'celebrated Hampton Court cartoons.' Raphael was a bird" (52). This sounds much like the narrator of *The Innocents Abroad*, although Twain's own view of art is quite different, or at least is not to be inferred from his books: in *A Tramp Abroad* the narrator has changed his mind about "The Old Masters" and their duplicators; he finds that "the copy is to the original as the pallid, smart, inane new wax-work group is to the vigorous, earnest, dignified group of living men and women whom it professes to duplicate. There is a mellow richness, a subdued color, in the old pictures, which is to the eye what muffled and mellowed sound is to the ear" (X, 221). This is a far cry from calling Raphael "a bird," and it is worth noting that in *A Tramp Abroad* Twain is at some pains to paint the glories of the "receptive" life, as in rafting down the Neckar and ascending Mount Blanc by telescope—that is, ascending aesthetically and not practically. The people in *The Innocents* are out to "do" Europe, and so they have no time, and certainly no real patience, for art.

To Hank, Raphael's art is a "nightmare," as, at first, is his own existence in the sixth century (XIV, 34). After a while, he accepts the reality of his transmigration, but "for a time, I used to wake up, mornings, and smile at my 'dream,' . . . but . . . at last I was fully able to realize that I was actually living in the sixth century, and in Arthur's court, not a lunatic asylum" (60). Of note are the terms in which Hank approaches the sixth century: "I wouldn't have traded it for the twentieth. Look at the opportunities here for a man of knowledge, brains, pluck, and enterprise to sail in and grow up with the country" (60). As the idea that he is dreaming fades, Hank sets out to educate the "nursery." He is going to bring "progress" and "productivity" to the wilderness: the old New England conscience is at work. But his program ends with race suicide.

In terms of the dream-motif, Hank, just before he dies, gives Twain—and the reader—his final view of what has happened to him. Mistaking Twain for Sandy, he speaks:

"Have I been sick long? It must be so; it seems months to me. And such dreams! such strange and awful dreams, Sandy! Dreams that were as real as reality—delirium, of course, but *so* real! Why, I thought the king was dead, I thought you were in Gaul and couldn't get home, I thought there was a revolution; in the fantastic frenzy of these dreams, I thought that Clarence and I and a handful of my cadets fought and exterminated the whole chivalry of England! But even that was not the strangest. I seemed to be a creature out of a remote unborn age, centuries hence, and even *that* was as real as the rest! Yes, I seemed to have flown back out of that age into this of ours, and then forward to it again, and was set down, a stranger and forlorn in that strange England, with an abyss of thirteen centuries yawning between me and you! between me and my home and my friends! between me and all that is dear to me, all that could make life worth the living! It was awful—awfuler than you can ever imagine, Sandy. Ah, watch by me, Sandy—stay by me every moment—*don't* let me go out of my mind again; death is nothing, let it come, but not with those dreams, not with the torture of those hideous dreams— I cannot endure *that* again." (449)

The reversal is complete. Not "progress" but "home" and "friends" now constitute "all that could make life worth the living." "Knowledge, brains, pluck, and enterprise"—the values of the "productive" society, of nineteenth-century America—belong to what is now the "nightmare." Hank's statement early in the book that he wouldn't trade the sixth century for the twentieth is still true, but how different are the terms of its truth!

One accepts the change in Hank's thinking without question; the "feel" of the book overcomes any intellectual perplexity, and this is brought about mainly through Hank's particular use of language and allusion. Part of the effect is, of course, communicated simply through "plot," or through what the other characters say. The massacre of the sand-belt is an event that would have its effect no matter how the story were told. When Clarence informs Hank of the causes for the outbreak that led to the Interdict, and thus to the massacre, his mention of the part played by " 'one of your modern improvements—the stock-board' " (414) would be effective irony no matter how the fact itself were presented. In this last instance, however, much is gained through our recollection that Hank has earlier presented Sir Launcelot's attentions to Guenever as reprehensible by Arkansas standards (24). So long as "happy-hearted [sixth-century] indifference to morals" is the only issue, the king's eyes stay closed; but when Sir Launcelot begins to manipulate the market like a nineteenth-century "bull," his victims take pains to inform the king of Launcelot's attentions to the queen, and Hank's empire is threatened by the ensuing civil war. Progress and passion don't mix, as Hank's "modern" judgment of the queen's infidelity foreshadowed.

It is when Hank speaks directly for himself that the sixth century stands out most clearly in its complex relation to the nineteenth. Merlin "cursed like a bishop—French bishop of the Regency days, I mean" (198). Sandy's endless sentences give Hank "a mysterious and shuddery reverence for this

girl; ... it was borne in upon me that I was standing in the
awful presence of the Mother of the German Language"
(204). Sandy at least is a warm woman, but what can be
said in favor of the awful German language, which Hank
here puts into the distant future, along with the blasphemous
bishops? This is not to say that Hank ever forsakes his allegiance to his own century before he is actually dying. He
doesn't. But as the book progresses, Hank's language moves
farther and farther from his smug equation of living in "the
sixth century" with living "among lunatics" (16). Hank's
advertising campaigns, for instance, work in two directions.
He makes "sandwich-men" out of various knights, sending
them around the country to acquaint the people with mer-
chandise through slogans, and, often, through demonstration.
The introduction to this notion is particularly revealing,
especially as there is nothing of ridicule in Hank's straight-
forward language. Approaching a knight, Hank

saw that he wore a plumed helmet, and seemed to be otherwise
clothed in steel, but bore a curious addition also—a stiff square
garment like a herald's tabard. However, I had to smile at my
own forgetfulness when I got nearer and read this sign on his
tabard:

"*Persimmons's Soap—All the Prime-Donne Use It.*"

That was a little idea of my own, and had several wholesome
purposes in view toward the civilizing and uplifting of this
nation. In the first place, it was a furtive, underhand blow at this
nonsense of knight errantry, though nobody suspected that but
me. I had started a number of these people out—the bravest
knights I could get—each sandwiched between bulletin-boards
bearing one device or another, and I judged that by and by when
they got to be numerous enough they would begin to look ridiculous; and then, even the steel-clad ass that *hadn't* any board would
himself begin to look ridiculous because he was out of the fashion.

Secondly, these missionaries would gradually, and without
creating suspicion or exciting alarm, introduce a rudimentary

cleanliness among the nobility, and from them it would work down to the people, if the priests could be kept quiet. This would undermine the Church. I mean would be a step toward that. Next, education—next, freedom—and then she would begin to crumble. (127-28)

For Hank, modern advertising methods ridicule the barbaric life of the sixth century, and lead, however indirectly, to social reform. But the soap-man, unaware of the Boss's double motive, takes his job seriously and is "much depressed," for a hermit he had washed, in order to demonstrate the harmless efficacy of his product, had lost him his sale by dying, "and would take his place among the saints of the Roman Calendar" (130). Hank consoles the knight and turns "'that Mount Washington defeat into a Matterhorn victory'" by adding to the advertisement, "'Patronized by the Elect',", and, says Hank, "'a body is bound to admit that for just a modest little one-line ad., it's a corker'" (131). Hank will use the methods and the ritual of the very institution he aims to overthrow in order to sell his soap. The increased ridiculousness contributed by this line—it was, after all, only through an unwilling "patronage" that the hermit had the chance to "prove" his election—reflects on nineteenth-century advertising as well as on sixth-century knight-errantry and church. Inadvertently, Hank is looking in two directions at once. His language itself suggests that he is perhaps acquiring a sixth-century frame of reference, for the "square garment" of the unknown knight immediately suggests to Hank "a herald's tabard." The simile is noticeably not of the nineteenth century.

A subsequent encounter with another victim of Hank's adaptation of this nineteenth-century technique to the non-acquisitive sixth century pushes both edges of the sword even deeper into the conflict. Hank and Sandy are resting "under some trees by a limpid brook":

Right so came by and by a knight riding; and as he drew near he made dolorous moan, and by the words of it I perceived that he was cursing and swearing; yet nevertheless was I glad of his coming, for that I saw he bore a bulletin-board whereon in letters all of shining gold was writ:

"USE PETERSON'S PROPHYLACTIC TOOTH-BRUSH—ALL THE GO."

I was glad of his coming, for even by this token I knew him for knight of mine. (167)

Hank's pastiche of Sir Thomas Malory's style is as much an inadvertent adoption of the language he has been hearing since his arrival at Arthur's court as it is a satire on that language. Sandy herself talks in this way, and since Sandy, immediately preceding the rest beneath the trees, has been relating the life histories of a group of captured knights, Hank's introduction to the toothbrush knight is, in context, more of an identification with the sixth century than a rejection of it. The ridiculous feature is in the mood-shattering contrast between hustling commercialism and the leisurely dignity of the archaic phraseology. The humor is complete when one learns that the unhappy knight is lamenting a false lead given him by Sir Ossaise, "the stove-polish man. . . . There were no stoves yet, and so there could be nothing serious about stove-polish" (168), explains Hank. The context of the episode adds further meaning, for Sir Ossaise had recommended as prospective toothbrush buyers "the five [toothless] patriarchs" (169) whom Hank has recently released from Morgan la Fay's dungeons. Toothbrushes and prison-reform are here incompatible. Twain, through his control of the events in the story, underlines the conflict in Hank while leaving Hank unaware of any problem within himself. Hank sees advertising and social reform in a cause-and-effect relationship (128, quoted above), but in this case the two are in direct opposition.

It is the increasing but unvoiced split, or "tension," in Hank's feelings that demands a first-person narrative and that is the most important single element in *A Connecticut Yankee*. Hank must not brood, must not even be aware that his social gospel is unavoidably a gospel of destruction, personal as well as social. Over and over, he tells the reader one thing, and then shows him that the opposite is true also—sometimes, true "instead." Hank sees no problem in taking over sixth-century England, for "I judged I would have the start of the best-educated man in the kingdom by a matter of thirteen hundred years and upward" (16). But when Hank's superior knowledge enables him to establish his position because of the eclipse, his use of that knowledge is sheer "bluff." When Hank discusses political economy with Dowley and the others, he sees himself as "the first statesman of the age . . . defeated in argument by an ignorant country black-smith!" Hank's pride is hurt: "Put yourself in my place; feel as mean as I did, as ashamed as I felt—wouldn't *you* have struck back below the belt to get even? Yes, you would; it is simply human nature. Well, that is what I did. I am not trying to justify it; I'm only saying that I was mad, and *anybody* would have done it" (329). Since Hank's "low blow" leads him and the king directly into slavery, "brains" and "human nature" are a dangerous mixture. That "brains" alone can lead to trouble is made explicit in the further troubles of Hank and King Arthur. At one point the angry mob sends a man up a tree near the stream down which the two have fled, and Hank, who has led the king to an adjacent tree,

was obliged to admire my cuteness in foreseeing this very thing and swapping trees to beat it. But, don't you know, there are some things that can beat smartness and foresight? Awkwardness and stupidity can. . . . Well, how could I, with all my gifts, make any valuable preparation against a near-sighted, cross-eyed, pudding-headed clown who would aim himself at the wrong tree and hit the right one? And that is what he did. He went for the wrong tree, which was, of course, the right one by mistake, and up he started. (344-45)

Hank's brains constitute his most important nineteenth-century "asset." He is proud of his intelligence, although he can recognize its occasional failure to help him. Significantly often, his intelligence appears to be that of an adult Tom Sawyer, avatar of nineteenth-century boyhood, especially in episodes dramatizing his love of adventure and of "style." After Hank's complicated escape-plot has partially succeeded, he is trying to stay clear of the law until he can get help from Camelot to save the king, who is still in captivity as a slave. Hank is caught after trying a most elaborate ruse on a police officer, and, as he writes, can see for himself that it was a

mistake. A double one, in fact. There were plenty of ways to get rid of that officer by some simple and plausible device, but no, I must pick out a picturesque one; it is the crying defect of my character. And then, I had ordered my procedure upon what the officer, being human, would *naturally* do; whereas when you are least expecting it, a man will now and then go and do the very thing which it's *not* natural for him to do. (376)

Hank is recaptured easily. Tom Sawyer's approach to freeing Jim leads to Jim's recapture, too. Seeking adventure along mechanically-determined lines is not profitable, any more than is a mechanical, ratiocinative anticipation of a human being's reactions. Whether Hank tries too hard for a sensation or relies on human intelligence to the exclusion of the irrational, he is trying to treat people like machines. Over and over again he recognizes, but fails to remember, that not everything can be predicted in the realm of human behavior, that even though "we have no thoughts of our own, no opinions of our own," but are mainly the final link in "a progression of ancestors that stretches back a billion years," still, there remains "that one microscopic atom in me that is truly *me*" (150). He meets a peasant who has a keen sense of injustice, and he knows that "a man *is* a man, at bottom. Whole ages of abuse and oppression cannot crush the manhood clear out of him" (301). But his sense of what makes a man is a very controlled, mechanical sense.

Brains and "literary" adventure are equally out of place in the "nursery" of sixth-century life. Nobody wants to "bait a fish-hook." No one is that deliberate. The training that Hank devises for his "West-Pointers" equips them to overwhelm Arthur's military examiners with "mathematical nightmares on the blackboard that would stump the angels themselves" (240); but where is the good in teaching a "nursery" lad "all about siege-guns, field-guns, Gatling guns, rifled guns" (239)? The result is the slaughter at the end of the book. "Educate!" is the nineteenth-century cry that rings through Hank's narrative, but Hank's greatest satisfactions come from being with Sandy, "the untutored infant of the sixth [century]" (204).

In Hank's final nightmare, his dream-talk reveals that he knows the meaning of his story, but nothing that he says during the narrative itself suggests any such conscious knowledge on his part. Twain has no political or economic remedies to propose as a solution to modern ills. His "answer" is in terms of his art, and we will need to go further into his art to find it. But he is saying through Hank that man is not built to live by the machine, nor is man's "soul" built to enable him to live like one. Between Hank's dedicated acceptance of the nineteenth century as he knows it and his presentation of the effects of nineteenth-century values on the primitive life of the sixth century, there exists a tension that is in the end unresolved. This tension gives life to the book, and at the same time gives the reader pause. The machine mentality may be destructive, but there is no going back to the womb of civilization. Huckleberry Finn is a boy, and he can dream of lighting out for the territory; Hank Morgan can only die. His story might be the story of any reformer whose view of humanity has become too simple.

III

Parodies and Burlesques

4

Form and Force

TWAIN DEVELOPED the comic frontier narrator into a fictional tool which the sophisticated writer could use to suggest to his reader differing attitudes toward the events of a story. The complacencies of Huck toward slavery, of Hank toward mechanical progress, through implicit contrast throw Twain's judgments into relief, while simultaneously vivifying the emotions that underlie the opposing evaluations of author and character. This advance beyond the merely humorous effect of a frontier strategy suggests Twain's concern with discovering to his reader the complexities and contradictions he finds in human experience. More is at stake than simple fun and simple realism. Twain's use of narrative point of view reveals the dynamic processes of his characters' minds as well as the surface of their world.

The comic narrator is just one of the important elements of contemporary storytelling that Twain could make use of for his serious purposes. Equally valuable is the imitation of sophisticated literary forms and of social stereotypes in parodies and burlesques. Just as Twain's narrators arise from the frontier tradition, so the lampooning impulse latent in parody and burlesque is an offshoot of frontier aggression against the eastern intruder. On the other hand, specific allusions to and variations on exclusively literary material derive from Twain's extensive contact with English and French literature during his California apprenticeship and subsequent eastern development. That much of Twain's allusion is to the Bible should be no surprise, but that so very much is to popular New York drama, the lesser works of Victor Hugo (as Franklin R. Rogers* has demonstrated), and, in general, to the standard patterns of sophisticated literature of his day, concretely suggests the distance that Twain traveled from the frontier.

Apart from organizing many of his works through the form of burlesques, Twain uses allusive materials in a way that has an important effect upon his reader. From his simplest biblical allusions to his most complex parodies and burlesques, Twain with great success creates a dual perspective by his contrasts between the situation he is describing and the source of the allusions he draws on. The oblique references to David and Goliath in Hank Morgan's tournament offer a case in point. The preparations for Hank's duel with Sir Sagramor are fittingly impressive, gaining much of their dignity from the biblical echo. As Hank and Sir Sagramor face the king and queen, Guenever exclaims, " 'Alack, Sir Boss, wilt fight naked and without lance or sword or —' " (XIV, 388). The contrast between the two warriors is underscored when Hank refers to his opponent as "an imposing tower of iron," "the iron tower," "the gorgeous bed-quilt," "the big knight" (387-89). After Merlin steals Hank's lasso, Sir Launcelot limps up to offer the unarmed man his sword. "But Sir Sagramor said: 'Stay, it may not be. He shall fight

*Franklin R. Rogers, in *Mark Twain's Burlesque Patterns: As Seen in the Novels and Narratives, 1855-1885* (Dallas: Southern Methodist University Press, 1960), shows at length how Twain's early experimentation with literary burlesque, encouraged by the San Francisco literati, eventually suggested various ways of organizing the material of long narratives. Mr. Rogers' well-documented study demonstrates how self-consciously literary this experimentation was, and explores the different ways in which Twain manipulated his narrators in conformity to burlesque patterns.

with his own weapons; it were his privilege to choose them
and bring them. If he has erred, on his head be it' " (393).
One can hardly read these lines without recalling the preparations for the combat of David with Goliath, and it is
probable that Twain remembered, too, for "David and
Goliath" was one of his favorite biblical references, used with
devastating effect when Tom Sawyer, in answer to Judge
Thatcher's Sunday-school query, names the warriors as two
of the twelve disciples.

David will not accept Saul's armor and sword, "for he had
not proved it" (I Sam. 17:39). Goliath taunts David for his
lack of arms. "Am I a dog, that thou comest to me with staves?
... I will give thy flesh unto the fowls of the air, and to the
beasts of the field" (I Sam. 17:43-44). So Sir Sagramor
taunts Hank for his lack of a weapon. In each case, the
"unpromising hero"—unpromising in the eyes of his opponent
and of the spectators—is fighting for something greater than
himself. David tells Goliath, "I come to thee in the name of
the Lord of hosts, the God of the armies of Israel, whom thou
hast defied." Hank's duel excites such great interest because
"all the nation knew that this was not to be a duel between
mere men, so to speak, but ... a final struggle for supremacy
between the two master enchanters of the age" (XIV, 385).
Just as David represents not only God but also the Jews, so
Hank sees himself not only as an "enchanter" but as representing a completely earthly force as well: "I was a champion,
it was true, but not the champion of the frivolous black arts,
I was the champion of hard unsentimental common sense and
reason. I was entering the lists to either destroy knight-
errantry or be its victim" (386). Hank presents himself as a
"modern" David; he knows that right is on his side, and when
he finally kills Sir Sagramor with a bullet from his revolver,
he feels no more remorse than David expresses after his stone
has ended Goliath's life. Hank's defeat, like David's, would

have meant not only his own death but the death of his civilization.

The biblical parallel adds dignity and importance to the episode. In contrast with the implied biblical setting, however, two discordant notes in Hank's presentation—pride and bluff—create an effect of irony. Hank's personal pride as he awaits Sir Launcelot's charge is expressed in terms that undercut the "sense and reason" of which Hank considers himself the champion: "Across my mind flitted the dear image of a certain hello-girl of West Hartford, and I wished she could see me now" (391). This is human nature, but it is precisely this side of sixth-century human nature that Hank is striking at in condemning knight-errantry. The other unbiblical note in the tournament is Hank's admission of his "bluff" (395). In proving the supremacy of "the magic of science" over "the magic of fol-de-rol" (396), he uses a bluff of "fol-de-rol" to eke out his bullets of science; he must pretend that his two revolvers are supernatural messengers of death, with inexhaustible powers, for "if I spent the eleventh shot without convincing these people, the twelfth man would kill me, sure" (395). David is never in a position of bluff, nor is he guilty of pride. His trust is in God, not in science, and he does not need to "show off" to anyone. Hank discovers that science alone—the revolvers—will not suffice, so he must bluff. He is guilty of pride because his reliance on his own scientific ingenuity prevents him from seeing himself as merely the servant of the force he worships. The suggestion that nineteenth-century Americans worship the machine and see themselves as God's Chosen People rounds out the irony of the implicit contrast between David and Hank.

However much this scene draws on the Bible, it is certainly no parody or burlesque, either of biblical language or of biblical action. It is simply a parallel, a literary use of biblical material. Twain here draws on the Bible for a serious purpose, but elsewhere he does not. In *Roughing It*, he tells us of his affliction with the tale of Hank Monk and Horace Greeley, a tale he later used for the substance of Nat Parson's wild ride in "Tom Sawyer Abroad." After several people have annoyed Twain by reciting the anecdote, he suggests that a fitting punishment for the story's originator will be found in "the sixteenth chapter of Daniel . . . Aha!" (III, 143). The Book of Daniel has only twelve chapters, the last of which details the punishment of the wicked, "in shame and contempt," when the world shall end. To suggest a punishment so severe that it can only be mentioned four chapters after the end of Daniel is merely to enjoy the humorous exaggeration of a minor annoyance. The humor and the annoyance are both expressed, but there is no connection between the Book of Daniel and the context in which Twain makes the reference.

Different, although related, is Jim's admonition to Huck that " 'we better let blame' well alone' " (XIII, 92). As the source for his advice Jim refers to "de good book," which uses no such language; the burlesque of "sufficient unto the day . . ." emphasizes the disparity between the appearance of Jim and Huck on the raft and the conventional view of Christian behavior. Jim's and Huck's behavior takes the form of anything but saintliness: they "borrow" whatever they can get their hands on, except, of course, for "crabapples and p'simmons" (91); and they are continuously in the act of stealing valuable property, as Jim is an expensive slave, "wuth eight hund'd dollars" (65). But just as Jim's words express the essence of the biblical phrases, so at heart Jim and Huck do make what Lionel Trilling has called "a community of Saints."[1] The serious implications of Jim's paraphrase can be enlarged upon, but as humor, his words serve the same purpose as the reference to the sixteenth chapter of Daniel:

both arouse laughter by presenting a solemn association in a context that is ridiculous or insignificant—although the passage in *Huckleberry Finn,* while it seems trivial, is not.

In casual reference and in detailed parallels, Twain uses biblical material to suggest multiple significance in scenes that seem unambiguous. This is the same effect he achieves through his combined use of parody and burlesque in a single episode. To distinguish between them, burlesque might be considered as an alteration of content within a given form; parody, a preservation of content in an altered form. The duke's version of Hamlet's soliloquy is a burlesque, as the form of the original is preserved despite the drastic alteration in content. The rituals of "Tom Sawyer's Gang" are parody, for Tom preserves the words that signify the machinations of a cutthroat band, while forcing them into a context, a form, of boyish pranks. Although satire is implied in these examples, and in the two forms themselves, consideration of humor and satire must for the moment give way to the problem of form.

Just as allusions can create a multiple effect, so too can parody and burlesque which are, in a sense, types of extended allusion. In "Legend of the 'Spectacular Ruin,' " a representative sample from Twain's work (see Appendix), elements of parody and burlesque are combined to achieve a complex evaluation of chivalry and science; the two forms suggest different ways of interpreting the story.

The contrast between the unloving, unsentimental hero of "The Ruin" and the heroes of legitimate legend is strengthened through a burlesque of the same material Twain was to use in Hank's tournament. The explicit presentation of his knight as the "unpromising hero" (2),* beginning with the castle itself and emphasized through repetition

*Numbers here refer to elements and themes enumerated in the Appendix.

right up to the combat, depicts in unflattering terms not only the hero but his science as well, "for science was despised in those days." David's reliance on God and Hank's and Sir Wissenschaft's reliance on science are presented in similar terms. The "David theme" (10) is here, however, a source of parody; the formal sequence of preparation, discouragement, and final victory is given a surprise fillip when the knight vanquishes his foe with such ease and certainty. Most legends are so organized that their climax comes with the battle. Here, however, the form that the story takes places the emphasis on the preparation, the combat itself occupying an insignificant part of the tale. Because of the upset to the reader's expectation, the explanation of how the battle was won is much more important than the mere fighting, and instead of leading one to share the hero's elation, the form throws one back to a more detached view of the events. The dragon very quickly "curled up and died"; there was no risk, and so no suspense; the victory was certain from the start.

The unheroic caution of this hero who "stole warily to a good position" is of the same stripe as his financial motive in asking "if the emperor's offer was still in force." The hero— the "tramp"—is in many respects admirable as a man of science, but his single-minded dedication to affairs of the "head" to the exclusion of the "heart" is at the center of the burlesque. The balancing of themes 1 and 7 is done in such a way that all the other themes brought into the legend can be organized around the pair. At the beginning, the very stones of the "monopolist's" castle enjoy a more loving relationship than any of the personages in the story, for the theme of money is triumphant over the theme of love. The equation of "daughter" with "pay" brings both themes together with a surprising bluntness—especially surprising because this is a legend, and one expects a king's daughter to be treated respectfully in legend. The formula, "My daughter

and half my kingdom," is familiar to all readers; through
the two gifts a king can deal separately with the warmth of
love and the cold financial prerequisite for any love nest.
The hero of this legend is at one point viewed as a "mother"
to the baby dragons he raises in his laboratory, but this
relationship is coldly experimental, not maternal: love *is*
money, and money is all. There is no separation.

The cash basis upon which the knight does business is
underscored by the unheroic, commonplace language used
throughout the piece (3). This strand of the language aims
at reducing emotional elements to materialistic value only;
the "procession" of knights, the "surplusage" and the "detachment" of daughters, assign a cash value, so to speak, to love
and glory, just as the raft-captain's narrative ability is
degraded by the word "stick" and the knight's lack of daring
highlighted by the nonfeudal "laboratory" in which he has
done his real fighting. Word-theme 3 is complemented by
theme 5, a use of modern expressions or words—such as
"knap-sack," "rail-way train," the "sale of spectacles," and
the bringing of "brains" to one's aid—which functions mainly
to play off the nineteenth century against the days of legend.
Understatement (4) and defeated expectation (8), apart
from their significance as popular humor-producing devices
of nineteenth-century American humorists, emphasize this
break between the legend-form and its parody, as does the
insistence on the ordinary quality of what usually pass for
the components of a sensational adventure (6). The legend-
theme itself (11) is burlesqued by attributing myth-over-
tones to a story that has dealt with such sordid things as
monetary reward and scientific research. The presence of
Christ-parallels in the knight's adventure (9) completes the
burlesque and parody qualities of the story.

The satire on unthoughtful acceptance of religious habit
is obvious enough: the "monopoly" of David-Christ-Wissen-

schaft originates a "widespread custom" and "a custom once established in these old lands is imperishable." The edifice commemorating the "monopolist," though "once stately and sumptuous," is "now called the 'Spectacular Ruin.'" The combining of myth with parody and burlesque is here satirical, and, as in Twain's best pieces, serves to organize the story and also to attack in two directions at once. The satire works not only against a vacant religiosity but also against the serious acceptance on the reader's part of the excitements of legend. The emphasis on the "customary"(6) presence of what is usually taken to be uniquely horrifying throws the whole legend-genre into a new light. Instead of being caught up in the archetypal qualities of the pattern, Twain's way of undercutting the excitement is to put his reader on a level of observation rather than of involvement. The emphasis on the "archetype" in this case makes one blasé about the particular instance. Also, however, this distance makes one less sympathetic to the "scientific" as well as to the "romantic" overtones suggested by the plot. The noble grace and high motivation of legendary heroes are superior to the base materialism of the monopolist, who seems a living burlesque of the old nobility of thought. His lack of bravery, his cold calculation, and his indifference to love contrast strongly and unfavorably with the "standard" knight of legend in a similar circumstance. On the other hand, his David-like steadfastness in the face of discouragement, his Christlike meekness under scorn, his scientific thoroughness and patience, to say nothing of his reduction of the price of spectacles, all operate as a deadly parody of the impractical impetuosity of the "renowned knights" and their infantile retirement. The parody and the burlesque point in different directions.

In most cases where Twain uses such a combination of parody and burlesque it cuts two ways: his attack on nine-

teenth-century materialism in *A Connecticut Yankee* is no
less strong than his condemnation of the "romantic" frame
of reference. In *A Tramp Abroad*, it is directly after "The
Lorelei" that Twain presents "The Spectacular Ruin." Twain's
approach to "The Lorelei" has been most reverent; yet "The
Ruin" is, among other things, ridiculing the legend-genre
itself, a genre in which Twain occasionally worked most
happily. "Baker's Bluejay Yarn," for instance, might almost
be the legend of an old, deserted house that happened to
stand in California, rather than by the Rhine: " 'Seven years
ago, the last man in this region but me moved away. There
stands his house—been empty ever since; a log house, with a
plank roof . . .' "(IX, 18). And so on. It is not the legend itself
that Twain is undercutting, but rather the sentimentality of
many legends. "The Cave of the Specter," also in *A Tramp
Abroad*, is archetypically sentimental, and its heroine is
as "chuckleheaded" as Baker's bluejay, so far as Twain
is concerned.

II

Any parody or burlesque implies the existence of a given
subject to measure itself against. Something, clearly, must be
being parodied or burlesqued. Through his use of overly
sentimental material earlier in *A Tramp Abroad*, for instance,
Twain provides something of a standard—at least in so far as
a general feeling can serve as such—with which to contrast
"The Ruin," with its unsentimental echoes of the legend
genre. Most of Twain's paradoxes and burlesques have as
their target something even more general than the sentimentality of the typical Rhine legend. "Romance" in one
form or another is the implicit standard against which much
of Twain's literary effort is to be measured. It will be necessary, therefore, to define briefly the essential meaning of
"romance" as it appears in Twain's writing.

In *Life on the Mississippi,* immediately after referring to
two representatives of nineteenth-century business practice
as "the two scoundrels" (XII, 330), Twain launches his fierce
attack on Sir Walter Scott as the man not only "in great
measure responsible for the [Civil] war"(376), but responsible as well for the postwar continuation of "maudlin
Middle-Age romanticism here in the midst of the plainest
and sturdiest and infinitely greatest and worthiest of all the
centuries the world has seen"(334).

In the parodies and burlesques, romance is, to Twain, the
source of an illegitimate excitement or sensation. This is a
broad definition, and calls for immediate distinction between
romance and melodrama. Melodrama implies the arousing
of an emotion, the causing of a sensation, for its own sake.
It implies a specific incident and the reader's reaction to
it. Romance usually implies a structure around which to
organize incidents. Mark Twain never seems very much
concerned about melodramatic excitement: he uses scenes
that might become melodramatic, avoids the potential melodrama, and in general does not attack melodrama as such.
When Huck Finn discovers that he and Jim are trapped
aboard the *Walter Scott* with a band of murdering thieves,
Huck "catched my breath and most fainted. Shut up on a
wreck with such a gang as that!" His next sentence, however,
destroys the melodramatic overtones he has just created. "But
it warn't no time to be sentimentering. We'd *got* to find
that boat now—had to have it for ourselves" (XIII, 98).
Huck's further dangers in this passage are needed as ballast
for the end of the book, but the matter-of-fact way in which
the threats occur and are passed over keeps the story from
becoming a series of excitements used for their own sake.

Huck's use of the word "sentimentering" and Twain's
naming of the *Walter Scott* in an episode that suggests
the excitement of melodrama are both relevant. While

melodrama is not necessarily romantic, nineteenth-century romance is usually melodramatic. How better establish the virtue of a prospective hero than by providing him with excitements to which he can react, or by making him react excitedly to events that are in themselves commonplace? However, the causes for the rise of the notion that to feel deeply was to prove oneself virtuous lie beyond the scope of this volume. It is enough to say that the fictional character's virtue could be established by showing his strong emotional response even to daily existence. Early in James Fenimore Cooper's *The Spy*, Harper, an apparently threatening stranger who will later turn out to be George Washington in disguise, reassures the heroine of the story, and the reader, of his real goodness by his response to nothing more momentous than a sunset:

"What a magnificent scene!" said Harper, in a low tone; "how grand! how awfully sublime!—...."
... There can be no danger apprehended from such a man, thought Frances; such feelings belong only to the virtuous.[2]

Frances will gamble the life of her brother on the strength of such evidence, and she will win. The Man of Feeling, as the title of Henry MacKenzie's book suggests, needs no more than his feelings to recommend him as a reliable moral entity. And the same equation persisted—perhaps, to a degree, still persists—in real life, for the reader's virtue is similarly established, at least in his own eyes, if he can react emotionally to the situation in the fiction he reads. This is melodrama, because the reader's virtue is quite outside the artistic point of any art. The exciting incidents of a romance, however artificial they may be, are thus morally acceptable, and in themselves imply no break with social convention. It is important to see this clearly: although the "adventures" of a romance often seem most unconventional, the form of the romance—as distinguished from its content—is, of all prose forms utilized in the early nineteenth century, the most conventional, the most conservative, and the most "social." Just as the dashing hero gallops back to the respectability of his social position, so the reader finds himself assured of his own virtue within the moral framework of his time and place. Virtue is, after all, social, and, in the words of Benjamin Franklin, "Nothing so likely to make a man's fortune as virtue."

But what exactly is romance? "Usually," says D. H. Lawrence, "a nice little tale where you have everything As You Like It, where rain never wets your jacket and gnats never bite your nose and it's always daisy-time."[3] But if the concept of romance is to be helpful, it needs to subsume more than mere subject matter. "Sentimentality of feeling and of language" is a possible definition,[4] but an insufficient one: the romance is a form, not a technique. Through this form, a writer can manipulate the forces with which society must deal by personifying those forces as characters in a story. As many critics and scholars have pointed out, the blonde, the dark-haired girl, the hero, the villain, all are representative, or archetypal, rather than individual.

Archetypes become stereotypes, stereotyped characters imply a convention, and conventions aim at conserving something. What exactly is it that the romance seeks to conserve? In the broadest terms, it is the social order as it exists. The contrast between the light-haired and dark-haired girls is only one element in a form that aims at combining the thrills of sin with the sanctity of legality. The romance structure takes the reader on a conducted tour from the safety and respectability of the fireside out into the no-man's-land of political, metaphysical, or sexual exploration. Then, because the tour is indeed "conducted," it brings him back again. Ivanhoe, for instance, may dally with Rebecca and

fight exciting battles, but in the end he must return to a life
of safe respectability with the fair Rowena, last of the Saxon
princesses. Since Ivanhoe's return is made possible only
because he has so struggled, and since he wants that return
to be what it is, this romance is conservation with a venge-
ance. In *The Gilded Age,* Philip Sterling—whose name tells
all—explores the West, struggles in the East, feels, in however
forced and temporary a way, the seductive influence of dark-
haired Laura, and suffers various physical and mental pains,
but in the end he is happy and rich and married.

Twain's use of romanticism in *The Gilded Age* is, in
general, serious. Guilty Laura's brokenhearted death is as
much a part of the romantic pattern as is Philip's marriage
to Ruth; even the light and dark hair of women is played
upon, as Laura's lawyer begins his defense of the dark-haired
murderess by announcing that " 'the story I have to tell is
of a lovely little girl, with sunny hair' "(VI, 239). Laura is
really acceptable, he seems to say; she became dark-haired
only after the steamboat explosion and is entitled to be
judged as though she were a blonde. Even in this clumsy
romance, however, there is some of Twain's typical mockery
of the romance itself, as when Laura "had just reached the
romantic age—the age when there is a sad sweetness, a dismal
comfort to a girl to find out that there is a mystery connected
with her birth, which no other piece of good luck can afford"
(V, 98). Twain goes on to admit that "to be human is to have
one's little modicum of romance secreted away in one's
composition" which will lead one to manufacture mystery
and excitement out of daily life. But any reader of Twain can
call to mind many examples of his satirically ironic use of
romantic excitement, as when Tom Sawyer glories in visions
of Becky Thatcher's reaction to his death: "This picture
brought such an agony of pleasurable suffering that he
worked it over and over again in his mind and set it

up in new and varied lights, till he wore it threadbare"
(VIII, 26-27). This excitement is part of a romantic structure
rather than merely melodrama, for with it goes the reader's
assumption that within the frame of romance Tom and
Becky will be happily reconciled, and all will be well. And
so it happens: Tom gets the girl as well as the gold, and ends
the book by urging Huck Finn to become a respectable
member of society in order to join Tom's gang.

The form of the romance gives organization not only to
Tom Sawyer and *The Gilded Age* but, through burlesque, to
such diverse works as "The Esquimaux Maiden's Romance"
and "Skeleton for a Black Forest Novel." Repeatedly, Twain
uses parody and burlesque to undercut the conventional
social values conventionally supported by conventional
romance. In the "Black Forest Novel," the struggling hero
wins the girl only after he returns to the social fold, and his
final respectability is guaranteed by his possession of a large
quantity of manure; in the "Esquimaux Romance," wealth
and social standing stem from the possession of fishhooks.
One remembers that, for Tom Sawyer, robbers occupy the
pinnacle of social respectability.

III

Although there is little sustained satire in Twain's works,
and none comparable to *Don Quixote* or *Gulliver's Travels*,
one continuous thread of satire running through most of his
writing is anchored to his use of parody and burlesque to
ridicule the sterile neatness of the form that most "romances"
take. The formal nature of Twain's quarrel with romanticism
can best be seen in the contrast between his preface to *The
Gilded Age* and Hawthorne's preface to *The Marble Faun*.

Hawthorne's conception of the "romance" involves at
least two elements. Of *The Marble Faun* he says: "The
author proposed to himself merely to write a fanciful story,

evolving a thoughtful moral, and did not propose attempting a portraiture of Italian manners and character. . . ." The "thoughtful moral" of Hawthorne's romance is never the "Ben Franklin moral" of a Scott romance, especially not in *The Marble Faun,* for in Hawthorne's eyes Hilda, although a blonde, is guilty of a great sin in her failure to accept evil as the source of man's brotherhood with man; the moral iconography of romance, however, pictures the blonde as innocent. The moral of which Hawthorne speaks is surely "thoughtful," for some sophistication is needed before one can commit oneself to the proposition that too great innocence is in itself culpable. As for the "fanciful" element of romance, its importance to Hawthorne is apparent. However Trollopian his notebooks, his romances are more concerned with "atmosphere" than with "portraiture." One remembers the celestial "A" in *The Scarlet Letter,* Zenobia's exotic flower in *The Blithedale Romance,* the bleeding portrait in *The House of the Seven Gables,* and Donatello's mystical sympathy with animals in *The Marble Faun* itself.

In his preface to *The Marble Faun,* Hawthorne goes on to lament the plight of the would-be romancer in unfanciful America, and commends Italy as a welcome stimulus to his own romancing:

Italy, as the site of his Romance, was chiefly valuable to him as affording a sort of poetic or fairy precinct, where actualities would not be so terribly insisted upon as they are, and must needs be, in America. No author, without a trial, can conceive of the difficulty of writing a romance about a country where there is no shadow, no antiquity, no mystery, no picturesque and gloomy wrong, nor anything but a commonplace prosperity, in broad and simple daylight, as is happily the case with my dear native land. It will be very long, I trust, before romance-writers may find congenial and easily handled themes, either in the annals of our stalwart republic, or in any characteristic and probable events of our individual lives. Romance and poetry, ivy, lichens, and wall-flowers, need ruin to make them grow.

Hawthorne's irony, here, is directed at America, not at the conventional excitement arising from the account of a "picturesque and gloomy wrong." To present life as a series of aesthetically pleasing relationships is, for Hawthorne, the artist's concern. He accepts without question the evil that accompanies the fitting conditions of romance, specifically itemizing physical and moral "ruin" as the prerequisites for romance. The irony is even more telling if one remembers Henry James's summation of Hawthorne's era:

The generation to which he belonged, that generation which grew up with the century, witnessed during a period of fifty years the immense, uninterrupted material development of the young Republic; and when one thinks of the scale on which it took place, of the prosperity that walked in its train and waited on its course, of the hopes it fostered and the blessings it conferred—of the broad morning sunshine, in a word, in which it all went forward—there seems to be little room for surprise that it should have implanted a kind of superstitious faith in the grandeur of the country, its duration, its immunity from the usual troubles of earthly empires. This faith was a simple and uncritical one, enlivened with an element of genial optimism, in the light of which it appeared that the great American state was not as other human institutions are, that a special Providence watched over it, that it . . . must come off easily, in the battle of the ages.[5]

It is obvious that Hawthorne's "faith" in the excellence of America was hardly "simple and uncritical," however much James wanted it to be so for the sake of his argument that Hawthorne had to struggle against an all-encompassing provinciality. Hawthorne makes his critical judgment of American morality in the guise of an aesthetic reaction only; since his own romances disprove—to Hawthorne's satisfaction though not to James's—his expressed view of America's

paucity of material for the romance, the only inference is
that America is not so light and airy and "sunny" as it might
seem to be, and that behind American efforts to appear
flawless lies a real depravity. So Hilda, the blonde in *The
Marble Faun,* is innocent and free and even "commonplace"
in her paintings, yet her failure of sympathy is a greater sin
than Miriam's and Donatello's "gloomy wrong."

Mark Twain in the preface to his work takes an equally
ironic stance with Hawthorne so far as an attitude toward
America is concerned. Like Hawthorne, Twain presents his
impatience with America's failings in terms of the problems
confronting the artist who must deal with the country in
fiction. But Twain's irony is double: not only is he saying
the reverse of what he means about his country, he also
insists that his story is not at all a romance by his patently
ironic claim to be writing as "fanciful" or "ideal" a tale as
Hawthorne—or any other romancer—ever penned:

> It will be seen that it [this book] deals with an entirely ideal
> state of society; and the chief embarrassment of the writers in
> this realm of the imagination has been the want of illustrative
> examples. In a state where there is no fever of speculation, no
> inflamed desire for sudden wealth, where the poor are all simple-
> minded and contented, and the rich are all honest and generous,
> where society is in a condition of primitive purity, and politics is
> the occupation of only the capable and the patriotic, there are
> necessarily no materials for such a history as we have constructed
> out of an ideal commonwealth. (V, xxi)

Twain's lamentations are expressed in terms of specific detail
that can serve as an artist's model. His irony suggests that
he is not concerned with the atmosphere of romance, but,
seemingly, only with the transcription of reality in as "realistic" a way as possible. As Leo Marx suggests,[6] Twain ultimately distrusts the "picturesque" arrangement of details so
prevalent in romance, even though he often labors to achieve

the picturesque himself. Even in the preface to so contrived a romance as *The Gilded Age,* Twain's statement implies a photographic rather than an impressionistic approach to his material.

In Laura's pleasantly gloomy discovery that she is an orphan with a living father for whom she can search, Twain presents a situation that, for Hawthorne, might have become the basis for a moral inquiry. Instead, Twain apologizes in the book's appendix for getting the reader "all stirred up" over the possibility of finding the missing man; through this apology he points to the meaninglessness of experience. Yet the insistence on life's lack of form is managed within the framework of a literary form. When Laura disappoints a young lady-friend by referring to the dinner menu instead of weeping over a "lost love," the parody and burlesque of a traditionally "romantic" situation reassure the reader that life can be lived without the props of romantic melodrama. If romantic meaning is lost, another sort of meaning is gained. Twain here rejects the romance as a means of organizing experience artistically.

Twain is careful to avoid Hawthorne's sort of romance, even when the material is given to him. In *Life on the Mississippi* he briefly tells the story of an old river-friend into whose life "had dropped a bit of romance." "George Johnson"—really Samuel A. Bowen (XXXVII, 185-86)—had lived with a girl, and the extralegal couple had informed the girl's fatherly employer that they were married. On the good man's death, the sole beneficiary of his large estate was "*Mrs. George Johnson.*" The couple then married, only to have the falsified date on the marriage certificate exposed by the dead man's relatives, "leaving," concludes Twain, "the Johnsons very legitimately, and legally, and irrevocably chained together in honorable marriage, but with not so much as a penny to bless themselves withal. . . . not all novels have for a base so telling a situation"(XII, 397). Again one imagines what Hawthorne would have done with such a *donnée*; Twain cannot deal with it unless he can burlesque or parody its romantic overtones. It is only in *Pudd'nhead Wilson* that he writes a successful tragedy.

Twain's objections to romance are objections to the arrangement of details to fit a preconceived pattern, or, rather, to fit a specific preconceived pattern, for Twain is not transcribing reality in the manner of a reporter. This specific pattern is expressed through the characters who, as archetypes, embody social forces. The force exerted by the dark-haired lady, for example, is always opposed to what is socially acceptable and materially productive, toward what is sensationally titillating and conventionally condemned. The hero may leave his blonde early in the book to sow his wild oats, but he returns to her in the end to raise a family and pay taxes. The intervening melodrama explores the various possibilities of rebellion against the conventions, but always with the assumption that the social order will somehow continue. The forces of anti-society, while temptingly embodied in the passionate brunette, must always be defeated. Generally, the dark-haired girl dies; in every instance, she is rejected by the hero.

The romance embodies forces in its characters. It is clear that even a rebel can use these fictionalized forces for his own antisocial ends, as Herman Melville did in *Pierre*. The romance itself can thus be an aesthetic force so long as any artist chooses to avail himself of its possibilities. Most superficially, James's *The Portrait of a Lady* might seem to escape the romance tradition simply because Isabel has dark hair and Madame Merle, the passionate plotter, is a blonde. The book does partially escape being "romantic" because the problems of its characters are worked out in personal, rather than in archetypal, terms: Isabel's decision to return to

Osmond is essentially a decision of personal morality and personal psychology; one thinks of Isabel's concern for the opportunity to choose, and one thinks of her fear of sexual experience as expressed in the recurring imagery of a "bolt" and "money in the bank." That her decision is conventionally acceptable is beside the point, for it represents an individual's efforts to come to grips with his own life. On the other hand, *The Portrait* is a romance to the extent that Madame Merle, Caspar Goodwood, Isabel herself, and the others are all presented as archetypes of social or psychological "forces." The force of Europe, the force of money, the force of American industry—all come to bear on Isabel, who is often allowed to appear as the force of innocence, or Eve in the Garden. It is in this sense that the romance is a potent aesthetic implement: its use commits the artist to a point of view. When Melville in *Pierre* allies his hero with the dark-haired girl and her symbolism of social anarchy, his "message" is antisocial, but the terms in which he expresses it are the terms of the romance. Isabel, Pierre's half-sister, is even more of a force than is Cooper's Isabella in *The Spy*, although Isabel's victory through death is, in terms of social meaning, very radical, while Isabella's death is in the conservative tradition. The point is that the romance framework, even when turned inside out as in *Pierre*, presupposes a basic order in the universe, an order in which clearly-defined social forces exert pressures on individuals in predictable ways and have predictable outcomes. The individual is not alone in an indifferent universe; even physical nature, in the romance, has his interests at heart. Melville's Pierre reacts to social conventions as though they still had validity and draws on physical nature for moral support; that his actions are in defiance of convention and that his gleanings from nature point to a malevolent universe are beside the point. Nature, however cruel, is not indifferent; society, however stifling, is orderly. The forces of rebellion and of cohesion can be measured, and depended upon.

For Mark Twain, the forces with which the writer had to deal were no longer measurable. Just as Henry Adams came to look back upon the world of *Mont-Saint-Michel and Chartres,* so Twain looks back upon the pre-Civil War South if not as a lost Eden, then at least as a world in which stable social patterns prevailed. For Henry Adams, a series of events led him to view Mont Blanc as "a chaos of anarchic and purposeless forces." Confronting these forces, "man became chaotic, and before the illusions of Nature were wholly restored, the illusions of Europe suddenly vanished, leaving a new world to learn."[7]

As the reaction of an artist confronted with the literary problem of delineating the breakdown of his world, Adams' method of dealing with forces suddenly turned chaotic is a helpful point of comparison from which to examine Twain's response. Both men avoided the Civil War. Adams was in England, and Twain, after a few weeks of masterly retreating —described self-mockingly in "The Private History of A Campaign That Failed"(1885)—went West with his brother. Amusingly enough, both noncombatants were serving their country as assistants to members of their families who held political appointments. Repeatedly, in his *Education,* Adams evokes the Civil War as anarchic fratricide, symbolic of the chaos of modern life. As Twain looked back in 1873, he saw that "the eight years in America from 1860 to 1868 uprooted institutions that were centuries old, changed the politics of a people, transformed the social life of half the country, and wrought so profoundly upon the entire national character that the influence cannot be measured short of two or three generations"(V, 176-77). Adams too was concerned with measuring changes and forces, as the *Education's* recurrent metaphors of balance, mathematics, and measurement attest.

Adams sees the war as a logical outcome of southern mentality, which he is at repeated pains to define in the *Education*. His Harvard classmate, Roony Lee, is "ignorant" and "childlike" and "helpless before the relative complexity of a school. As an animal, the Southerner seemed to have every advantage, but even as an animal he steadily lost ground."[8] As for Roony's seniors,

The old and typical Southern gentleman developed as cotton-planter had nothing to teach or to give, except warning. Even as example to be avoided, he was too glaring in his defiance of reason, to help the education of a reasonable being. No one learned a useful lesson from the Confederate school except to keep away from it. . . . it was overshadowed by the cotton-planters, from whom one could learn nothing but bad temper, bad manners, poker, and treason.[9]

This is indeed the mentality of a child, similar to that of Arthur's court as Twain presents it through Hank Morgan. The knights are children, and it is knighthood and its conventions as presented by Scott that Twain holds responsible for the Civil War.

Both men, then, agree not only on the fact of chaos, but also on the immediate sources of the event that spelled chaos for their society. Faced with this irruption of old standards and values that is equally devastating to them both, each takes a characteristic literary pose in confronting chaos. For Adams, the pose in the *Education* is one of exaggerated self-mockery, and of emphasis on a sense of his own inadequacy. Adams is a "begonia," as Senator Howe tells him, and he is eager to agree. Not only does he elaborate on the flower's connotations of ostentatious ineffectuality,[10] but he also uses the reference to bind together the two chronological sections of the book: on his way back from Europe, Rudyard Kipling "dashed over the passenger his exuberant fountain of gaiety and wit—as though playing a garden hose on a thirsty and faded begonia."[11] Adams is unable to understand the banking crisis of 1893;[12] in fact, to hear him tell it, he cannot really understand anything at all. He is a failure as a teacher—a failure, indeed, as a nineteenth-century man. Faced with such abundant confession of inadequacy, the reader can only smile wryly at himself and wonder what chance of intelligent survival he has if so well-endowed a personality as Henry Adams can find no haven of security. Adams mocks himself and by so doing draws the reader ever deeper into despair. There is no hope. Multiplicity is ever more multiple. Man is doomed.

Twain's pessimism, as we shall see later, needs to be distinguished from Adams', and Twain's approach to chaos is not the self-mockery of Henry Adams, either. But Twain's symbols of disruption are no less devastating than the implications of Adams' contrast between the Virgin and the Dynamo. The ending of *A Connecticut Yankee* is the immeasurable explosion of all forces, social, political, moral, and industrial, as well as simply mechanical. Darwinian evolution, a focal point of chaos for Adams, suggests to Twain a sort of impersonal order which is nevertheless very upsetting to the ego-satisfying world-picture of boyhood, "when the happenings of life were not the natural and logical results of great general laws, but of special orders . . . usually local in application"(XII, 434). At the end of Evolution, the "procession of ancestors that stretches back a billion years to the Adam-clan or grasshopper or monkey from whom our race has been so tediously and ostentatiously and unprofitably developed"(XIV, 150), we find the third of Twain's main symbols of dissolution, the American Congressman, equal in symbolic weight, however comically applied, to Darwin and to Industry. "It could probably be shown by facts and figures that there is no distinctly native American criminal class except Congress"(XX, 80). Philip Sterling and Colonel Sellers strongly resent any suggestion, however innocently intended, that they are fit to join the highest legislative body in the land (VI, 193, 208), for morally it is a putrid corpse.

In a world of such instability, a world in which the only thing to be taken for granted is that everyone is corrupt or corruptible, a cipher before the rush of Progress, Adams retreats into isolation and self-mockery, but Twain's response is to attack. He is concerned with seeing exactly what the forces are that create so chaotic an era, and for his purposes, romance as a tool of measurement must be done away with. At the same time that romance is destroyed, an active attack, satirical in its nature, is launched against the more obvious evils of the day. Each gains its point from the other.

The heavy irony in Twain's parody of the preface to *The Marble Faun* gains meaning simply because it is a parody. That is, even if the reader has never encountered *The Marble Faun* and its preface, his acquaintance with the viewpoint of romance strengthens the force of the irony in Twain's preface to *The Gilded Age*; he is especially impressed by the ironically presented insistence on the realistic nature of the story to follow. The "romantic" repudiation of America is ignored in favor of one that is, seemingly, much more damaging; so far as the reader can at this point tell, he is about to be introduced to the chaotic world of contemporary chicanery and immorality. At the same time, the preconceptions of romance demand that a "pure" society be a "primitive" one: in *A Connecticut Yankee* the knights are referred to as "children" in a "nursery," and are ignorant and amoral rather than shrewdly corrupt. America, as presented in *The Gilded Age,* is both primitive *and* corrupt. The characters may follow the line of romance, but the social commentary in the book includes a renunciation of a favorite

romantic cliché. Twain's ironic reference to "primitive purity"
is especially devastating because only half of it is irony:
primitive impurity has even less to recommend it than the
more sophisticated kinds, and from the Knobs of East Tennessee to the drawing rooms of the "Oreillé" (formerly
"O'Reilly") family, the primitive and the corrupt are inevitably linked.

The Gilded Age is a weak book; were it not for the life
and gusto of Beriah Sellers no one would ever read it. Form—
what there is of it—and content are hopelessly at odds. Still,
the ironic parody in the preface is a gallant effort to pull the
book together by a tour de force. By assuming that all his
readers recognize and distrust romance, Twain persuades
them to accept his parodies and burlesques in the course of
the action as the real meaning of the story, and encourages
them to take less seriously the sentimental claptrap of Philip
and Ruth and Alice, which one blames partly on the long-
suffering Charles Dudley Warner and partly on nineteenth-
century literary habit.

The corrupt world of *The Gilded Age,* inartistically presented though it is, shows in skeleton form the essence of
Twain's difference from Adams, so far as presenting that
world is concerned. Adams' self-mockery drives each reader
farther into isolation; there can be no common ground of
security when even an Adams is lost. Twain's use of humor
to meet chaos has an effect opposite to that of Adams'
mocking humor. Twain uses parody and burlesque to assume
a common moral ground, to unite his readers and himself
against the threatening world. Twain uses these forms satirically, as we have seen, and it is important to recognize
this use in dealing with his works, obvious though it be.
Equally important—probably more important—is the assumption behind every parody and burlesque that all readers agree
on exactly what the standard is against which they are to

measure the distortion of form or content. Twain's burlesque of Thomas Moore's "Those Evening Bells" is effective because Twain prints Moore's poem along with "Those Annual Bills" (VII, 56-57). The reader sees the same form filled with different contents. The Sailors' parody of the Pilgrims' address to the Emperor in *The Innocents Abroad* gains immeasurably from a view of the starched and proper Innocents as contrasted with the grimy sailors, each of whom excuses his grotesque disarray with the formula that opened the address: "We are a handful of private citizens of America, traveling simply for recreation—and unostentatiously" (II, 119-21 vs. 105-7). The content of the address is indisputably retained, but the form is wonderfully varied.

Readers and author share a common knowledge of a standard. Such agreement may seem to be a bulwark against chaos, but what it amounts to at times is an obligation for the reader to mock his own preconceptions or beliefs. Adams mocks himself, but Twain's use of parody and burlesque is a subtle mockery of the reader. If one is to continue in the author's company, he must assume what Twain assumes. He must, almost unthinkingly, participate in Twain's desecration of what the reader himself might not be quite ready to abandon. In looking at "The Spectacular Ruin," we have seen that Twain played parody and burlesque off against each other in order to satirize both aspects of the "knight's" behavior. But so far as effect on the reader is concerned, and apart from satirical function, these two forms that are so exactly opposite in construction are identical in force as they unite to bring into question patterns and standards, whether of romance or otherwise, that the reader might prefer to hold dear.

IV

The Hoax

5

Revelation

PARODIES AND BURLESQUES, then, cast ridicule upon social habits, or emotional attitudes, or literary forms that the reader is persuaded to belittle. The reader is led to question what he has perhaps accepted without question, because, to read at all sympathetically, he must identify with the author's particular point of view. Humor arises because the reader has assumed a familiarity with an absolute standard—the author's —against which to measure the deviations of the parody or the burlesque. In the gap lies the humor.

Twain's parodies and burlesques sometimes derive their humor from an element different from any inherent in the nature of the parody or burlesque itself: the hoax. The parodies and burlesques of legends in *The Innocents Abroad, A Tramp Abroad,* and *Life on the Mississippi* are, in a sense, hoaxes as well: Twain pretends that he is going to present a real legend in "legendary" form; when he pointedly fails to do so, the reader realizes that he has been tricked into expecting, and even approving of, the very thing that Twain is satirizing. The reader, instead of sharing the author's point of view, is fooled by the author.

A common form for Twain's hoaxes to take is that of the incomplete, or purposely unresolved, story. At the end of "A Medieval Romance"(1868; VII, 198-208), Twain blandly tells his reader that "the remainder of this thrilling and eventful story will NOT be found in this or any other publication, either now or at any future time." He has worked his heroine into a situation from which she cannot possibly be extricated, while simultaneously encouraging the reader to believe that the unfortunate girl will manage to live happily ever after. Faced abruptly with Twain's abandonment of the trapped heroine, one must re-evaluate his concern for her fate in the light of the hoax which seems to say that what happens next doesn't really matter.

In *Following the Equator,* the usefulness of such a hoax in upsetting an unthinking complacency is more explicit. The contest on board ship to complete the story of shy John Brown (XX, 19, ff.) is never won, because nobody can concoct an ending that will be both plausible and happy. The reader's interest in Brown, as his interest in the medieval heroine, has been built up through the romance-pattern of the tale. But then one sees that such a pattern is illegitimate; it cannot possibly fit the facts of life as the central character experiences them. Faced with the sudden denial of an expected conclusion to the story, the reader must decide that the grapes were sour, that the story didn't matter after all. Instead of allowing the reader to assume blithely that of course he sides with Twain against the romance and its implications, such a hoax avoids the easy flattery of parody and burlesque, and shows all readers that they are not the sophisticates they thought they were. The reader is thrown off balance and shown a part of himself that he perhaps never expected to find. What ever *did* happen, one wonders, to that poor girl in "A Medieval Romance"?

One subspecies of the hoax to be found throughout Twain's work has to do with the use of language, of the words themselves, as they mislead a gullible reader. The hoax of terminology is important in that it suggests the formal prerequisites of any hoax. The "esophagus" of "A Double-Barrelled Detective Story" is of this variety, satirical as it is of a sappily conventional "gush" about weather and landscape:

It was a crisp and spicy morning in early October. The lilacs and laburnums, lit with the glory-fires of autumn, hung burning and flashing in the upper air, a fairy bridge provided by kind Nature for the wingless wild things that have their homes in the tree-tops and would visit together; the larch and the pomegranate flung their purple and yellow flames in brilliant broad splashes along the slanting sweep of the woodland; the sensuous fragrance of innumerable deciduous flowers rose upon the swooning atmosphere; far in the empty sky a solitary esophagus slept upon motionless wing; everywhere brooded stillness, serenity, and the peace of God. (XXIII, 304)

When the story first appeared (in *Harper's Magazine* for January, 1902), numerous readers wrote to Twain about the strange bird, but failed to object to the other oddities of natural lore in the passage. Commenting on one such communication, Twain wrote (Springfield *Republican,* April 12, 1902), "Do you notice? Nothing in the paragraph disturbed him but that one word. It shows that that paragraph was most ably constructed for the deception it was intended to put upon the reader"(XXIII, 305).

The use of words in contexts that render them nonsensical appealed to Twain. In *Life on the Mississippi,* he introduces his reader to the involved process of making sugar. His poker-faced recital of the successive steps followed by the raw cane is mundane enough until the final detail: "Then through the vacuum-pan to extract the vacuum" (XII, 385). Coming at the end of a series of highly technical terms, this sounds well, and the reader does not immediately perceive that anything is the matter. Twain himself, in his "First Interview with Artemus Ward"(1870), is tricked into

believing that he is drunk, after taking a midmorning cocktail, because he cannot understand Ward's simple question
about

"the sulpherets—I believe they call them sulpherets, though why
they should, considering that, so far as I can see, the main depen-
dence of a miner does not so lie, as some suppose, but in which it
cannot be successfully maintained, wherein the same should not
continue, while part and parcel of the same ore not committed to
either in the sense referred to, whereas, under different circumstances, the most inexperienced among us could not detect it if
it were, or might overlook it if it did, or scorn the very idea
of such a thing, even though it were palpably demonstrated as
such. Am I not right?" (VII, 336-37)

As Prince Agge says when he finally understands the point
of Mike Van Dyke's double-talk in Fitzgerald's *The Last
Tycoon*, " 'I see. It is like your Gertrude Stein.' "[1] In each
case, the double-talk requires the reader—or hearer—to ask
a question, to start the conversation over again. In another
form, this is a part of frontier humor, as Constance Rourke
points out (*American Humor*, Anchor edition, p. 68). The
asking of a question in answer to another question, supposedly typical of Jews and of Yankee peddlers, is especially
common among frontiersmen who long for company and
conversation. A precise and lucid answer ends social inter-
course. Twain himself complains of an especially brisk waiter
that "the essential element of discussion had been left out
of him; his answers were so final and exact that they did not
leave a doubt to hang conversation on"(XIX, 291). The form
of "beginning again," of Gertrude Stein's "continuous present," is at least latent in the structure of *Huckleberry Finn*,
a book that ends where it began, whose episodes succeed
each other in a repetitive pattern of commitment and
betrayal.

The use of double-talk as a hoax on the reader has the effect of stopping him, of making him go back over the ground just covered. Something, he feels, has gone wrong, and the result is that he reads more carefully, more perceptively—unless he is one of the many who took the "solitary esophagus" at face value and never began again, never questioned the elaborate sentimentality and falseness of the scene in which the strange bird appears.

The care with which the esophagus' presence is prepared for suggests that even double-talk requires more than a spontaneous overflow of humor to work properly. The function of the "vacuum-pan" comes at the end of a legitimate series; Artemus Ward's successful fooling is effective for the reader only because Twain prepares one for it by detailing his fears about taking a cocktail so early in the day. This last example, however, is simply good fun; it has no profound effect upon the reader beyond amusing him. The reader must himself be victimized, at least to a degree, if the hoax is to be significant as revelation.

A hoax, then, is not merely a "trick" or a "deception"; it can be a literary form as well. Huck Finn's wily representation of his own murder, despite all its literary overtones, is the hoax as action, not the hoax as literary form. Huck is perpetrating a hoax that will fool all the other characters in the book, making them believe what is not so. The effect on the reader, however, is simple: just as at any frontier humor trick, the reader laughs to see the gullible crowd taken in, but the reader is himself never made to question the validity of his own interpretation of reality. As the St. Petersburg ferry stands in close to Jackson's Island and fires its cannon to bring Huck's body to the surface of the river, we laugh at the passengers and chuckle with Huck when he reminds us that "if they'd 'a' had some bullets in, I reckon they'd 'a' got the corpse they was after" (XIII, 53).

The principal effect of Twain's successful hoaxes is to jolt the reader. Although the hoax can be used primarily as incident, to create a humorous effect,* Twain's use of it as a literary form is generally satirical as well. This is why Twain's hoaxes often come as the climax to a parody, or a burlesque, or a tall tale, for the reader's expectation must be committed in a false direction if the surprise attack is to be effective.

II

To see exactly what Twain does with his hoaxes, and to appreciate the deliberate art behind them, it will be helpful to contrast his use of the form with that of another nineteenth-century specialist, Edgar Allan Poe. Poe and Twain both wrote parodies and burlesques, and each found special value in narratives that take the form of a hoax. More specifically, both men use the hoax, as well as parody and burlesque, to work against a love of sensationalism for its own sake and as embodied in romance. " 'There was "The Dead Alive," a capital thing!' " says Mr. Blackwood to the Signora Psyche Zenobia in Poe's "How to Write a *Blackwood* Article." " 'The record of a gentleman's sensations when entombed before the breath was out of his body—. . . sensations are the great thing after all. Should you ever be drowned or hung, be sure and make a note of your sensations—they will be worth to you ten guineas a sheet.' "[2] Silly Psyche hangs on his every word, and in "A Predicament" tries to follow his formula in a burlesque startlingly related to Poe's own serious efforts in "The Pit and the Pendulum." After hilarious adventures in a church tower, Psyche loses her head to the slowly descending hand of the steeple clock.

---

*B. J. Whiting, in "Guyuscutus, Royal Nonesuch, and Other Hoaxes," *Southern Folklore Quarterly*, VIII (December, 1944), 251-75, has documented precisely and extensively the widespread use of the hoax in pre-Civil War American humor. In each case that he adduces—and in many that he does not—the hoax is simply part of the "funny-man's" working equipment.

The hoax on the reader's sensibilities in "The Premature Burial" is effective because of the elaborate preparation within the convention of a sensational tale: the sensitive narrator with a monomania presents his fear of living inhumation, detailing the precautions he has taken to insure a speedy rescue should he by some accident be buried alive, as he so psychotically fears that he will be. Having established firmly in the reader's mind the reality of his obsession, the narrator then relates his adventure, in the course of which he awakens to find himself a victim of the fate he has so long and so obsessively dreaded:

So far, I had not ventured to stir any of my limbs—but now I violently threw up my arms, which had been lying at length, with the wrists crossed. They struck a solid wooden substance, which extended above my person at an elevation of not more than six inches from my face. I could no longer doubt that I reposed within a coffin at last.[3]

One's flesh crawls as one experiences with the narrator the horror of his predicament, and then one discovers that the narrator has simply fallen asleep in the narrow bunk of a river-sloop. The horrors he has recounted have arisen entirely from his own fevered imagination; the reader's sympathies have been falsely stirred.

After the hoax is revealed, the narrator confesses that his whole view of life has been changed by his experience. "I thought upon other subjects than Death. . . . I read no . . . bugaboo tales—*such as this*" (italics Poe's). The reader, of course, should do likewise, but it is doubtful if any reader did, or ever will. Mark Twain complains at the end of his account of "My Bloody Massacre" that "we never *read* the dull explanatory surroundings of marvelously exciting things when we have no occasion to suppose that some irresponsible scribbler is trying to defraud us; we skip all that, and hasten

to revel in the blood-curdling particulars and be happy"
(VII, 296-97).

Both men have many characteristics in common in the
construction of their hoaxes. Twain often likes to leave the
reader "up in the air," as he does figuratively at the end of
"A Medieval Romance" and quite literally in a balloon hoax
omitted from the final version of *Life on the Mississippi*. The
simple device of leaving a story "open" at the end is not
frequent in Poe, but it does appear. Indeed, the ending of
Narrative of A. Gordon Pym is, in a sense, patterned in this
way, especially if one chooses to read *Gordon Pym* as culminating in a gigantic hoax on the reader with the disappear-
ance of the last chapters of Pym's adventures.

As a part of their use of the hoax to ridicule the reader's
penchant for collecting thrills, both writers build their hoaxes
around issues that, perhaps inadvertently, become completely
secondary by the time the hoax has been completed. Thus
Twain's "Massacre" was meant to be an attack on and a
warning against the "cooking" or "watering" of dividends
by unscrupulous boards of directors. As a result of one such
fraud, a placid family man commits the grisly massacre.
Poe's stories, "Hans Pfaall" and "The Balloon Hoax," give
expression to Poe's indignation at the inaccuracy of earlier
writers who had misjudged the optical effects produced by
the spatial relationship between a rising balloon and the
spherical surface of the earth. But both fraudulent stock-
manipulation and faulty science fail to claim any part of a
reader's attention.

Even the development of a hoax from a tall tale—so
common in the work of Twain the westerner—is not completely missing from Poe's "Hans Pfaall," with its extrava-
gances and its deception of the respected and pompous
"intellectuals" of the community. But the differences are
striking. Twain laments the readers' desire to be "happy"

(to enjoy sensationalism) as the cause for their failure to detect a hoax. Poe too is aware of this human failing, but the terms in which he refers to it in his "Note" to "The Unparalleled Adventures of One Hans Pfaall" point to an important difference in emphasis: the public's "gross ignorance,"[4] rather than the desire to enjoy excitements, causes them to miss the guideposts to the hoax. Although Twain is as articulate as Poe about the stupidity of the mob, he stresses the universal, human desire to "be happy" rather than the selective, and hence pejorative, failing of low intelligence.

Furthermore, Poe, by his own testimony as ardent an opponent of sensationalism as Twain, makes use of the identical craving he wishes to destroy. "The Balloon Hoax" itself has nothing in it to keep the reader from excited speculation on the possibilities of balloon travel; indeed, a common element in many of Poe's hoaxes is the encouragement of open-mindedness at the same time that the open mind is being hoodwinked. The ironic use of romantic clichés in "Ligeia" does not prevent the story from arousing all the sensations of a less self-conscious presentation of the romance elements. Poe's use of the macabre in *Gordon Pym* forces the reader to participate in the thrilling horrors of the derelict-bound sailors who must descend to cannibalism or die. The approach of the ghost-ship, with its skeleton passengers, involves the reader in the raised expectations, the horrid realizations, and the intensified oppression experienced by the protagonist, just as the protagonist's burning thirst, so minutely described earlier in the story, makes the reader reach for a glass of water. There is no such participation in Twain's "My Bloody Massacre." Twain makes one enjoy the aesthetic, not the immediate, in the sensations latent or explicit in his hoaxes.

The importance of these and other differences can best be explicated through a careful look at an elaborately-arranged hoax written as the second part of a chapter in

Life on the Mississippi that was to follow what is now Chapter XXXIV. In setting, buildup—every technique of the hoax—Twain's "balloon hoax" (see Appendix) is a perfect example of what Twain does with the form, and it furnishes a contrast with Poe's use of the same material. The noteworthy observation is not in the fact that Twain seems to be borrowing from Poe, but that he borrows "with a difference."

"Mr. Harvey," whose identity as a steamboat mate was established in Chapter XXXIV, has been shown as a whimsical man who enjoys tall tales and the convivial participation in helping them to grow. He tells beautiful "whoppers" about the Arkansas and Lake Providence mosquitoes, which resemble the traditional exaggerations of "The Big Bear of Arkansas," Thomas Bangs Thorpe's immortal yarn of 1841. Then Mr. Harvey's friend picks up the narrative thread, but Mr. Harvey insists that his friend's statements be discounted, and admonishes the irresponsible fellow to " 'stick to the cold facts; what these gentlemen want for a book is the frozen truth' " (XII, 295). The chapter ends as Mr. Harvey gravely warns Twain and his party that the friend is not to be trusted. " 'I will not deceive you; he told me such a monstrous lie once that it swelled my left ear up, and spread it so that I was actually not able to see out around it; it remained so for months, and people came miles to see me fan myself with it.' " The impulse behind this innocent talk is that of the tall tale; it has nothing to do with the hoax, it has nothing to do with satire or with revelation or with any of the effects that a hoax is capable of achieving.

The "mournful episode" mentioned in the first sentence of the balloon-hoax passage is a reference to a tale told by an unknown Mr. Dunham at the very start of the suppressed chapter. Mr. Dunham's performance differs from that of Mr. Harvey, and the change in tone is especially marked. Mr. Dunham tells a coherent story, rather than a series of anecdotes, and presents his story of a young man's military experience in such a way that the use of a Bible bound in iron as a seat-guard serves to mock sentimental reliance on scripture in time of danger; Mr. Harvey's stories have not been at all satirical. Also, Mr. Dunham is completely detached from the events of the tall tale he tells—he had merely known the young man whose adventure he relates— in contrast to Mr. Harvey, whose personal relationship to the "facts" of his stories gives them their particular tone, their authority, and their charm.

The reader returns to Mr. Harvey, with his first-person narrative style, in anticipatory pleasure; the reader knows him and understands— or thinks he does—Mr. Harvey's point of view; and when Harvey talks not of natural history again but of himself directly, the reader is pleased. The tall tale pattern is here especially attractive, because the reader has been made a part of the group that is not fooled but rather solidified in its sharing of the yarns. He wants another tall tale, and he expects one.

Poe, in his two principal balloon stories ("Mellonta Tauta" is not primarily concerned with the balloon locale of the story), carefully contributes all the scientific data of which he is capable. Almost any page of "Hans Pfaall" and "The Balloon Hoax" is sure to contain some substantiating fact. Twain's method is quite opposite. The form of the whole piece is of the tall tale from the beginning, for, wonders the reader, how could anyone get out of that belt of "dead air" which, by definition, is inescapable? Each suggestion of an insurmountable difficulty—"What did you live on?" "How had the balloon and gas managed to last?"—is raised by the auditors and passed over by Mr. Harvey. By ignoring these matters of circumstantial fact, Mr. Harvey increases one's certainty that he is telling a tall tale. One is encouraged not to identify with the feelings Mr. Harvey describes, because

Twain makes a point of providing no plausible grounds for
the reader's being carried away. One certainly does not
believe that Hans Pfaall went where he says he went, but
the sensations he describes are such as he might have had if
his tale were true. One shares the feelings while one disbe-
lieves. In Twain's tale, we are asked to share no feelings,
to believe nothing, but merely to join in the fun of piling
up tall facts, as Christopher Newman had done around his
western campfires. The hoax at the end of "Hans Pfaall"
is on the reader for giving way to his love of sensation. But
one smiles at Mr. Harvey's grisly skeletons, which surely are
descendants of the "twenty-five or thirty human bodies . . .
in the last and most loathsome state of putrefaction"[5] that
appear to Arthur Gordon Pym as the final symbols of the
hopelessness of his situation.

Mr. Harvey's story encourages the reader to take lightly
the sensations that Harvey plays upon. One sees that there
is no attack on sensationalism, because the reader has no
sensations. But a hoax of the incompleted-ending variety is
clearly being perpetrated. The hoax is aimed at the assumptions that make the romantic appreciation of sensationalism
possible. This hoax arises from the tall tale formula, for in
telling a tall tale, the narrator must satisfy the listener of the
aesthetic validity of the tale. That is, one does not demand
a convincing resolution of the tale's impossibilities, but one
does demand a resolution that will be consistent with the
point of view from which the tale is told. From the very
beginning the reader has been waiting for Mr. Harvey to
delight him with an account of how he managed to get back
into the earth's atmosphere. The reader is sure that the
explanation will be ingenious and funny and highly impossible. In the anticipation of this final entertainment, the
reader has been willing to laugh at horror. The permanently
frustrated wedding-party (does it include Poe and his child-

bride?) would reduce an Emmeline Grangerford to damp
grief, but it gives the reader quite another sensation. Life
is to be viewed aesthetically; the pattern of events has been
contrived for his particular enjoyment, and he can ignore
the particular detail as he hurries on to the climax—which
in this case never occurs. Poe uses the macabre and the
bizarre to entrap one in "what happens next," to engulf one
in the sensation of events. He may then pull the rug out
from under, or not, as the case may be. So Twain in "A
Medieval Romance." But here something subtler is taking
place. Instead of the explicit lecture of "My Bloody Massacre," Twain balances his reader between an enjoyment
of the literary pattern and a condemnation of that enjoyment.
His closing words not only express for one one's own good-
humored disappointment, and enjoyment of that disappointment, at not hearing Mr. Harvey's explanation, but also
suggest that in an overeagerness for the literary solution,
the reader paid too little attention to what was happening
in the story. One looks back and notices the combination of
humor and horror with which the bony priest is further
dehumanized. As the dance of death goes on, as others join,
and join to watch, the effect is of an audience at a theater,
all looking on "as if from opera boxes." Thus do the citizens
of Bricksville regard the death-agonies of old Boggs in the
drugstore window. If the false sentimentality of a premature
involvement is romantic and worthless, then so is a complete
withdrawal from participation.

Huck Finn both acts and watches. The readers of Mr.
Harvey's tale are forced to watch only. Whether events are
viewed as producing romantically pleasing sensations, to
be used for emotional enjoyment and proof of virtue, or as
forming insignificant patterns whose contemplation can
provide pleasure, the result is the same, so far as the reader's
insulation from real experience is concerned. Poe's hoaxes

lead one to project oneself into new experiences; Twain's balloon hoax leads one to react as disinterested observer of material and situations which the typical romancer would have his reader participate in and uncritically react to, for the sake of the reaction alone. These effects are obviously different: Poe emphasizes his own control over the events of the hoax, in contrast to which the reader's helplessness is marked. Poe seems bent on laughing at his reader. Twain, while no less in artistic control, wants the reader not to be overpowered but to look around himself with care.

III

Before going on to the particular value of Twain's technique, we will do well to look briefly at the development in Twain's ability to do with the hoax what he wants. The balloon hoax from *Life on the Mississippi,* for example, is a successful application of principles which Twain had tried to embody in earlier efforts, but with less success. Arousing in the reader an expectation of an intriguingly ingenious explanation, only to omit the explanation, is the basis for the hoax concerning Mr. Erikson in *Roughing It.* Erikson, Twain is told, has been driven insane as a result of his good intentions and a young man's request for advice. A series of letters to Erikson from Horace Greeley is presented for Twain's edification by people who know the case well. At the end of the episode, Twain confesses that he has enjoyed talking to Erikson and the others. "But they did not say what drove him crazy. In the momentary confusion, I forgot to ask" (IV, 242). This conclusion is very much like the ending of the balloon hoax, in form, but the point has been blurred. The frenetic and fantastic correspondence, enough to drive anybody crazy, slaps playfully at Horace Greeley's insufferable handwriting, but by the time a reader finishes the correspondence, he no longer cares about Erikson and the cause of his madness. He has lost sight of Erikson to such a degree that Twain's "punch line" succeeds neither as a satire on bad penmanship nor as a hoax on the reader for swallowing the correspondence whole. Later in his career Twain showed an awareness of the dangers involved in this sort of hoax. In a more thoughtful approach to the problem than that in "My Bloody Massacre," he reflects that "one can deliver a satire with telling force through the insidious medium of a travesty, if he is careful not to overwhelm the satire with the extraneous interest of the travesty" (1881).[6]

The episode from *Roughing It* fails to be a hoax because the material it makes use of is too interesting. It becomes all "art," all aesthetic delight, with no "point," no satire. Conversely, Twain is just as likely in his early works to attempt a hoax that functions perfectly as a mechanism, yet fails ultimately because it is all "point" and not at all artful. In *The Gilded Age*, the reader is told of Laura's fate: "The verdict of the jury having left no doubt that the woman was of an unsound mind, with a kind of insanity dangerous to the safety of the community . . ." (VI, 267), the judge follows the only course open to him and sends her off to "the State Hospital for Insane Criminals." One sees her there. The foulness and the horror of the scene are enlarged upon, and finally their effect on Laura's mind: " . . . she recalled the testimony regarding her lunacy. She wondered if she *were* not mad" (268). The reader is touched; he is made sorrowful over poor Laura's plight; and then the rug is pulled out from under him. The authors reveal that they were only pretending, that the law of the land would never suffer so fair a maid to endure so cruel a fate. No indeed. Despite the fact that her acquittal for murder was on the grounds of insanity, "Laura left the courtroom . . . amid the congratulations of those assembled" (269). The authors apologize for fooling the reader, but now they must tell the truth, for "this is history and not fiction." Nevertheless, the reader is reminded, "the novelist who would turn loose upon society an insane murderess could not escape condemnation" (269). The point is made, but one is forced to forget completely about any emotional involvement in the story. Intellectually one admits the justice of the social criticism, but since the story itself has succeeded in putting the reader on Laura's side, the hoax fails to move him. It is too extraneous, too much like the architecture that is added after the building has been completed. One really does not care.

As we shall see, the later Twain will avoid both pitfalls.

6

Fooling Poor Old Huck

ONE OF THE EFFECTS of any art is to teach one something about himself on the level of emotion, of feeling. In this sense, great art presents experience in a new perspective, because only as one reacts to experience of some sort does he feel. Twain's use of the hoax is, as we have seen, often satirical, but in the long run the specific issues of his satire do not in themselves interest his readers. Nobody cares whether or not Twain finds the pomp of chivalry ridiculous; the antislavery sentiments in *Huckleberry Finn* are hardly at the core of the book. But when, in *Life on the Mississippi*, Twain says that the southern whites are still slaves, and then goes on to describe the one-party system and southern lawlessness in the light of this remark, not only is he waving the "bloody shirt" of northern Republicanism, but also he is beginning to interest us because he is forcing us to "feel," psychologically, our way through an aspect of our own lives, no matter where we may live. Twain has no "answers" to the problems of his society. His insights are aesthetic; they come to one in the terms of art, as perception: it is the nature of a hoax to displace very suddenly one set of perceptions by another.

The hoax-as-satire becomes especially important in Twain's works when it serves to reveal the hidden truth

159

about the reader himself. Ourselves in particular, not people in general, are stripped of pretensions and made to stand self-revealed by Twain's most effective hoaxes. Because the ending of *Adventures of Huckleberry Finn* has been so often maligned, it is a particularly helpful place to examine the difference between satire and hoax. Surely the satiric elements of the ending are obvious; the romance and its conventions are pilloried unmercifully. If these chapters were merely an antiromantic satire, however, all the harsh words directed at them would be justified. But the ending is a hoax, not only on the characters in the book but, in effect, on the reader as well. It is a well-organized section of the book, not a spontaneous overflow of high spirits on the part of an amateur, however "divine."

Hoax based on human love of sensation underlies the book as a whole; from the town's reaction to Huck's "murder" to "The Royal Nonesuch," this is clear enough. The ending must be read as hoax, not simply as parody and burlesque; and yet it is as simple—and simple-minded—burlesque that the ending of the book is usually received. Occasional kind words have been spoken about the "formal" justification of allowing Huck once more to take a back seat to Tom's excited and phony outlawry, and readers have recognized the ironic juxtaposition of Huck's real adventures with Tom's labored effects; but neither consideration excuses the superfluity of detail with which Twain loads down the concluding portion of his book. In the last ten chapters of *Huckleberry Finn*, however, the hoax becomes important enough to support the weight of narrative stasis Twain burdens it with.

This hoax is effective in a variety of ways, and on two distinct levels. Indeed, it is really two hoaxes in one: a gradually unfolding succession of deceits perpetrated against the other characters in the book by Tom and Huck, and a sudden blow aimed at the reader's opinion of himself when the author deliberately withholds and then reveals his—and Tom's—mendacity in fooling the reader, along with Huck, into thinking that Tom Sawyer will help to free a slave. The hoax against the reader, like Mr. Harvey's balloon story, derives its force from the reader's assumption that the author (or narrator) is "on his side." In addition, the reader's reaction is heightened through his expanding sense of what Tom's escape plot means to the other characters in the book, and also through the evocative power of the final chapters as they call to mind important incidents and conflicts developed earlier in the book.

The groundwork of the hoax's effectiveness is carefully laid. Far from being a chaotic afterthought, the closing ten chapters are bound together by themes and patterns that forcibly communicate to the reader the significance of Tom's escapade in all its ramifications. Repeatedly, the contrast between Huck and Tom is underscored. Continuously the scope of Tom's hoax broadens out to involve more and more people, just as Tom's initial inspiration of calling himself "Sid" and Huck "Tom" itself implies the proliferation of minor hoaxes. Gradually there emerges a distinct pattern that charts Tom's, Huck's, Jim's, and "society's" reaction to the hoax. Finally, the hoax's meaning to the people in the book acquires a growing satirical effect for the reader as he becomes increasingly aware of precisely what is in the minds of the fictional characters, both victims and protagonists.

At the very start of Tom's pretense that he will help free Jim, the reunion of Tom with Huck reminds one of the earlier reunion of Jim and Huck on Jackson's Island in a way that underscores Tom's craving for romantic excitement and distinguishes it from Huck's concern for life as it is lived by ordinary human beings. Tom, confronted by what he takes to be Huck's ghost, reacts much as Jim had back on the Island. Says Tom, " 'I hain't ever done you no harm.

You know that. So, then, what you want to come back and ha'nt *me* for?'" He hears Huck's voice and is still shaken: "'Don't you play nothing on me, because I wouldn't on you. Honest injun, you ain't a ghost?'" (XIII, 312). Jim's response has been only slightly different: "'Doan' hurt me—don't! I hain't ever done no harm to a ghos'. I alwuz liked dead people, en done all I could for 'em. You go en git in de river ag'in, whah you b'longs, en doan' do nuffin to Ole Jim, 'at 'uz alwuz yo' fren'"(58). But the difference, in that it points to different ways of relating oneself to other people, is important. The first thing Jim and Huck talk about is the practical matter of breakfast; only after "we had got pretty well stuffed" (59) does Jim ask Huck to explain his miraculous resurrection to him. Huck, on meeting Tom, once more has practical problems: his identity at the Phelpses' and the freeing of Jim. But this time the sensational "murder" comes first, for Tom "wanted to know all about it right off, because it was a grand adventure, and mysterious, and so it hit him where he lived" (313). Only with effort does Huck persuade Tom to "leave it alone till by and by," thus bringing Tom out of the romantic past to the problems at hand. To Tom, excitement comes first, brotherly affection second.

The contrast between the two meetings points not only to Tom's romanticism but also to his egoism. Huck and Jim in search of breakfast work together: "'Now you kill sumfn en I'll make up de fire,'" says Jim. "So we went . . . and while he built . . . I fetched . . . I catched . . . and Jim cleaned . . ." (59). Huck's sense of openhearted identification with Jim is most fully revealed when Huck blurts out his warning on his return to the Island after visiting Judith Loftus: "'Git up and hump yourself, Jim! There ain't a minute to lose. They're after us!'" (86). Tom Sawyer but rarely can think in terms of "us." Indeed, his response to Huck's problem is to ask Huck to "let him alone a minute, and don't disturb him"

(313). His solution remains his own secret, and even in its working out Huck is not in Tom's confidence. Huck accepts Tom's leadership out of an innate respect for respectability, but as Tom's disguise as his own respectable half-brother Sid disguised as William Thompson from Hicksville, Ohio, goes on and on, Huck can't help "getting a little nervous, and wondering how this was going to help me out of my scrape" (316).

The contrast between the boys follows a definite pattern. Huck's practicality and Tom's romanticism come closer and closer together, until finally, in the episode of Aunt Sally, the rats, and "that meddlesome cub," the young Phelps who lets the rats loose in his mother's room, Huck can lament the escape of the rats and bemoan the inferior quality of the second batch just as Tom might: "I never see a likelier lot of rats than what that first haul was" (366). Huck's point of view here is exactly what Tom's would be. Tom, too, has come closer to Huck, in that he accepts Huck's advice to climb up the stairs " 'and let on it's a lightning-rod' "(342). The contrasts and similarities between the two boys are kept before us, always; finally, the ultimate contrasts explode the tenuous union: Tom, seriously wounded, wants to go on playing his romantic game, "but me and Jim was consulting —and thinking" (381), and Huck, instead of "manning the sweeps," goes for the doctor. Subsequently, the two boys are as far apart as they were at the start of the hoax, for the reader learns that while Huck was in earnest, Tom wanted to "free" Jim only for the " '*adventure*' " (400).

Bound up with the shifting relationship between the two boys is the succession of hoaxes that keeps the plot moving and also explicates the social meaning of the whole affair. When Huck returns to the Phelpses' after Tom has agreed to help free Jim, Huck, by forgetting to dawdle on home in order to allow enough time to elapse to simulate a complete trip to town and back, inadvertently deceives Uncle Silas as to the speed of his horse. " 'Why, this is wonderful!' " he says. " 'Whoever would 'a' thought it was in that mare to do it? I wish we'd 'a' timed her. And she hain't sweated a hair—not a hair. It's wonderful' " (314). This mistake underlines both Huck's subservience to Tom and Uncle Silas' role as gentle scapegoat, but also it suggests the rapidly expanding scope of Tom's hoax. Tom at first fools only Huck, when he responds to Huck's plea for help with the exclamation, " 'What! Why, Jim is—' "(313) and fails to finish the sentence. But society is the ultimate victim of Tom's hoax, as we infer from Huck's reaction to Uncle Silas' failure to question the mare's perform- ance: "It warn't surprising; because he warn't only just a farmer, he was a preacher, too . . . . There was plenty other farmer-preachers like that, and done the same way, down South" (314-15). Uncle Silas is a representative of a whole class.

Tom's subsequent double-hoax of identity on Uncle Silas and Aunt Sally—he is first a stranger, then Sid—and repeated exploitation of "nigger" Nat's superstitions widen the social range of his hoax's effectiveness. Tom as a stranger astonishes the Phelpses by kissing Aunt Sally "right on the mouth." Under cover of the storm raised by this seeming abuse of " 'Southern hospitality' " (316), Tom's claim to Sid's name is unhesitatingly accepted. Love is used to further deceit. By fooling Nat, Tom not only emphasizes that a Negro is an emotionless piece of property but also by his mention of "witch pie" prepares the reader for the successful delivery of the pie in Uncle Silas' "noble brass warming-pan which he thought considerable of, because it belonged to one of his ancestors with a long wooden handle that come over from England with William the Conqueror in the *Mayflower*" (355-56). This evocation of the *Mayflower* suggests that Tom's plot is going to affect all of society, since it completely ruins the pan that symbolizes society's beginnings. Tom's efforts will spread out to involve more and more people, culminating in the assembling of fifteen men with guns in Aunt Sally's parlor, and, subsequently, the dinner-table gossips. The hunters and the talkers represent society's failure to understand Tom's plot for what it is; instead of recognizing the romance-elements, both groups take the hoax in all seriousness, and by so doing suggest that the power of a romance-hoax to deceive is almost limitless.

Not merely the fact of the hoaxes, but their effect as well holds the closing chapters together. As Tom and Huck hurry to town to try to warn the duke and the king, they exchange information about the two great hoaxes of the book, so far (320), Huck's "murder" and "The Royal Nonesuch." In each case, society has reacted to the hoax by losing its human qualities. The citizens of St. Petersburg had endeavored to lynch Huck's Pap for "killing" him (79), and the duke and the king turn society into "a raging rush of people with torches, and an awful whooping and yelling, and banging tin pans and blowing horns" (320). Huck and Tom have to jump to one side to avoid being trampled. As a result of Tom's plot to free Jim, society once more goes berserk, shooting Tom in the leg and threatening to hang Jim. Society becomes dehumanized. By evaluating a human being as either an object to shoot at or a piece of property to be paid for, society en masse loses its own sense of human dignity. Jim escapes hanging not through any moral awakening on the part of the irate crowd, but because "the people that's always the most anxious for to hang a nigger that hain't done just right is always the very ones that ain't the most anxious to pay for him when they've got their satisfaction out of him" (393).

The Phelps family—and later their neighbors—come to stand for all of society, and the upsetting of society by Tom's hoax rises to a crescendo of chaos. From the minor disturbance of Aunt Sally's household arrangements over a missing sheet and spoon to the complete demoralization of Aunt Sally herself and of her children's discipline, first with snakes and rats and then, more devastatingly, with Tom's "nonnamous letters," society is increasingly befuddled and metamorphosed by the hoax. The movement of the chapters is away from the purely personal effects of the hoax and toward society's involvement in it. At the same time, the effects on individuals are always important. Although society as a whole derives every possible sensational thrill from the hoax—especially the gossips at the dinner table—Aunt Sally is singled out as too concerned about Tom, who is missing, to enjoy herself. She tucks Huck in for the night, "and mothered me so good I felt mean, and like I couldn't look her in the face" (390). This is the closest Huck has come to a mother-relationship since we have known him. No longer caught up in the sham glitter of Tom's romantic hoax, he resolves that he will "never do nothing to grieve her any more" (391).

This change in Huck's view of the hoax points in two directions. It contrasts with Tom's final reaction to the hoax (397 ff.), when he feels no remorse for the pain he has caused Aunt Sally, and it underlines the dehumanizing effects of the hoax as it takes us back to Huck's acquiescence in Tom's plan to change the sex of all the members of his cast:

"All right, I ain't saying nothing; I'm the servant-girl. Who's Jim's mother?"

"I'm his mother. I'll hook a gown from Aunt Sally."

"Well, then, you'll have to stay in the cabin when me and Jim leaves."

"Not much. I'll stuff Jim's clothes full of straw and lay it on his bed to represent his mother in disguise, and Jim'll take [Aunt Sally's] gown off me and wear it, and we'll all evade together." (371)

No one involved in the hoax can retain his identity, but Aunt Sally's maternal feelings toward Huck are not part of a disguise. Another perspective is offered if we remember Huck's previous assumption of the robes of femininity on his illuminating visit with Judith Loftus: Huck's search for the information that saves Jim's life necessitates the transformation, but Tom's shenanigans simply add troublesomeness to Jim's condition, while doing nothing essential to change it.

Finally, the progression of the last ten chapters leads the reader from Tom and Huck to Jim and then to society, as the hoax takes shape. Turning from one character to another, the text gives one a growing sense of what the hoax means and does to those involved in it. As the reader sees the hoax's effects on the characters in the book, he comes more and more to a sense of the satire in the episode. Early in the scheme, Tom is "romantical"(326) in Huck's eyes, and for the first time this is to Huck a defect. Huck is not the blind follower he was at the start of the book, as the terms in which he expresses his attitude toward Tom's plan suggest: "I see in a minute it was worth fifteen of mine for style, and would make Jim just as free a man as mine would, and maybe get us all killed besides"(324).

At first, though, Huck is bothered more by what will turn out to be Tom's hoax on the reader than by the parody-burlesque romance of the escape-plot itself: he returns again and again to "the thing that was too many for" Huck to understand—"Tom Sawyer was in earnest, and was actuly going to help steal that nigger out of slavery"(324). But eventually, like Jim, practical Huck objects strongly to the conventions of Tom's romance. Only when Tom concludes that " 'we can *let on*, to ourselves' "(338-39) is Huck enthusiastic: " 'Letting on don't cost nothing; letting on ain't no trouble; and if it's any object, I don't mind letting on we was at it a hundred and fifty year' "(339).

Huck will tolerate Tom's need for romance, but he has the possible troubles clearly in mind. Not only do the incidents probe the Tom-Huck relationship, but they do so in terms of the boys' responses to the Phelps family—society— and to Jim. The hoax will affect both: " 'Jim ain't got no use for a rope ladder. . . . we're going to get into trouble with Aunt Sally, just as sure as you're born' "(333). The Iron Mask may have scribbled messages on his dinner-set, but " 'Jim ain't got no tin plates.' " Besides, " 'What's the sense in wasting the plates? . . . it's *somebody's* plates, ain't it?' " (335). Tom is in his own private world, but Huck knows that wherever there is excitement, there is someone who has to pay for it. One sees that Huck's sense of responsibility is truer than Tom's.

Huck's sense of property and of the responsibilities of ownership suggests not only a satire on Tom's impractical romance but also a reversal in Huck's attitude toward Jim. When the two boys outline Tom's elaborate escape-plot, with all its possibilities for Jim's romantic discomfort, "Jim he couldn't see no sense in the most of it, but he allowed we was white folks and knowed better than him; so he was satisfied, and said he would do it all just as Tom said"(344). "We" is now Tom and Huck; on Jackson's Island, it was Huck and Jim. Jim here puts Tom and Huck in the same category: they are both "white folks" and owners. In his own eyes, Jim is a slave, a "nigger," and he expects both Tom and Huck to treat him as property, even though they are at the same time helping to set him free. Huck presents the hoax's first specific effects on Jim in terms that satisfy Jim's expectation and reveal it to the reader. Tom initiates Jim into the romantic glories of his plot by smuggling a piece of candlestick to him inside some corn-pone, and Huck is pleased with the way the device works: "It just worked noble; when Jim bit into it, it most mashed all his teeth out"(345). Any pain or degradation the property might have felt is unmentioned; Huck's imagination has been stirred enough by Tom's nonsense to enable him to forget his own sensitivity to Jim's feelings on the raft.*

Huck, as he becomes involved in the plot despite himself, comes once more to see Jim as merely property. He reverts to feelings he has outgrown. Just previous to the corn-pone trick, he has approved Tom's change from case-knives to picks, from romance to practicality, in terms that take us back to Huck's first struggle with what to do with Jim: "'When I start in to steal a nigger, or a watermelon, or a Sunday-school book, I ain't no ways particular how it's done so it's done. What I want is my nigger; or what I want is my . . .'" (341), and so on. Like the Sunday-school book that Joe Harper captures during Tom's romantic raid on the "rich A-rabs"(17), the "nigger" is just another piece of property to Huck. Jim's plan to steal his children from captivity troubled Huck, for, after all, they were "children that belonged to a man I didn't even know; a man that hadn't ever done me no harm"(124). Huck has since then undergone a change of heart, so far as Jim individually is concerned, most clearly signaled when he wonders over the undoubted fact that Jim "cared just as much for his people as

---

*Huck's attitude toward Jim during the escape-chapters is the product, in other words, of Twain's "romance," in Henry James's sense of the word. Huck's association with Jim, one feels, would be expected to change Huck so that he could not possibly accept Tom's debasement of Jim. In Chapter XV, "Fooling Poor Old Jim," Huck has even lowered himself to apologize to the "nigger" who has become his friend. Huck has shown Jim respect as well as love, and one expects that Huck's feelings will persist. But Twain, for his special purposes, has made Huck's river-experience somehow "exempt from the conditions that we . . . know to attach to it." (See *The Art of the Novel* [James's preface to *The American*], ed. Richard P. Blackmur; New York: Charles Scribner's Sons, 1934, p. 33.) Huck's complicity is intellectually meaningful, but, realistically speaking, it is also a violation of Huck's character. Twain's break with realistic character-portrayal in this instance costs him the critical approval of many careful readers—but the risk, calculated or not, offers impressive benefits, too.

white folks does for their'n," even though "it don't seem
natural"(215). But Huck has changed identities so many
times during the course of his adventures that it is difficult
to keep track of just who or what he is at a given moment.
In his most recent rebirth, Huck has discovered that he is
supposed to be Tom Sawyer, and so overjoyed was he upon
learning of his providentially assigned name that "it was like
being born again, I was so glad to find out who I was" (310).
By the very end of the book it is painfully clear, once more,
that Tom Sawyer is precisely who, or what, Huck isn't, but
with Tom's name forced upon him, Huck becomes more and
more like Tom. Now the value most typical of Tom Sawyer
—or, for Twain's purposes, of Tom's society—is the equation
of "nigger" with "property."

If Tom's plot is really going to subvert the social order
by freeing Jim, then the plotters' ideas about Jim ought, we
might legitimately expect, to be different from society's. Yet
because of his commitment to Tom's plot, Huck's view of
Jim conforms more and more to society's. As the romantic
trappings multiply, the satire broadens out to ridicule other
aspects of this relationship between stable society and the
world of romance. Tom Sawyer has been pretending to be
in revolt against society, but he depends upon society's
accepted conventions for every suggestion and addition to
his scheme. When he advises Jim to play music on his jew's-
harp to the animals the boys intend to infest him with, he
suggests that Jim " 'play "The Last Link is Broken"—that's
the thing that'll scoop a rat quicker'n anything else' "(364).
When Huck joined the Grangerford household, "nothing was
ever so lovely as to hear the young ladies sing 'The Last
Link is Broken' and play 'The Battle of Prague' on ... a little
old piano ... that had tin pans in it, I reckon"(144). These
references to maudlin music of the day had special meaning
to Twain. An Arkansas bride at the Jungfrau Hotel, in *A*

Tramp Abroad, "turned on all the horrors of the 'Battle of Prague,' that venerable shivaree, and waded chin-deep in the blood of the slain . . . . it was the worst music that had ever been achieved on our planet by a mere human being" (X, 29-30). Twain's description in *Life on the Mississippi* of the "best dwelling, finest dwelling" in a typical river town includes on the music-stand, among other selections, " 'Battle of Prague' " and " 'The Last Link is Broken' "(XII, 318). Tom's grand revolt against society makes use of the parlor musicale and bookshelf, as well as of parlor morality.

Tom's whole plot is a romance, and its satirical emphasis makes us laugh at romance. There is no movement away from society; instead, society increasingly comes to control the action and to exert pressure on the supposed rebels. In order to achieve more thrills, Tom has deliberately warned the society he ostensibly hopes to rob. Since he knows all along that Jim is free, he is never trying to change the *status quo,* in the manner of a true rebel, but instead wants nothing more than a brief period of "howling adventures . . . for a couple weeks"(XIII, 404) before returning home, a socially accepted hero, "with a torchlight procession and a brass-band"(403). After Tom finally admits that he was merely pretending to free a slave, for the adventure of it all, Aunt Polly enters to reveal the true identity of Aunt Sally's guests. As in any romance, the melodrama concludes with the triumph of law and order on the western frontier. With Huck's "nothing more to write about"(405), we have come full circle, for Huck is ready again to challenge society, to "light out for the territory," just as he had been ready to steal Jim, and to remain an outcast, at the start of the book. Huck is once more alone. Even though Tom is a hero, with "his bullet around his neck on a watch-guard"(405), and Jim is free, Tom's elaborate machinations have had no permanent effect on anybody in the book.

II

The rescue-chapters oscillate between the effects of Tom's "romantic" plot on Jim, Tom, and Huck, and on the Phelps family, culminating with its effect on society as a whole—the fifteen men with guns, and the dinner-table gossips. Because we are, after all, concerned with the hoaxes and plots only as they do something to us, this pattern is intrinsically important because of its effect on the reader. First of all, we notice that while Tom's pretended revolt against society has stirred up all manner of sensational reactions, Huck's really significant split with society, through his struggles with his conscience and his determination to go to hell, has absolutely no effect on that society, because Jim (as Tom, of course, knows) has been free almost from the beginning.

Tom's "appearance" seems to have more force than Huck's "reality," and the problem of differentiating between what is true and what is false has been a central theme through the book. Huck is "antiromantic," in our special, literary sense of the word, and Tom lives for romance. But in terms of a romantic point of view more widely recognized as such, Huck is more nearly the true romantic than Tom, who is merely a nineteenth-century hero of romance. Alex Comfort, in his short treatise on *Art and Social Responsibility*, presents the romantic as the man whose responsibility it is to fight for freedom, and "the war for freedom," he maintains, "is the war against society. There is no other enemy."[1] By this definition, Huck is not really a romantic either; he makes the reader question society, but he himself never does. It is true that when, in *Tom Sawyer*, Huck and Tom discuss what they will do if they are successful in their hunt for buried treasure, Huck's vote is for pie, soda, and "every circus that comes along," while Tom, disdaining such carefree extravagance, plans, as befits a solid member of the community, to "save" and "get married" (VIII, 203). Huck's words constitute an attack on society, perhaps, but only if the reader puts himself in Huck's position and spells out the unproductive and irresponsible implications of his preference. In *Tom Sawyer*, the reader is not encouraged to do this. In his own book, Huck finds himself at every turn in opposition to society, but he is no Prometheus whose revolt is open and in his own eyes justified. The effect of the ending of his story is to force one to an awareness of overtones more finely shaded than the simple reversal of appearance and reality. This reversal is only the framework within which the ending unfolds.

The reader is compelled to accept the revelations of the closing chapters because of the way the story is told. The forms of humor discussed so far all play their part in driving the reader ever farther into the implications of the final hoaxes. Tom Sawyer is the poker face personified. Quite literally, he possesses a good poker face, bluffing everyone he wishes to. The Phelpses believe that he is William Thompson, Nat believes that he and Jim are strangers to each other, and so on. But Huck also has the same ability, as we have seen throughout the book; both boys are characterized as the little southwesterners that they are, although Huck really needs to hide his true position, his "hand," while Tom only wants to do so, for fun. Tom doesn't know when to stop playing; it is Huck who goes for the doctor when Tom would still retain the pose of a hero. More important, Tom's penchant for grouping the sublime with the ridiculous, for imposing the devices of royalty upon a defenseless slave's flight from a woodshed, reminds one of Simon Wheeler's poker-face technique. Tom's introduction into Jim's coat of arms of a " 'crest, a runaway nigger, *sable*, with his bundle over his shoulder on a bar sinister' "(358) is, among a number of other things, a combination of incongruities that causes Tom no amusement at all. It is the reader who balks at such matter-of-fact transitions from the dignified to the ludicrous. When Huck accepts without question Aunt Sally's implicit equation of Negroes with nonhumans—" 'Well, it's lucky; because sometimes people do get hurt' "(306-7)—his lack of selectivity is different from Tom's deliberate imposition of undiscriminating artifice into a simple problem of escape; but in each case, what starts out as humor becomes a critique of unawareness.

Tom's bluffs, and Tom's incongruous lumping of the real with the pretend, come to us through Huck's point of view. It is here that the effect of Tom's hoax is most clearly felt by the reader. Like Huck, indeed with Huck, we are incredulous when Tom announces that he will help free Jim. Tom's abbreviated ejaculation, " 'What! Why, Jim is—' "(313) puts the reader in Huck's position. In this particular area, we have no more knowledge than Huck has; we are all taken in by Tom's hoax. But even as we share Huck's bewilderment, we are aware of Mark Twain's point of view as it emerges through Huck. Huck is shocked at Tom's statement of intention; Twain—who, after all, is perpetrating Tom's hoax—misleads us still farther because he seems to applaud it. We understand Huck's surprise at Tom, because we too have been led in the opening chapters of the book to see Tom as the representative of respectability. Huck is surprised, and he condemns Tom's decision; we are equally surprised, but, with Twain, we approve. To us, at first, comes the notion that Tom's romanticism can help him to transcend his society's attitudes toward slavery. Certainly we sense Twain's nudge as our thoughts take this direction. Throughout the close of the book, Twain's wit behind Huck's naïveté helps us to see the true meaning of Huck's observation. Tom's suggestion that Jim play "The Last Link is Broken" on his jew's-harp acquires the sardonic weight of the reference in *A Tramp Abroad* only because we have felt Twain's condemnation behind Huck's enjoyment of the Grangerford girls' music.

The reader accepts Tom's boyishness because he has been watching it through Huck's eyes, but his impatience with the plot to free Jim stems from more than Huck's common-sense dissatisfaction. Tom's "romance" is held up against three standards, and this makes the parody and burlesque especially potent as they lead one farther into the hoax. On the one hand, we have Twain-the-author's implicit attitude toward romantic excitement, as communicated by the mere presence of the derelict *Walter Scott;* on the other hand, there is the standard of Huck's real adventures with which to contrast Tom's maneuvers. In between these points of view are Tom's literary examples, the tales of kings, princes, and knights, which contrast so strongly with Nigger Jim in a wooden shack. The reader, with so many guideposts, is unthinkingly swept along in a tacit agreement that of course we all condemn Tom's extravagance: the degradation of Jim, the burlesque of Huck's escapes and adventures, the parody of Tom's models—yes, of course—we all get the point, there is surely no problem. But why, one who stops here may ask, does Twain bother so much with what is so obvious? The parody-burlesque, as transmitted through Huck's point of view, helps us to see the overall structure of the book, to be sure; we can balance St. Petersburg with the Phelpses' plantation; we can watch Tom Sawyer as he almost ties up Jim the slave "for fun"(7) and fails in his attempted delivery of Jim when Jim is already free. None of this, however, has much to do with Tom's concealment of his knowledge that Jim is free, and it is the revelation of this knowledge that comes at what ought to be the climax of the book. If the hoax as Twain uses it is an instrument of self-knowledge, of shock, why do we need it at the end of the book when the parody-burlesque has already made us annoyed with Tom's romantic games and aware of their foolishness? Why, indeed?

III

The revelation of importance in the ending of *Huckleberry Finn* is concerned with neither Tom nor Huck, but with society and—by a parallel structure—with the reader. Most simply, the reader is hoaxed into believing that Tom Sawyer is going to triumph over the romance-pattern; that is, one sees that Tom is intent upon experiencing every romantic sensation that he can engineer, but one feels that the end result of Tom's romancing will be the freeing of Jim and, therefore, a significant rupture with society. If Tom really helps to free a runaway slave, he becomes a rebel in earnest rather than a hero of romance, and until we learn that he is wounded, we see no reason why even his overly-elaborate plan should fail. " 'Why,' " complains Tom—and we know that he is right—" 'we could work with a torchlight procession if we wanted to, *I* believe' " (331).

It is important for the meaning of this hoax on the reader that he be made to react to Tom. If there is any weakness in the ending of the book, it is Twain's failure to make some of his readers think about Tom enough. It would seem, though, that one is made to think about him a good deal. Huck's narrative focuses almost completely on Tom. Jim, of course, and Huck are both important to us because we have followed them so far; Tom is an intruder, and because his presence is so annoying to us, we come to watch him more closely. Huck slides into the background not only because he must put himself outside of society, but in order to make us focus on Tom. We may not like Tom—we very definitely do not—but we are made aware of him and we follow with interest what we take to be his true revolt against society. That this revolt takes on all the trappings of the literary romance makes it even more satisfying; it is as though we could assure ourselves that there is something real behind our romantic daydreams. Sensationalism, we think, can lead to something antisocial. We succeed in forgetting that the basis of sensationalism as Tom enjoys it is a social basis, depending on accepted conventions for its effect.

Just as we believe in the truth of Tom's revolt despite its romantic form, so the people in the book—Aunt Sally, Uncle Silas, and their neighbors—believe that a "gang of cutthroats from over in the Indian Territory"(372) is about to steal Jim, but that they can kill the members of the gang at their "leasure." In view of the preceding events, no real Uncle Silas and Aunt Sally would ever believe Tom's "nonnamous letters." With two boys around the house? The supposition is silly. But the fact of society's credulity is one of the elements of the ending of the book that causes the reader no trouble at all. He can accept the popular belief in Tom's hoax because he has been prepared for it by the episode of "What Royalty Did to Parkville"(Chapter XX). Here, society has accepted without question a hoax as unrealistic as Tom's, and the king is a great success as a reformed Indian Ocean pirate. "He said it warn't no use talking, heathens don't amount to shucks alongside of pirates to work a camp-meeting with" (184-85.) Realistically, the reader can object that no Indian Ocean pirate would wander through the Mississippi Valley, so no one would believe the king's claim. In *Mark Twain's America* Bernard DeVoto has summed up the realist's objections to the incident:

The scene at the camp meeting is one of the book's climactic passages. . . . But also the scene provides an instance of Mark Twain's literary judgment betrayed into error. Here, as in so many other places, his imagination—or his discretion—goes wrong and forces him out of realism, out of satire even, into extravaganza. His effect is something damaged by the repentant Dauphin's decision to set his evil-doing among the pirates of the Indian

Ocean and his exhortation for funds with which to convert them.
A scene of corrosive realism loses credibility in this touch and
recedes into burlesque. . . . A high moment in "Huckleberry Finn"
would have been better if Mark Twain had adhered to the scene
that unquestionably produced it . . . Chapter X of Johnson J.
Hooper's "Adventure of Simon Suggs."[2]

The objection is to the pirates, yet if one looks at the
psychological realism of the scene, one finds that to make the
king pretend to be a pirate is the most effective pretense
Twain could possibly adopt, as Twain himself must have
sensed when he made the trick work perfectly. If we ask
ourselves why it works we need look no farther than Twain's
own writing for the answer. The pirate combines elements
of excitement and respectability as no other romance-object
could. The Indian Ocean is far away, and distance lends
enchantment; but even more explicit than this are statements
all through the body of Twain's work. Tom Sawyer, "exalted
into the vague august realm of the romantic" (VIII, 74),
considers the advantages of becoming a clown, or a soldier,
or an Indian. "But no, there was something gaudier even
than this. He would be a pirate!" (75). Joe Harper, set on
living the life of a hermit, quickly changes his mind on hearing Tom's description of piracy (112). As Twain later said,
"Celebrity is what a boy or a youth longs for more than for
any other thing. He would be a clown in a circus, he would
be a pirate, he would sell himself to Satan, in order to
attract attention and be talked about and envied. . . . it is
the same with every grown-up person" (1906).[3] Huck Finn
equates Captain Kidd with George Washington, so far as
reputation is concerned ("Tom Sawyer Abroad"; XIX, 89),
and the boyhood wish most often referred to by Mark Twain
is that of becoming a pirate (XII, 32; XXVI, 82; passim).

Not only is piracy the career dreamed of by romantic
youth, it is also the epitome of respectable sensation, of

romance, to adult society. A New Orleans graveyard finds its way into *Life on the Mississippi* because it holds the ashes of a celebrity:

He was a pirate with a tremendous and sanguinary history; and as long as he preserved unspotted, in retirement, the dignity of his name and the grandeur of his ancient calling, homage and reverence were his from high and low; but when at last he descended into politics and became a paltry alderman, the public "shook" him, and turned aside and wept. When he died, they set up a monument over him; and little by little he has come into respect again; but it is respect for the pirate, not the alderman. Today the loyal and generous remember only what he was, and charitably forget what he became. (XII, 356)

This is more than just another one of Twain's mocking attacks on American legislators. The pirate is adored, worshiped; he is the symbol of all the romantic longings of people who find their own lives unbearably dull and who long for the excitement of romance to brush against their humdrum existence. The citizens of Pokeville believe that the king is a pirate because they so desperately want to. Because Huck, the narrator, is outside the hoax, looking on, we can laugh, and we do laugh, at the king's successful deception. The hoax-within-the-hoax at the end of the book, however, arouses no laughter. Lifted out of context, the notion that fifteen grown men should respond with such dogged earnestness to a boy's prank is surely amusing. But while we are amused by Huck's entrance into the parlor with a lump of butter under his hat, the fifteen men with guns do not amuse us at all. We see the comic side of Huck's situation—an "evoker of the horse-laugh," as Satan in *The Mysterious Stranger* would call it—but we miss the "high-grade comicality" implicit in the delusion of society.

Since we have already laughed at such situations, as when Huck hides from the ferryboat (XIII, 53), our failure

to notice the humor here must mean something in terms of
the double hoax. We, after all, are being imposed upon just
as much as the farmers, for if they believe in the cutthroats'
existence, we believe in Tom Sawyer's rebellion. So, as we
shall see, in reading "The Man That Corrupted Hadleyburg"
we do not react to the humor latent in the townspeople's
efforts to guess a remark that was never made in order to
gain gold that does not exist. The hoax in "Hadleyburg"
strips the characters of their pose of innocence; the hoax in
Huckleberry Finn strips the reader of his own pretensions.

For Twain, for any humorist, a major source of humor
is in the sudden revelation of a discrepancy between appearance and reality. In a sense, a bluff is "called"—by the reader
—and humor is the result. For some reason, we are compelled
not to call the bluff at the end of Huck's book, and we do not
laugh at a situation that is, potentially, among the most
ridiculous in Twain's writings. Society accepts the hoax
at face value, because it wants to believe that life on "one of
these little one-horse cotton plantations" that "all look alike"
(303) can still partake of romantic excitement. And what
does that society do as a result of its participation in romance?
It goes out en masse and shoots a bullet into the leg of its
most undisguised avatar. Society believes that Jim is property; Tom Sawyer believes that Jim is property, and only
because he does so believe is his elaborate and brutal hoax
possible, for, clearly enough, no one who looked upon Jim
as a human being possessing human dignity could subject
him to such indignities. Because it hungers after sensation,
society, in effect, shoots itself. Then the "property" saves
Tom's life by helping the doctor.

Jim is the focal point around which Twain organizes both
society's respectability and its love of romantic excitement. On
the one hand, Jim's status as property forces society to show
a sense of responsibility toward him. He must be fed and

housed; his owner must be found. If he were to be hanged, he would have to be "paid for." Likewise, Huck's failure in his own eyes to measure up to the expectations of respectable society is defined in terms of his decision to aid and abet Jim, the runaway slave. On the other hand, Tom's whole romantic plot has for its center the disposing of Jim. Without Jim, there could be no escape, and society could not be titillated. Both respectability and romance, in other words, derive their ultimate thematic statement from the same object: Nigger Jim. When society shoots itself in the leg, therefore, we do not laugh, because we ourselves have been guilty of pandering to our own desires just as society has done. If the farmers have been too eager to share in any available excitement, we have been too eager to believe that the excitements of romance could lead anywhere except straight back to the society against which they seem to be (but are not) organized. We cannot "call the bluff" and laugh at the men with guns, because, until Tom tells us that he was thinking only of the "*adventure*," since Jim was already free, we are as badly fooled as they are.

We have been fooled because we have assumed too easily that we agree with the parody-burlesque of the escape as it satirizes the falseness of Tom's contrived adventures; we have unthinkingly assured ourselves that we see through the excitement-for-its-own-sake that characterizes romance, that we understand well enough that it is meaningless humbug. But we do not. Nobody does. Twain isn't trying to tell us that we should expect so much of ourselves. "To be human," we remember, "is to have one's little modicum of romance secreted away in one's composition"(V, 98). Our mistake is in assuming a self-knowledge that we do not really possess. We think that we are impervious to the temptations of romance, but we are mistaken in ourselves. The farmers do not know themselves well enough, either; they do not see that

their eagerness for excitement can lead only to self-destruction, just as the citizens of Pokeville lose their money for the
sake of romance. The essential truths for man are truths of
self-knowledge, and a lack of self-knowledge is a target for
pity—or for laughter. "There are many humorous things in the
world; among them the white man's notion that he is less
savage than the other savages"(XX, 192). In self-deception
lie most of the "high-grade comicalities" of this world, and
Twain's humor at its core is organized around the hoax which
operates to reveal to ourselves the discrepancy between what
we assume we are and what we are in truth.

The comic attitude enables us to hold two or more points
of view simultaneously; it permits us to laugh, however
grimly, at ourselves and still to respect ourselves. The farmers
at the end of *Huckleberry Finn* are funny, but they are also
people. Just as Jim and Huck share a common humanity,
despite Huck's preconceptions about slaves and property,
so the reader shares the assumptions and gullibilities of the
farmers, despite the facile antipathy organized by the parody-
burlesque. Twain once drew a picture of a tower with a flag;
on the tower he placed an out-of-scale man. "I composed the
picture from two points of view," he explains; "the spectator
is to observe the man from about where that flag is, and he
must observe the tower itself from the ground. This harmo-
nizes the seeming discrepancy"(IX, 86). This seems as naïve
as any of Huck's reactions to Mississippi social convention,
but just as Twain's wit lurks behind Huck, so here there is
something hidden. No one can be at the top and at the
bottom of a tower at the same time; to do so would be to
transcend human limitations. When we smile at Twain's
advice for viewing his picture, we smile from a context of
shared limitations of which we are all aware, and there is
nothing cruel in our amusement. If we were to laugh at the
farmers, we would be separating ourselves from them. They

are not meant to receive a "horse-laugh," but rather the smile of shared amusement, because, like ourselves, they have human weaknesses as well as strengths. They are duped, but so are we all. They are victims, yet some notion of free choice is inescapable after reading of Huck's choice of hell over respectability. Through his use of the hoax as a form rather than as a series of incidents, Twain pushes the reader farther and farther toward the self-knowledge that will enable him to live in this world. The recurring theme in Twain's major fiction—we think of *The Prince and the Pauper, A Connecticut Yankee,* and *Pudd'nhead Wilson,* as well as of *Huckleberry Finn* and *Tom Sawyer*—is that of the discovery of identity. The recurring form of his humor—for most of his mature humor leads to the hoax—is one of sudden revelation.

The ending of *Huckleberry Finn* is the most thoroughly worked out example of the hoax-as-revelation in Twain's writing, and we should read it as such. It is easy for us to ignore the climax toward which the form of the ending pushes us. Certainly it is difficult to accept the temporary eclipse of Huck's newfound sensitivity to Jim; so, perhaps, we tend to read the parody-burlesque as the final meaning of the episode, and thus to malign *in toto* the ending of the book. It is easy to agree with Twain that Tom's eagerness for romantic excitement leads him to do what all writers of romance do: Tom imposes upon reality a preconceived pattern that simply does not fit, that is dangerous and immoral in its implications. Tom's hoax on society points so clearly to this conclusion that we ignore the larger hoax on the reader, and so question the validity of the ending. Tom's hoax on the reader operates to make the reader aware that he himself possesses that "modicum of romance" present in all human beings, no matter how vociferously he may join in the condemnation of Tom's romantic nonsense.

Many readers will object that they, at least, never for one

moment were misled into taking seriously Tom's expressed intention to free a slave. Their sensitivity to the true meaning of romantic excitement serves to emphasize Twain's effect, for their insight emerges from the action that Twain has presented. As for those not so astute, one must remember that Huck Finn is persuaded of Tom's good faith, and it is with Huck that the reader has been encouraged to sympathize. Perhaps it is Huck's newfound respect for Jim that leads him to assume that Tom, despite the pretenses of the robber gang, will himself respect Jim's dignity enough to refrain from merely empty sensationalism. But the reader who recognizes that Tom will go to any lengths to create adventure will also realize immediately that in the hands of respectable Tom, romance-excitement will be totally impotent as a weapon against social order. Those who share Huck's view of Tom will certainly be taken in, to be disabused by Tom's final revelation of duplicity. In any case, these last chapters of the book demolish romantic excitement not simply because its appurtenances are ridiculously out of place, incongruent to real life, but because such excitement can have only a harmful effect on those who give themselves up to it. The people at the king's camp meeting lose their money; the Royal Nonesuch victims lose money and self-respect; Tom Sawyer is shot in the leg—the clearest example of all that in pursuit of thrills society injures only itself.

Twain is not telling us through his hoax that we must despise ourselves if we, too, love sensation and chase after Christians or Communists or "cutthroats from over in the Indian Territory"—depending upon the hysteria of the moment—mainly to satisfy our hunger for excitement. He has no evangelical message; he expects no sudden reform. "Habit is habit, and not to be flung out of the window by any man, but coaxed down-stairs a step at a time"(XVI, 44). Nor is Twain suggesting that we have no real dangers to fear, for Huck himself, one remembers, has had to deal with con men, thieves, and murderers—to say nothing of all the well-meaning people who would enslave him. It is toward self-knowledge that Twain's humor leads, and at the core of this humor is not the parody-burlesque we so often and so easily notice, but the hoax. Any situation in Mark Twain's writings that appears out of context to be funny yet inspires no laughter is worthy of attention. We need to call Twain's "bluffs" as we find them; we need to see ourselves as caught in the hoax. "There are few things that are so unpardonably neglected in our country as poker .... It is enough to make one ashamed of one's species."

V

Calling the Bluff
Images of Darkness and of Light

7

Was Hadleyburg Corrupted?

There are few things that are so unpardonably neglected in our country as poker. The upper class know very little about it. Now and then you find ambassadors who have a sort of general knowledge of the game, but the ignorance of the people is fearful. Why, I have known clergymen, good men, kind-hearted, liberal, sincere, and all that, who did not know the meaning of a "flush." It is enough to make one ashamed of one's species.[1]

MARK TWAIN's quarrel with the damned human race appears at its most violent in "The Man That Corrupted Hadleyburg" and *The Mysterious Stranger,* the most important works of his last years. In each, the human community seems to be a brush-heap of ants that deserves only to be set afire. This appearance, however, is deceptive. The disgust for life and for the living of it that one feels to be so characteristic of the elderly Twain does doubtless underlie the fiction of this period, but Twain's art is other than, or at least more than, a mere reflection of his spiritual weariness. Both stories express a bitterly satirical despair, but "The Man That Corrupted Hadleyburg" presents an understanding of how we damned humans come to damn ourselves that makes any consideration of "despair" beside the point, and *The Mysterious Stranger* carries one from the darkest sort of fatalistic hell to the bright world we all might create for ourselves. In each case, the quality of Twain's understanding reaches us only as we call his bluff.

By questioning the surface of the image Twain presents, one discovers that his narratives are scarcely as straight-forward as they might seem. The town of Hadleyburg, for example, is not simply an object of scornful attack. Twain explores the psychological defenses of the citizens with a precision almost clinical, so that by the end of the story the reader is less appalled at the town's dishonesty than aware of how the townspeople are constituted as human beings. To understand all may not be to forgive all, but the empha-sized effect of the story is to make us understand even while we condemn.

"The Man That Corrupted Hadleyburg" is the story not of a man but of a hoax. An explication of the hoax will in large measure be an explication of the story as well, although the two do not exactly coincide. The story is about a hoax, though, and one might ask, who is the victim of the hoax? Is the hoax played on the innocent characters, or is the inno-cent reader the true object of attack? As in *Huckleberry Finn,* both character and reader become involved in different ways.

From the beginning, the virtuous innocence of Hadley-burg is stressed in a way to contrast it with the rest of the world. But if Hadleyburg is the "most honest and upright town in all the region"(XXIII, 1), it is also "proud." We learn that "throughout the formative years temptations were kept out of the way of the young people, so that their honesty could have every chance to harden and solidify," and the townspeople's complacent faith in this regimen warns us that trouble lies ahead. John Milton could not praise a "fugitive and cloistered virtue," and neither can we. We cannot even trust it. Mary Richards puts into words the new

insight she has gained after regretting her husband's honest
haste to report possession of the sack of "gold coins" delivered
to their house in the dead of night, and her insight into the
nature of the town's virtue is no more than the reader has
known from the start:

"It's *artificial* honesty, and weak as water when temptation comes,
as we have seen this night. . . . It is a mean town, a hard, stingy
town, and hasn't a virtue in the world but this honesty it is so
celebrated for and so conceited about; and so help me, I do
believe that if ever the day comes that its honesty falls under
great temptation, its grand reputation will go to ruin like a house
of cards." (15-16)

Mary's insight is soon confirmed; the townspeople have been
fooling themselves.

   Into the innocent town of Hadleyburg, into the Richards'
very parlor, the Stranger drops his sack of "gold"—at the end
of the story we find that it is filled with lead discs—together
with written instructions to find the right man and reward
him for his past generosity and advice to the Stranger. In
this "hard" and "stingy" town the only conceivable claimant
for the sack would be Mr. Goodson, but he is dead, as Mary
and Edward Richards remember after Edward has hurried to
publicize the Stranger's trust in the town's honesty. The
Stranger's letter has suggested either a public or a private
inquiry, but after the public announcement of the Stranger's
"trust," only a town meeting will do to award the money, if
there should be a claimant, with fitting pomp. The claimant
of the sack is to deposit with the Reverend Burgess a letter
containing an illuminating remark made to the Stranger by
the unknown man whom the Stranger wishes to reward and
relies upon the town's honesty to find. Prior to the meeting,
the head of each of the town's nineteen leading families
receives a letter from "Howard L. Stephenson" (22) revealing

the remark and telling each man that *he* should have the money, because, since Goodson is dead, the man who had done Goodson "a very great service once" is Goodson's legitimate heir, and Goodson, as all have suspected, had helped the Stranger. Each of the nineteen sends Burgess a letter with the remark enclosed, and only Richards escapes public disgrace at the meeting, as the Reverend Burgess withholds his letter. A final letter inside the sack explains that there never was a "test remark," that the purpose of the whole plot from the beginning was to damage the town on as large a scale as possible. The Stranger, amazed that even one man could withstand temptation, pays Edward Richards the full face value of $40,000 for the sack of lead discs, but at the end even Edward's guilt becomes known. The whole town, as Mary predicts, has fallen.

Like any new convert, Mary has overstated her case. Stingy and vain though the town as a whole is, there are individual exceptions to her general condemnation. The late Mr. Goodson, the Reverend Burgess, and the irreverent Jack Halliday are neither innocent nor vain nor stingy. The two still living have looked with understanding on the horrors the town has committed in the name of righteousness, and Goodson, we are told, had repudiated on principle any link to the professed innocence of his fellow-citizens. The minister and the loafer—the two extremes of respectability—are neither horrified nor surprised by the citizens' loss of integrity. Both men are merely "puzzled"(31) by the outward signs of the town's moral disintegration, and Burgess is even able to lie for the Richardses at the meeting (63). Even more telling is Burgess' ability to live in a community which considers him guilty of a crime he never committed (8); the paradoxical irony of this simple fact is played upon throughout the story. Since Burgess never knows that Edward Richards could have cleared him, he feels only gratitude to

Richards for having saved him from the angry crowd of long ago, a gratitude that makes Richards feel even more guilty for not having had the courage to tell the truth. In one sense, Burgess might thus seem to be the most "innocent" person in the story, for not only is he not guilty of whatever it is he was charged with, but he is also above the false accusers and the silent witness. But to accept human nature deeply enough to be able to live under the shadow of false accusation is to have a deep knowledge of evil, and Burgess is far from innocent when as chairman of the meeting (36) he feigns surprise upon "discovering" that more than one citizen of the town has claimed the reward money.

The cynicism of Jack Halliday's assumptions about human motivation (29) indicates a departure from innocence as great as Burgess', and yet Halliday too seems innocent. He is a "loafing, good-natured, no-account, irreverent fisherman, hunter, boys' friend, stray-dogs' friend, typical 'Sam Lawson' of the town"(18).* What could be a more childlike and innocent depiction? Jack is an idle joker, too (20), totally irresponsible; but just as the supposedly errant Burgess is designated by the Stranger's letter as the man to conduct the town meeting, so Halliday is approved by the town to auction off the bogus gold coins for Richards' benefit (54).

Burgess and Halliday, though at opposite poles so far as social status is concerned, have more in common than a seeming innocence and a real knowledge of evil. If Halliday is a "no-account" in the townspeople's eyes, the Reverend

*The allusion to the "Sam Lawson" of Harriet Beecher Stowe's creation is particularly apt. Twain is not so much paying tribute to a long-time neighbor as he is summoning up in the reader's mind allusions especially useful to his purpose. Chapter IV of *Oldtown Folks* (1869), "The Village Do-Nothing," presents Sam Lawson as the idle man of insight whose kindly, intuitive psychological sense is the only comfort offered to the small-boy "narrator" on the death of his father. "Of course no one thought of looking after me," the second paragraph begins: only Sam Lawson, the village do-nothing. The title of *Sam Lawson's Oldtown Fireside Stories* (1871) suggests that Mrs. Stowe's Sam had found quick favor with the public.

Burgess is without exception " 'the best-hated man among us' "(7); Halliday is not respected; Burgess " 'will never get another congregation here' "(7), and Mary thinks it " 'odd that the stranger should appoint Burgess to deliver the money' "(8). Yet at the town meeting, "when the Rev. Mr. Burgess rose and laid his hand on the sack he could hear his microbes gnaw, the place was so still"(32). His words about the sack and the town's reputation are respectful and friendly, and are greeted with applause. He controls the meeting as though he were the most popular and respected man in town. Yet he has been pictured almost as the town's scapegoat (10-11); a pariah although innocent, he is put in charge of the ceremony that will disclose the town's rottenness to itself as well as to the outside world. Considering the strong emphasis early in the story on the town's hatred and lack of respect for Burgess, one wonders why he is matter-of-factly accepted and obeyed at the meeting, especially as Mary's explicit questioning of the Stranger's wisdom in appointing him (8) has the force of representing the townspeople's reaction in general.

A related fact is Halliday's rise in position. After the town has demonstratedly fallen, the saddler—not of Hadleyburg's top nineteen families—moves that Burgess " 'appoint Jack Halliday to get up there and auction off that sack ... and give the result to the right man—the man whom Hadleyburg delights to honor—Edward Richards,' " the " '*one* clean man left ... out of the late aristocracy' "(54). Clearly, Halliday's will be a position of trust, but is the man trustworthy?

When Jack Halliday is nominated and accepted as the right man to reward Edward Richards' adamantine virtue, the town is satirizing itself, and the action helps sustain the mood of the meeting, which has become one of almost joyful acceptance of the disillusioning truth. But to stop with this easy summary of the effect of Jack Halliday's rise is to divorce his change of role from Burgess' change, and is also to ignore the two qualities of Halliday that are most emphasized. He "always noticed everything; and always made fun of it, too, no matter what it was"(19). Not only are we told about Halliday's roles as observer and debunker, but we are also shown them. Faced with an unsmiling populace, as the worried people try to imagine what the golden remark might have been, Halliday not only laughs at the sudden loss of risibility, but also "carried a cigar-box around on a tripod, playing that it was a camera, and halted all passers and aimed the thing and said, 'Ready!—now look pleasant, please' "(20). Halliday is the cameraman; he sees everything; Twain emphasizes this fact to make his reader remember it. It is understandable that the town, in wry self-criticism, should elevate the loafer, but it is strange that the one man in the story who is supposed to "notice everything" fails to notice—as does the rest of the audience—the discrepancy between Burgess' announcement that " 'there are nineteen' " (47) letters and the minister's failure to read Richards' letter after, as Mary mentions quietly to her husband, " 'he has read eighteen' "(50).

If "The Man That Corrupted Hadleyburg" were a detective story or a "realistic" narrative, one would object to the inconsistency of Jack Halliday, who "notices" and "makes fun of" everything, but neither laughs at nor sees through Richards' apparent honesty. With the spectacle of the town's acceptance of Burgess as mediator one would have no patience at all. These inexplicable events would be the two most disturbing in a series that begins with Mary Richards' immediate and even reflexive fear of robbers in a town so proud of its honesty and extends through the inexplicable failure of anyone to examine the contents of the much-coveted sack and so discover that the "gold" is really lead. But such details do not bother a reader as he reads; one

senses that there is a deeper reality involved, a reality into
which these odd facts will somehow fit.

Because the Man who corrupts Hadleyburg tells Mary
Richards what she wants to believe, that the sack is filled
with gold, neither she nor anybody else in town questions
the honesty of his statement. Amidst the innocence of Eden,
Eve believed the serpent. Mary—and the town—believes the
Stranger's words not only because she is innocent, but also
because she (and the rest of the town) is at the same time
not innocent at all: her (and their) thoughts are guilty. This
paradox is presented through Mary's fear of being robbed.
She believes the Stranger unquestioningly, and at the same
time is filled with panic. She fears that in the most honest
town in the world the spurious treasure will be stolen. Since
Mary's second thoughts are that she and her husband ought
to steal the sack themselves, we see that her fear is merely
the projection of an as yet unaccepted wish. Mary's belief
and fear are complemented by her husband's response to
the adventurous connotations of the sack. The gambler and
his loot, the material solidity of the reward, the sudden
emergence into Hadleyburg of the sordid side of life—all
these elements are summoned before the reader when
Edward learns of the sack and the letter, and exclaims,
" 'Isn't it an adventure! Why, it's a romance; it's like the
impossible things one reads about in books, and never sees
in life' "(6). Mary's reaction to the responsibility of the
sack has been to fear for its safety; Edward's is to say,
"humorously"(6), that all they need do is hide the sack,
burn the papers, and " 'we're rich, Mary, rich.' " In context
it is clear that he is speaking in jest. His joke and Mary's
fear reveal the same desire, and the same unexpressed break
with innocence. Mary never jokes; her reaction to the sack
centers around her unexpressed guilt. Edward, when he
leaves Mary alone with what they believe is $40,000, has

no fear of robbers; he is intent on savoring the "romance" of the situation. Edward can suggest robbery, but only in jest; Mary can think of thieves, but only in fear. They deceive themselves about the nature of their deepest feelings.

Just as Mary and Edward fool themselves, so does the rest of the town. Everyone wants to believe the Stranger, and not only for the "romance" of the affair. Punishment is due the people of Hadleyburg, and through the structure of the story Twain shows that they know it without being aware of it. Only on the deepest levels of personality do their feelings exist; but, Twain demonstrates, such levels are potent. The people are guilty. Mary's fear of robbers and Edward's joke have shown us their guilt. No matter how conscientiously the town tries to foster innocence in its citizens, evil impulses remain part of humanity. Although we are told of the town's care to protect its children, significantly enough there are no children in the story. Every one is a guilty adult.

"Lead us not into temptation"(69) is the town's motto. For an insight into Mark Twain's attitude toward established Christianity in this story, the timing of the revelation of this motto from the Lord's Prayer is most important. Its appearance only at the very end, after we know all, shows us that the town has consciously tried to deny the existence of evil. Like so many other Christians in Twain's works, the people have perverted Christianity. Absolute innocence is impossible if one is to live in this world. The town's motto is futile, even hypocritical, for the love of money corrupts and destroys the whole pretense of innocence. Hadleyburg, the pure community, with a motto that is the prayer of every Christian, suggests that the Christian creation itself is a gigantic hoax. The Christian overtones in the story lead the reader to measure the town's fate against the myth of the Fall. How can fallen man deny evil? Yet this is what Hadleyburg tries to do. The hoaxes in the story work because innocence is everyone's expectation. But the supposed innocents are all concerned from the beginning with the getting of money. Richards laments his hard lot in life, and the nineteen families spend their "reward" money before they even see it (30).

Throughout his work, Twain makes his readers realize that no one engaged in making or spending money can be innocent. No matter how innocent a man may appear, if he is active in the world of getting and spending, then he must first have fallen. Colonel Sellers is the most "innocent," or otherworldly, character Twain created, yet the good Colonel proposes schemes that would oppress millions of people (*The Gilded Age*; V, 76-81) and assumes that climate has always been a ready source of income, no matter who suffered: " 'Take the glacial period. Was that produced by accident? Not at all; it was done for money' " (*The American Claimant*; XV, 248). After Philip Sterling has lost his innocence in the worlds of politics and finance, he "had to look about him for something to do. He was like Adam: the world was all before him where to choose"(VI, 186). The point of view here expressed is not unique with Twain, of course. The combination of guilt and innocence suggested by the closing lines of *Paradise Lost* was seized upon by Americans throughout the century as particularly expressive of the American experience. If the Puritans saw themselves as the chosen people of God, led by him to a New Canaan, their nineteenth-century successors often looked on the relationship between God, country, and self as Adam-like. Samuel E. Moffett, in his biographical sketch of Twain written in 1899, expresses surprise at the inability of Twain's migrating parents to make a fortune, because, after all, "The whole Western empire was before them where to choose" (XXII, 388). In 1837, Robert Montgomery Bird opened

Nick of the Woods, his horrific tale of "the early settlers in Kentucky," with a direct quotation of the last four lines of Milton's epic. Isabel Archer, suddenly become a sought-after heiress, wanders through the London fog: "The world lay before her—she could do whatever she chose."[2] In general, the Miltonic overtone might seem to emphasize American innocence rather than American guilt. But this is not unequivocably true, despite nineteenth-century optimism and lightheartedness. Isabel Archer's real fall may be ahead of her, yet how innocent is she really as she moves on to greener pastures? How innocent are the American settlers of Kentucky who clear away the forests and the Indians with equal callousness? "Well, take your choice . . . as Goethe says in his Paradise Lost" (*A Tramp Abroad*; X, 284). The point is that Twain uses Miltonic echoes to suggest that life in this world is incompatible with innocence, that innocence and life are, indeed, mutually exclusive. Innocence doesn't really exist, except perhaps in sentimental young women, and then only as convention: Sophia Grangerford, as sweet as she can be, uses the church to arrange the assignation that leads to mass slaughter. As in much of Twain's writing, through the story of Hadleyburg runs the theme that innocence is merely a worthless pose. This is explicit in Mary's tirade (XXIII, 15-16), in the Stranger's letter (52-53), and in the town's climactic revision of its motto to "Lead us into temptation" (69).

Innocence such as Hadleyburg's is especially vulnerable to a hoax; the townspeople are unable to express any knowledge or sense of evil, and because they are human beings they have impulses and thoughts that must remain hidden, especially from themselves, or else their whole self-image would break. They are guilty in their thoughts, but because they hide their guilt from themselves, they cannot possibly atone for what they are not aware of. They are self-prepared and even eager for punishment. Indeed, according to one psychoanalytic school, *"only that unconscious expectation of punishment makes the criminal action possible,"*[3] an insight which explains why each of the nineteen is able to claim the money by "remembering" the nonexistent test remark, without realizing that if he is capable of such an action, then so are his fellows. They all want to be caught, although they don't know it.*

Their desire for punishment stems not from the immediate misdemeanor of remembering a remark they never made, but from years of living with their own unacknowledged thoughts and desires. Their acceptance of Burgess as their spokesman is the reader's clue to this state of mind, for the reader knows that Burgess, though judged guilty, is innocent of the specific, but nameless, crime for which he has been made to suffer. Burgess reflects the town's unexpressed feelings about its moral life prior to the Man's arrival with the sack. So far as deeds are concerned, Burgess is innocent, but he has been forced to live as though he were guilty. He has been the repository of all the guilts that the townsfolk have never been able to accept in themselves.

The town's desire for punishment is seen most clearly in its reaction to the sudden disclosure of evil at the public meeting. The townspeople themselves joyfully accept the destruction of their reputation. Led by Jack Halliday, they absolutely revel in their degradation. Not only does Jack set the note of hilarity that prevails through the entire scene, but in his eagerness to proclaim the virtue of the Richardses he sets up the town's final disillusionment when even this last straw turns out to be rotten (67-68). The contrast

---

*Just how conscious Twain may or may not have been of such an insight is beside the point. That he sensed how to work it into his fiction is demonstrated by the fact that we do accept his characters' actions as we read. What those actions "mean," what they reveal, is the subject of this inquiry. Twain, to be sure, was not a psychiatrist.

between the Richardses and the other eighteen families at
first serves to emphasize the guilt of the fallen while giving
the town one remaining beacon of innocence: " 'There's *one*
Symbol left, you bet!' "(51). But at the end, "the last of the
sacred Nineteen had fallen a prey to the fiendish sack; the
town was stripped of the last rag of its ancient glory. Its
mourning was not showy, but it was deep"(68).

Halliday's attitude has punished the townsfolk, but not
enough to be completely satisfying to the communal conscience. He has laughed at the false front from the very
beginning, and by refusing to take seriously either the pretensions or the wickedness of the town, he has taken some
of the sting from the town's sense of guilt. The intensity of
the town's desire for serious punishment is revealed in its
submission to Burgess' authority at the meeting. Burgess'
ability to punish the town, to increase the severity of the
Stranger's hoax, depends on the two conditions that the town
itself is most careful to provide. Burgess must first of all
want to damage the town, and as an outcast, ostracized and,
for practical purposes, defrocked, his motive for pretending
ignorance at the meeting is clear enough. He holds back his
advance knowledge of the town's dishonesty in order to
inflict as great a shock as possible on the people in front of
him. His introductory speech flatters his hearers by telling
them that " 'To-day your purity is beyond reproach—see to
it that it shall remain so. To-day there is not a person in
your community who could be beguiled to touch a penny
not his own—see to it that you abide in this grace' "(33). The
speech, contrasting Hadleyburg with other communities, to
the advantage of Hadleyburg's honesty, repeats in various
ways the adjuration that the citizens of Hadleyburg preserve
their town's fair name, an adjuration that serves to emphasize
the fairness, the nobility, of Hadleyburg's repute. But Burgess
knows as he speaks that there are at least eighteen persons

"in your community" who have been all too easily "beguiled to touch a penny" to which they have no right, for "When the great Friday came at last, he found that he had nineteen envelopes"(31), each purporting to contain the remark worth $40,000. Nevertheless, he is the picture of injured innocence when he draws from his pocket a second letter; he "looked surprised and worried, and stood silent a few moments. Then he waved his hand in a wandering and mechanical way ... "(36). Coming as the sequel to Burgess' explicit summary of Hadleyburg's past glory, this second letter, even without its fellows, is enough to blast forever Hadleyburg's pose of innocence. Burgess wants to punish, and he succeeds. The desire is the first condition, which Burgess meets; the second is that he must be in a position to punish, and as chairman of the meeting he is, clearly enough, perfectly placed.

Burgess becomes, then, the harshly punitive side of the conscience. Spurned by the town, by those who try to deny the dual nature of humanity, he rises to hold the town to strict account—which is exactly what the town unknowingly wants. It might seem that Burgess is exceeding the requirements of his office; his feigned surprise at finding more than one letter and his dramatic buildup to the implications of there being many claimants for the sack (44) point to an intention to inflict as much pain as possible. But according to the psychoanalysts, this is the way of conscience. Twain's own conscience tells him the same thing: " 'We do it simply because it is "business." It is our trade. The *purpose* of it is to improve the man, but *we* are merely disinterested agents. We are appointed by authority, ... But I am willing to admit this much: we *do* crowd the orders a trifle when we get a chance, which is most of the time. We enjoy it' " ("The Facts Concerning the Recent Carnival of Crime in Connecticut"; XIX, 315). The community demands that Burgess exercise this severely punitive function of conscience. They want, of course unconsciously, to be able to recognize and accept their own guilt as human beings, and to suffer for it so that they can live with it. Burgess' accusing finger and sharp voice bring the relief that the people have been wanting. "Lead us into temptation," the town's new motto (XXIII, 69), is the humanistic equivalent of the theologian's *felix culpa.* Humanistically speaking, "sin" is "happy" because the existence of evil gives man a choice. By welcoming temptation, the townspeople show both their acceptance of the sinful nature of man and their readiness to assume the existential dignity which humanity attains by exercising the power of choice that only the acceptance of evil can posit.

"The Man That Corrupted Hadleyburg" has for its theme not the corrupting of a town but the awakening of the town to a sense of its innate depravity. It is a story not of a man at all, but of a hoax, or a succession of hoaxes, by means of which human corruption is laid bare. The checks that Richards finally receives from the Man " 'came from Satan. I saw the hell-brand on them, and I knew they were sent to betray me to sin' "(67). The revelations engineered by the devil-stranger come to the reader as characters are forced, by the nature of the hoax in which they are involved, to look at themselves. Mary and Edward have accepted the notion that they and their morality are important; moral responsibility is completely real to them, and because they cannot place the hoax in any sort of perspective *sub specie aeternitatis,* they are overwhelmed by it. The others in the town can laugh at themselves. Lawyer Wilson, angry at his personal discomfiture, has the reassurance that others have been taken in as well as he, so he can rise with humor to the occasion: " 'You will allow me to say, and without apologies for my language, *damn* the money!' "(54). The town as a whole is caught in the hoax, and as a social unit can admit that it is. Jack Halliday is the conscience of the fraternity of the trapped, while the Reverend Burgess speaks to and for the isolated sinners whose self-imposed isolation springs from their failure to face their neighbors and themselves. Public opinion means nothing to Halliday; he can laugh, and in so doing he can destroy the importance to the town of the town's self-righteousness and at the same time protect the town from a too-intense involvement in its guilt. The Richardses cannot share the town's reaction, and they go down before the hoax; the rest of the community puts up a united front. They lose their empty reputation, but in the end they achieve a moral victory. "It is an honest town once more, and the man will have to rise early that catches it napping again" (69).

Through their reactions to the hoax, the people in the story reveal themselves to us. The hoaxes serve not only to set the action going and to measure the characters but also to organize the story. The hoax-as-revelation focuses on the discrepancy between the appearance and the reality of the town's moral nature. The hoax leads to an understanding of the inevitable split between ideals and actions, with the sack of "gold" pieces as the central symbol. With the right words, the sack can belong to the lucky winner. The Richardses and the Coxes lie awake that first night trying to think what Goodson's remark might have been, "that golden remark; that remark worth forty thousand dollars, cash" (17). In light of our subsequent knowledge, there is something humorously futile in this vision of four people tossing and turning all night in an effort to guess at a remark that was never made in order to win money that doesn't exist. This is the closest we come to something really funny in the story, for the function that the hoax most often performed in frontier narrative is missing here. There is no humor that arises directly from the working out of any of the hoaxes in the story. Jack Halliday enjoys his own jokes, and the townspeople laugh at their own downfall, but the reader rarely even smiles as he reads. The disillusion is too great for laughter.

The satire of "The Man That Corrupted Hadleyburg" is Swiftian in its bite; we are in the presence of an attitude similar to that expressed by the King of Brobdingnag when he confesses that he "cannot but conclude the bulk of your natives to be the most pernicious race of little odious vermin that nature ever suffered to crawl upon the surface of the earth." As we shall see, not even in *The Mysterious Stranger* does Twain abide by so final a statement of black despair; even when he approaches it, as he does here, the hoax, without evoking laughter but still suggesting latent humor, raises a dimension of meaning, a quality of insight, that leaves a reader almost optimistic about the human species: men may at times be vile, but man can understand man.

8

The Ills of Humanity

THE SACK around which the story of Hadleyburg's corruption is built sums up the futility of combining idealism and action, a theme common throughout Twain's works and usually presented in terms of money. Tom Sawyer can't make a fortune out of Sahara Desert sand, because the tax-duty will take all the profits, and Tom refuses Huck's suggestion of simply flying over the frontiers in their balloon. Saladin and Electra cannot enjoy even in imagination their $30,000 bequest, because they unite dream and action to the extent of allowing the two to overlap: the loving couple fall apart over dreamworld differences. Money itself as exerting a magnetic force is rare neither in Twain nor in American literature nor in the novel-in-general, as has been noted by others. Even Cooper, romancer of the wilderness, wrote his first book—*Precaution*—around the financial eligibility of various English noblemen, and the motivation of Ishmael Bush as he rushes westward in *The Prairie* is to collect a ransom for Inez. Melville's Ishmael hunts whales in hopes of profit, and in the Hollywood botchery of the chase Starbuck characterizes Moby-Dick as "120 barrels of oil, men, so pull away."

For Twain, only in a dreamworld can money and compassionate idealism or love go together. This dreamworld takes, in Twain's works, two forms, in each of which it is a world of romance. In one form, the hero is spotlessly rich, and the author has given himself up to romance, either innocently or for satirical effects. *The Gilded Age* follows the romance-pattern with no reservations on the authors' part, so far as the hero is concerned, and "The Loves of Alonzo Fitz Clarence and Rosannah Ethelton"(1878) works within the pattern in order to attack it. The other form of the romantic dreamworld in which the love of money corrupts nobody is exemplified in "The £1,000,000 Bank-Note"(1893), a romance that offends no one because the combination of love and dollars is so patently a dream of wish-fulfilment. Even in the sweet intimacies of courtship, says our hero, "we talked salary; never anything but salary and love; sometimes love, sometimes salary, sometimes love and salary together"(XXIII, 131). The sudden transfer of the narrator from one continent to another, the even more surprising rise from literal rags to tangible riches, the nightmare quality of his anxieties as he waits for the month to end, the sudden arrival of the old friend with the mining property to sell— all are events that have no internal logic to them outside of a dream. The poor American, named—and this, perhaps, forces the issue—Henry Adams (122), literally conquers his world, including the upper reaches of English society. The reader is able to react to the story as though it were a dream because Twain has taken care to give the plot-explanation at the very beginning. One does not have to puzzle over *why* the "vest-pocket millionaire" received the £1,000,000 note; thus, one is free to participate in the "dream," which has been given a certain plausibility.

It is within this context of total unreality that money and love, with all their symbolic overtones, come together to the satisfaction of all concerned. In "The Man That Corrupted Hadleyburg," the dream turns nightmare, and money and love are mutually exclusive. After Mary and Edward receive "Stephenson's" letter assuring them that the $40,000 is theirs, "it was a happy half-hour that the couple spent there on the settee caressing each other; it was the old days come again—days that had begun with their courtship and lasted without a break until the stranger brought the deadly money"(22). But when the $40,000 is actually in their possession, "they began to piece many unrelated things together and get horrible results out of the combination"(65), and instead of bringing them together the money drives them both into the isolation of insanity and death.

The $40,000 in the story of Hadleyburg reminds one in more than simply a numerical way of the ubiquitous $40 in *Huckleberry Finn* (XIII, 127, 293, 403). The emphasis that Twain puts on these sums of money leads one to contemplate society's love of sensation, to marvel at some people's attempts to substitute cold cash for love, and to recoil in disgust from man's disloyalty to man. Moreover, the symbolic overtones that Twain works into his treatment of these dollars enable one to become aware of the necessary connection that Twain sees between his attitudes toward love, loyalty, and sensation, and thus lead one directly to Twain's diagnosis of humanity's ills.

First, and most clearly echoed in "Hadleyburg," is Huck's attitude toward the "forty dirty dollars"(294) for which the king sold Jim. Judas' thirty pieces of silver come to mind, and in a sense all the citizens of Hadleyburg are ready to sell out the town's reputation for one thousand times the price of Jim. Huck's use of the word "dirty" makes this overtone clear. There is an element in Huck's thought that is missing from "Hadleyburg," however; Huck condemns the king and the duke "because they could have the heart to serve Jim such a trick." Huck expects people to show compassion, an expectation that Edward Richards has outgrown by the time he is confronted with Burgess' kindness at the end. *Huckleberry Finn* preserves the point of view of the boy who can still condemn people not only for lack of gratitude "after all we'd done for them scoundrels," but for lack of love, of "heart." Betrayal for money implies a confusion of values that overwhelms the people of Hadleyburg and threatens to unbalance even Huck, until he takes his stand against society and determines to go to hell. Money is the force directly opposed to loyalty and compassion in both "Hadleyburg" and *Huckleberry Finn,* although the theme of compassion is more explicitly developed in the latter.

The gap between love and money is widened when money is used in an effort to compensate for a lack of love. Again, the angle of vision is wider in *Huckleberry Finn.* In "Hadleyburg," possession of the sack leads Richards and his wife to lose all remnants of their self-love, and, consequently, their separateness at the end of the story is emphasized. Their momentary happiness in the expectation of wealth makes the contrast all the more severe. In *Huckleberry Finn,* two men who refuse to help Huck "tow the raft ashore" because his "Pap" has "smallpox" contribute twenty dollars each in lieu of more personal service (127). The reader notices the inadequacy of money to provide the sort of help Huck has asked for (he has said that he cannot manage the raft alone), but the power of the episode stems more from Huck's view of life than from the actual contrast between money and compassion. Since Huck actually wants the men to stay away from the raft, because of Jim, he asks them to approach, carefully leading them to believe that his father is stricken. Huck has gauged human nature to a nicety; the men offer money not only to salve their consciences, but also to keep Huck at a distance, lest he contaminate them. Huck's earlier ruse involving the night watchman of the ferry, with the quick invention and insertion of "Miss Hooker," niece of wealthy "Jim Hornbeck"(103), again picks up the popular importance of money and the futility of society's attempt to make dollars do the work of humanity. The richness of Huck's point of view—as used by Twain—takes one farther into the contradictory values of money and compassion than does the impersonal satire of "Hadleyburg," but the theme is present in both stories.

One further symbolical use of the $40 and the $40,000 is to tie together idea and action, the abstract notion of a split between ideals and action, appearance and reality, and the specific, nonabstract events of a story as presented in a hoax and in a "sensational" plot. Edward Richards hurries on his ruinous way to have the Stranger's message publicly printed, because to carry out a private inquiry " 'would spoil the romance' "(XXIII, 6); the $40,000 is used to create as large a sensation as Richards can manage. At the end of *Huckleberry Finn*, "Tom give Jim forty dollars for being prisoner for us so patient, and doing it up so good"(XIII, 403). Tom will pay for his hoax, and in his own eyes the hoax is one of sensation. When Aunt Sally wonders "what on earth" he wanted to go to so much trouble for, he thinks her question is " '*just* like women! Why,' " says he, " 'I wanted the *adventure* of it' "(400).

This love of sensation goes with the assumption that money can pay for anything, and Huck has his reservations. "The first time I catched Tom private I asked . . . what it was he'd planned to do if the evasion worked all right . . . . And he said, what he had planned . . . was for us to . . . have adventures plumb to the mouth of the river, and then . . . pay [Jim] for his lost time . . . . But I reckoned it was about as well the way it was"(403). Huck, finally, is too involved with the life he seems to be merely watching to be able to view aesthetically the dangers of someone he loves. By the end of the book, Huck repudiates Tom's love of sensation; even his decision to "light out for the territory" is different from Tom's. Tom wants to "go for howling adventures amongst the Injuns . . . for a couple weeks or two," but Huck wants to escape civilization for life: "I can't stand it," he finally confesses. "I been there before"(405).

Just as Huck accepts slavery without moralistic questioning, so, too, he never inveighs against the evils of money; indeed, he is himself rich. But we rarely see him spend any of his wealth, nor does he daydream about its purchasing power. Instead, he is quick to evade its entanglements; he gives it to his father or to the king in order to pacify them—they will accept money instead of love—but he is not at all eager to exchange silver for sensation. He has money in his pockets, but when he goes to the circus, he "dived in under the tent"(204). Those who paid to get in laugh at the clown on horseback, but Huck—not a paying spectator—is, as usual, compassionate. The contrast is central to Twain's writing. In fact, the sense that a love of sensation is the root of most evil is expressed by Twain in one of his few allegories, "The Wild Man Interviewed," in the Buffalo *Express* for September 18, 1869. The Wild Man tells Twain of some of the hoaxes he has taken part in, and sums up his career by confessing that " 'I have been compelled by base men to create fraudulent history, and to perpetrate all sorts of humbugs.' " Much disturbed by the Wild Man's recital, the interviewer finally asks, " ' . . . what—what is your name?' " And the reply comes back, " 'SENSATION!' "[1] Men exploit their fellows for financial gain, but the sensation-seeking that makes possible the exploitation is Twain's target.

The love of sensation will induce people to part with their money, their self-respect, their loyalty—with almost any possession or worthwhile human quality. Man's inhumanity to man is not, to Twain, a product simply of economic forces. His eyes were by no means closed to the evils of industrial, and other, interests that claimed so much attention in the writings of other nineteenth-century commentators on the human condition: the rapacity of church and state in *A Connecticut Yankee,* of corporation directors in "My Bloody Massacre," and of congressmen in *The Gilded Age* leads to more than sufficient misery for the hapless victims. But Hank Morgan and Tom Sawyer, each in his own way, manage to bring ample destruction and indignity, respectively, into the lives on which their sensational effects impinge. Not outside forces primarily, but the subjective nature of man itself accounts for the ills that humanity suffers. No wonder, then, that Twain's characters so often come to grief through a desire for thrills as well as for cash.

9

The Hoax as Cosmology

This crown of the man who knows laughter, this rose-
chaplet crown: I have placed it on my head, I have con-
secrated laughter. But not a single soul have I found strong
enough to join me.[1]

THE LOVE of sensation is in Twain's works often symbolized
by the love of money, and is in turn symbolic of the greatest
evils in human nature. What in theological terms is called
"innate depravity" and in psychoanalytical terms "regression"
or "unresolved conflict," is expressed in Twain's writings as a
love of sensation for its own sake. The antidote for innate
depravity is divine grace; neurotic regression may on occasion
be cured by psychotherapy. Twain's cure is less specific but
more readily available to the unaided individual. Through
the objective vision that humor alone provides, man, Twain
seems to suggest, can see himself, and therefore his world,
clearly enough to preserve his own sense of proportion—
clearly enough, indeed, to force his world so to his soul's
conceit that his existence takes on the balance of perfect
architecture. Such a vision is hard to come by. There is no
guarantee that a would-be architect of the temple of life
will not inadvertently construct a chamber of horrors. The
attempt, however, does offer a palliative to the sense of chaos

that so overwhelms Henry Adams and that appears to Twain himself as a grim satire on the preconceptions of romance. In *The Mysterious Stranger* Twain's conclusions finally appear. They are, considering his western roots, startling. In any case, they are worth discovering in the context of his art itself.

In *The Mysterious Stranger* Mark Twain formulates his final diagnosis of the human condition. He also proposes a remedy. In answer to the narrator's claim that the human race possesses a sense of humor, Satan says that most people have only a "'mongrel perception of humor,'" enabling them to

"see the comic side of a thousand low-grade and trivial things— broad incongruities, mainly . . . evokers of the horse-laugh. The ten thousand high-grade comicalities which exist in the world are sealed from their dull vision. Will a day come when the race will detect the funniness of these juvenilities and laugh at them—and by laughing at them destroy them? For your race, in its poverty, has unquestionably one really effective weapon—laughter. . . . Against the assault of laughter nothing can stand. You are always fussing and fighting with your other weapons. Do you ever use that one? . . . No; you lack sense and the courage." (XXVII, 131-32)

Van Wyck Brooks says of Twain, "It was satire he had in mind when he wrote these lines." Brooks defines satire, justly, as "a criticism of the spirit of one's age," and then adds: "If this is true, Mark Twain cannot be called a satirist."[2]

It is unnecessary to enter at length into an argument with Brooks. His complaint that Twain fails to question the spirit of his society while indulging in the safer castigation of some of the "facts" of his times is worth answering, but this is not the place. Simply, literature that explores the discrepancy between what people-in-general think themselves to be and what they really are certainly criticizes the spirit of its age. And it is precisely this discrepancy that Twain in *The Mysterious Stranger* articulately and consciously explores. In the course of the book, the evils in the world have not come about through social, political, or economic conditions, although, significantly enough, a sack of gold pieces is once more at the center of the story's plot. The monarchy, feudalism, and other obvious and conventional targets of easy satire have not been responsible for the burnings and witch-hunts and assorted cruelties of human being to human being. The blame rests explicitly with what Satan calls "the moral sense," and evil has occurred repeatedly in the form of an action rationalized as morally "right," or "dutiful," but really expressing a striving for sensationalism. The laughter that will correct this part of the human condition is laughter that leads to self-awareness rather than to the debunking of something external to the self. The spirit within, not the "facts" without, constitutes Twain's target. Satan's purpose in talking to three sixteenth-century boys has been to make them more aware of themselves, and Satan is the artist, the creative imagination: "'My mind creates! . . . I think a poem, music, the record of a game of chess—anything—and it is there'" (80); when Theodor complains that, according to Satan's theory of determinism, man "'is a prisoner for life . . . and cannot get free,'" Satan's response is: "'No, of himself he cannot get away from the consequences of his first childish act. But I can free him'"(83). How post-Freudian this sounds!

Satan does succeed in "freeing" young Theodor, but he does so in a way totally unrelated to the sort of laughter that one associates with any petty satire. Satan, to be sure, exposes the corruptions of the world to Theodor's astounded provincial eyes, but understanding rather than laughter itself is the "weapon" with which the world of things-as-they-are is destroyed. In so far as laughter implies emotional distance, Satan might be said to teach Theodor to laugh, but the specific lesson taught is the lesson of awareness. Theodor finally understands both himself and the world, but he is not moved to laughter by what he sees.

II

In *The Mysterious Stranger,* Mark Twain develops to its logical conclusion the view of the world that he has fragmentarily suggested in his earlier works. Although any attempt to impose a consistent progression of intention upon Twain's writings will fail through its oversimplification, a consistent pattern of interest—repeated amid variations—is apparent. The uses of the novel to recapture the lost boyhood idyll of *Tom Sawyer* and to present the corruptions of the present *Gilded Age* coalesce increasingly in *The Prince and the Pauper, Huckleberry Finn,* and the sixth century of King Arthur's court, until *The Mysterious Stranger* presents Twain's final view of both boyhood and corruption. The poker-faced narrator exists less and less to draw attention to a conflict between western and eastern experience, more and more to direct the reader's vision, through parody and burlesque, to some of the paradoxes of life in general. Life as it is, in turn, becomes other than it seems; values taken for granted are exploded; even self-evaluation must go by the board as self-delusion. Finally, society itself, and then the universe, become gigantic hoaxes, imposing themselves on credulous man only so long as he will accept them at face value.

The hoax becomes, then, an element that takes one to the center of Twain's thought. Although hoax first appears in Twain's works as an element of entertainment, of humor, and (as in "The Empire City Massacre") a sugarcoating for specific political or social satire, more and more the terms in which Twain's hoaxes are perpetrated become the very terms of their satiric thrust. There is no relationship between the "facts" of the "massacre" on the one hand and the voting of false stock dividends on the other, except the weak one of plot, whereby the crazed victim of a stock fraud is driven to commit gloriously hair-raising crimes. But in *Huckleberry Finn*, Tom's pretense that Jim is not free is, as we have seen, specifically a part of Tom's satiric function, which is to hold up to the readers an exaggerated image of their own thirst for excitement on the one hand, their commitment to social convention on the other.

In Twain's final phase, literature might almost be said to exist for the purpose not so much of communicating experience as of forcing the reader to an awareness of the discrepancy between what he thinks he is and what he in truth turns out to be. In *The Mysterious Stranger* the revelation is pushed even beyond the individual's consciousness, for the world, life itself, is revealed to be a hoax, in that, though it would seem to exist, it has no existence beyond the mind of the observer; man's credulity gives reality to what, in essence, isn't there.

The suggestion that what most readers think of as "reality" may not in truth be real is not a sudden addition to the tone of Twain's fiction. The money-centered civilizations in both *Huckleberry Finn* and "The Man That Corrupted Hadleyburg" are, in so far as the moral meaning of their cash basis is concerned, as unreal as the elaborate dream-structure reared in "The $30,000 Bequest." Sally and Aleck Foster come to see "all things dimly, as through a veil" (XXIV, 42); their immense imaginary fortune, accruing from skilful management on paper of the $30,000 that they expect but never do receive, exists only in their minds; "and how soon and how easily our dream life and our material life become so intermingled and so fused together that we can't quite tell which is which, any more" (XXIV, 19). Their world is based upon money, and their money—hence their world—is nonexistent. So in *Huckleberry Finn*, in a less fantastical way, is the world that is anchored to money unreal. Of what practical good to a young boy with a sick father, alone in the

middle of the Mississippi and in need of specifically physical
aid to tow a raft ashore, is the gift of two twenty-dollar gold
pieces? Tom Sawyer, whose imaginary adventures culminate
in a real enough bullet-wound, pays Jim for being so patient,
but what monetary payment is possible when human dignity
has been outraged? How real, in other words, is the moral
fabric of a society that measures all things by money? Hank
Morgan, wondering at Morgan La Fay's blithe assumption
that her willingness to pay for a young page she has killed is
"a large and generous thing," must ask himself, "How could
she *pay* for him! *Whom* could she pay?" (XIV, 151). Similarly,
the moral collapse of Hadleyburg when confronted with
the temptation of the spurious gold underlines the artificiality
of a financial standard. Civilization is organized around
money, but standards of real worth are divorced from money.
The Richardses are respected as one of the nineteen leading
families, despite their poverty; their moral worth seems
secure. But honesty and desire are both measured against
money, rather than against human compassion, and the
money-civilization of Hadleyburg turns out to have no moral
reality.

     This point of view is hardly original with Twain; had he
stopped here, he would merely have been following in the
satirical footsteps of other men who also saw the moral
insufficiency of material standards. We have seen, though,
that in "The Man That Corrupted Hadleyburg" Twain goes
much farther. The social exterior is not alone in its hollow-
ness; sham lies at the heart of society as well as at its periph-
ery. Man is not deliberately corrupt—he cannot help himself.
Morgan La Fay, in brutally slipping a dagger into the young
page and then still more brutally offering to "pay for him,"
is "a result of generations of training in ... unexamined and
unassailed belief.... We have no thoughts of our own, no
opinions of our own; they are transmitted to us, trained into

us" (XIV, 151, 150). If humankind is its training, if men do not create the standards that uphold their opinions, then where do those standards come from? Mark Twain is not working his way systematically through this weighty problem; intuitively, however, he leaps to the imaginative conclusion that any solidified tradition must, at bottom, be a snare and a delusion, a hoax, a repository and simultaneously a promulgation of petrified training. "Hoax" has so much this sense in "Hadleyburg" that one almost forgets that the hoax is a device of the humorist. There is nothing especially funny in seeing Christianity exposed as but one more delusion of man.

Christian standards are, by Twain's implication, as unrelated to the realities of human nature as are money standards. "Lead us not into temptation" is Mary Richards' pious prayer early in the story (XXIII, 11, 23), first, when the idea of keeping the bag of "gold" is translated into action and her husband rushes (but too late) to retract the public announcement of the Stranger's faith in the town's honesty, and, second, when Edward tells her his first lie after receiving "Stephenson's" letter designating him as *probably* the rightful possessor of the sack because of his great but nameless service to the late Mr. Goodson. Never having helped Goodson in any way whatsoever, Edward can but haltingly reassure Mary that he is indeed the proper person to benefit from the deceased Goodson's kindness to the Stranger. Mary and Edward, sheltered from temptation all their lives, are, with the rest of the community, easy marks for the Stranger's revenge. Their Christian code has had no reality for them when they needed it most; it is just words.

So, too, is one of the central tenets of one branch of traditional American Christian doctrine, the belief in predestination. "It was so ordered," whimpers Edward (XXIII, 15), when Mary upbraids him for his honest haste in reporting the existence of the sack. "It was ordered," he laments again (60), trying to excuse the dishonesty of his and Mary's silence in the face of the community's applause for the Richardses' supposed virtue in failing to claim the sack. Passive honesty and passive dishonesty, both in their ways "ordered" by training and reflex, are contradictorily linked to divine fiat. The Christian words are merely an excuse, man's conditioning projected into a conception of God that can have no real meaning in its context. The Christian cosmology is a hoax that man has imposed upon himself. Man is doomed, compelled by training and by the nature of things as they are to stumble from one half-defined goal to another. Man's practical values—money and material gain—and his philosophical values—Christianity—are simply delusions.

It is at this point that *The Mysterious Stranger* becomes especially interesting to any close student of Mark Twain. To begin with, the values of both a money society and a Christian society are responsible for the evil that emerges from beneath the placid surface of sixteenth-century Eseldorf, seemingly as much "a paradise for us boys" (XXVII, 4), as was the St. Petersburg of *Tom Sawyer*. Tom encounters murder, starvation, greed, and Christian hypocrisy, but is able to triumph over them, even dealing with impunity in Sunday-school tickets. His book is a boyhood idyll; in it, Twain's purpose was not to reveal the insubstantial nature of the foundations of boyhood's world. Evil in Eseldorf, however, is triumphant, and significantly so in that the values which are expected to lead to the good life instead directly destroy or maim all life.

In so far as the story concerns Eseldorf, it is organized around the astrologer's attempt to defraud Father Peter of his mysteriously discovered money, and consists of related glimpses of village life in which, in the name of Christ, children are tortured and embittered, women are stoned and burned, and men are intimidated by the force of public opinion. In *The Innocents Abroad,* Twain had remarked upon the enmity between religious folk, especially at the Holy Sepulchre: "Christians of different sects will not only quarrel, but fight, also, in this sacred place, if allowed to do it" (II, 299). The Prince of Peace provokes bloodshed; theology becomes absurd. So in Eseldorf. Father Peter is accused of "talking around in conversation that God was all goodness and would find a way to save all his poor children." This, of course, "was a horrible thing to say," as young Theodor Fischer was well aware, but at least "there was never any absolute proof that Father Peter said it; and it was out of character for him to say it, too, for he was always good and gentle and truthful" (XXVII, 5). Here, the language itself, the individual words that Twain puts into Theodor's mouth, carry the meaning beyond the surface intellectual content. The idea that Theodor expresses is, in terms of one line of orthodox Christian belief, unexceptional, for the concept of hell may be as much a part of orthodoxy as that of heaven. Twain, though, makes his emphasis plain by having Theodor contrast "goodness" in God with the "good" Father Peter's reported heresy. Would Father Peter be truly "good" if he were to speak of God's sinfulness rather than of his "goodness"? Apparently, the answer is "yes." This is no more absurd, Twain reminds us, than is the burning of flea-bitten girls to drive the devil from their bodies. How real is the Christianity that prescribes such behavior? How real is the God in whose name such barbarities are practiced?

This brings us to the other part of what *The Mysterious Stranger* is about. Although the setting is Eseldorf, thickly shrouded in a dreamy past that but partially conceals the thematically related horrors of money and Christianity, the substance of the story concerns the effects of the Stranger—the angel named "Satan," nephew to the Fallen One of the

same name—on life in Eseldorf and on the attitude toward
life held by the narrator of the story, one Theodor Fischer
of the village. Satan first appears to Theodor and his two
friends, Nikolaus and Seppi, in the second chapter as the
three boys are idly lounging on the grass, talking companion-
ably about the supernatural revelations of Felix Brandt,
keeper of the local castle, and lamenting their lack of flint
and steel with which to light their pipe of friendship. Satan,
a nattily turned-out young man, makes a fine first impression
on the boys:

We wanted to be friendly with him, but didn't know how to
begin. Then I thought of the pipe, and wondered if it would be
taken as kindly meant if I offered it to him. But I remembered
that we had no fire, so I was sorry and disappointed. But he
looked up bright and pleased, and said:
    "Fire? Oh, that is easy; I will furnish it." (XXVII, 10-11)

Reading Theodor's mind and blowing the pipe into flame
are only the first of the "miracles" the Stranger performs. He
creates for the boys' amusement a miniature city with miniature people, and, more to the story's development, he leaves
a bag of gold pieces in Father Peter's absentminded way, so
that Father Peter and Marget, his daughter, are saved from
being dispossessed. The subsequent accusation of robbery
made by the astrologer forces Father Peter into jail, and
Satan's willing aid to Marget, because it is magical, brings
the still more deadly accusation of witchcraft from the feared
and respected Father Adolf. Satan enables Marget's fiancé
to defeat the astrologer's case, and he also strikes Father
Adolf dumb, thus silencing the accusation of witchcraft, not
only literally but also because what happens to Father Adolf
suggests to the people that the accuser is himself possessed
by the devil.
    Between these large events, Satan explains the determinis-

tic "facts" of man's moral nature to Theodor and the boys, laughing at man's "moral sense" and taking Theodor to various parts of the world to see human nature at its moralistic worst. Also, Satan has, in response to the boys' wishes, changed the fates of several of the townspeople. Finally, after Nicholas has died "now" rather than after forty-six years of bedridden hell, "praying night and day for the blessed relief of death" (85), and after Father Peter has been driven insane because, says Satan, "No sane man can be happy" (130), Theodor concludes that Satan "didn't seem to know any way to do a person a favor except by killing him or making a lunatic out of him. I apologized [for questioning Satan's judgment], as well as I could; but privately I did not think much of his processes—at that time" (131).

Satan's explications of the human condition to Theodor are in part identical with the Old Man's revelation to the Young Man in Twain's philosophical dialogue, *What Is Man?* Twain finished *What Is Man?* shortly after working on *The Mysterious Stranger,* in 1898, but he had been considering the ideas expressed for over thirty years and experimenting with the writing for about twenty. *The Mysterious Stranger,* among other things, was in part an attempt to push through on an artistic level the rather obvious doctrine of determinism that Twain's intellect had laboriously put together from his reading and his sense of guilt and responsibility. This sense, reflected in autobiographical accounts of his boyhood, finds imaginative expression most obviously in Huck's ceaseless soul-searching and in his vain attempt to hold his background responsible for his sinfulness. Determinism neatly absolves man from all blame—and from all merit. In the form of a dialogue between a young man and an old man (Twain), *What Is Man?* takes heredity and environment as the only two influences that determine a man's decisions. Man is an engine, limited in capacity by the kind of "metal" from which he is made: gold, silver, iron, and so on, each kind of engine having its place in the world. The engine that drives the lathes and presses of a huge factory wins more respect than the engine that runs a sewing machine, perhaps, but certainly there is no question of personal merit involved. The maker of the engine deserves all credit and all blame. There is, however, a difference between man's mental and moral machineries, a difference that distinguishes free will from free choice. Man has the latter, but not the former. Man's intellect—a part of the machine—acts as thermometer, measuring the degrees of right and wrong in any given situation, accuracy obviously dependent on the excellence of the instrument. Man's moral machinery, in charge of action, not of thought, is responsive to, and the product of, man's temperament—which he inherits—and his training, which includes every one of the billion influences that operate on him. This moral machinery determines whether he will actually make the right and the just choice that his intellect has pointed out to him. Twain is not very specific as to how the object of choice can fail to conform to the will to act, since both "machineries" are made from the same materials, but the point is not essential for our purposes. Twain simply knew that men often do what they know is wrong, and he was trying to embody the observation in his "system."

Behind every decision that a man makes, whether in conformity to his sense of the right or not, Twain saw a common motivation which was for him the center of his thinking on the subject: man's desire for his own inner self-approval. Sometimes the approval of neighbors is necessary to one, sometimes a break from convention is the needed satisfaction: whatever it is that will give a man his own self-approval at any given moment is what he will do, even though he sometimes repents afterward for the rest of his life. The repentance itself is in obedience to the drive of self-approbation. Whether this drive can be satisfied by good or by evil, so called, depends again on the heredity and environment that have acted on the man. All motivations that seem to have a physical or intellectual basis are in reality, Twain held, the results of the drive for inner, spiritual approval. Man is a whole being, not compartmentalized in his motivational system. No such thing as an altruistic act is possible; no matter how he sacrifices himself for others, he does so because such sacrifice brings with it its particular satisfaction.

There is, therefore, no personal merit possible in human action. This assertion riles the Young Man, the foil for the Old Man as Theodor is Satan's foil in *The Mysterious Stranger*. He wants to know how this doctrine, if it be true, can leave any use in the business of living, and why man should bother, when there is nothing that can be done, to try to change for the better the attitudes or conditions of his fellow-men. Twain's answer is especially important in view of the pessimism usually attributed to his last works. The Old Man explains first of all that no one is naturally inclined to be either good or bad. Association, or training, can turn him either way. However, his temperament does limit the possibilities for training, as he is born gold or silver or iron. Inside the limitations of temperament, though, training is possible. Since everything exerts an influence, each book, each word, has its power to sway a person to better himself— provided, as Twain never bothered to say, one knows in the first place what will be "better." Twain's words are:

Diligently train your ideas upward and still upward toward a summit where you will find your chiefest pleasure in conduct which, while contenting you, will be sure to confer benefits upon your neighbor and the community. (XXVI, 59)

Since the only motivation is the desire for self-approval, the "you" must come first. The idea of training "yourself" is

Twain's intellectual justification for writing, for working, for living. That admonition to "train yourself" will be an added influence to some people to choose more justly between courses of action, always remembering that only in consonance with all the millions of previous influences on those people can there be such an effect. Some people Twain can never hope to reach, but others are undoubtedly open to his particular influence: thus the use in writing and in living. Since man is here, why shouldn't he have the best life possible for so small and insignificant a creature? No need to be angry with anyone, to blame anyone; simply understand, try to help; the race will pull through, on the whole cheerfully, with exceptions.

What Is Man? is as full a statement as Twain ever made of what might be called an explicit philosophy of life. It is optimistically deterministic in its bias, and the only thing wrong with it as an "explanation" of its author's fiction is that Twan's emotional energy in most of his writing is committed to the problem of affixing blame. Poor Huck Finn, trying "the best I could to kinder soften it up somehow for myself by saying I was brung up wicked, and so I warn't so much to blame" (XIII, 295), must finally accept responsibility for his sinful deed of nigger-stealing and acknowledge to himself that he is bound straight for hell. The problem does, for Twain, exist: Christianity holds man responsible for his sins. Mere training is not a sufficient guarantee of virtue, as Mark Twain sees when he reverses the motto of Hadleyburg. But Twain also insists that the question of blame is irrelevant: Huck's guilt is all in his mind, and both *Pudd'nhead Wilson* and *Those Extraordinary Twins* culminate in trials that underscore the implausibility to Twain of attaching blame: the serious trial of Wilson's story affixes guilt for a crime that is the result of a long chain of environmental causes, and the comic trial of the Siamese twins ridicules the whole process of determining guilt, for although the drunken idiocy of Luigi is caused by the drinking of sober Angelo, both parts of the Siamese twins are punished when Luigi is hanged. The contrast with the "Monkey-Rope" chapter of *Moby-Dick* comes immediately to mind, for where Ishmael derives great comfort and a sense of universal brotherhood from contemplating the "siamese connection" of mutual responsibility that binds each man to "a plurality of other mortals," Twain uses the tie between the Twins to underscore the emptiness of a world that insists on holding people accountable for what they cannot help.

Twain might convince himself intellectually that "training is everything. The peach was once a bitter almond; cauliflower is nothing but cabbage with a college education" (XVI, 37), but throughout *The Mysterious Stranger* Satan condemns the human race for its faults in much the same terms that Colonel Sherburn had employed in *Huckleberry Finn*. Philosophically, logically, the contradiction between Satan's statement of man's inexorable bondage to a pattern determined by his experience of life, and Satan's relentless castigation of man for acting as he apparently is forced to do, is a disastrous one. Aesthetically, it is no contradiction at all, but a necessary step on the road to Theodor's—and the reader's—enlightenment. For the most salient feature of *The Mysterious Stranger* is that Theodor's point of view changes, and changes radically. He is brought in successive stages to examine and to change his assumptions about man's lot in life (sorry rather than glad), about the springs of human action (not altruism but the desire for self-approval), about man's moral worth, about man's freedom of moral choice, about man's image of deity, and, finally, about man's view of life as a whole. At the very end of the story, Satan announces that "there is no God, no universe, no human race, no earthly life, no heaven, no hell. It is all a dream—a gro-

tesque and foolish dream" (XXVII, 140). Satan has also
admonished Theodor to "Dream other dreams, and better"
(138), a bit of advice to which we shall return. Of interest
at this point is that Theodor is writing his story long after
the event. Satan's "processes" for making humans happy
seemed ridiculous, we remember, "at that time." But "with a
lifetime stretching back between to-day and then" (94),
Theodor now agrees completely with all that Satan has said.
Satan, then, is a dream-projection of Theodor's developing
imagination, so it is reasonable—in fact, it is necessary—for
Satan to condemn the human race, for Theodor revises his
estimate of life on earth only as he becomes aware that it
needs revision. Since there is nothing in the world around
him to reveal the social facts, and since Theodor is himself
so completely at one with his world, consciously, at least,
then Satan must be Twain's dramatic device for making
present to the reader—and to Theodor—the buried part of
Theodor's temperament which will clarify through calumny
the society that Theodor's conscious self simply takes for
granted.

Theodor's initial attitudes are, so far as Twain's intention
can make them, clearly the conventional ones of his sixteenth-
century day. Father Adolph, rather than kindly Father Peter,
is his religious spokesman, because "Father Adolph had
actually met Satan [devil, not angel] face to face more than
once, and defied him" (5). The peasant's respect for the devil
is strong in Theodor. Similarly, his attitude toward respectability is clearly defined: even though the Stranger is an
angel and has himself created the miniature town as well as
the earthquake that destroys it, Theodor's reaction to the
"massacre" is to feel "sick to see that awful deed . . . . we had
seen these murders done and it was our duty to tell, and let
the law take its course" (17). Just what the law might be
able to do to an angel with the power to disappear at will

does not occur to Theodor, who is simply outraged at the affront to the morality of respectability.

The keystone of Theodor's "respectability" is his unthinking evaluation of "the Moral Sense." Satan "seemed to trust anything that hadn't the Moral Sense" (71), Theodor finally observes, and in reminding Theodor of the gap between human and angelic nature, Satan suggests that man's possession of the sense is in itself conclusive evidence of the incomparable superiority of the angels. Theodor "merely knew that we [humans] were proud of having it" (26), without knowing what exactly the moral sense might be. He subsequently asks Father Peter for a definition and learns that " 'it is the faculty which enables us to distinguish good from evil' " (33).

It threw some light, but not a glare, and I was a little disappointed, also to some degree embarrassed. He was waiting for me to go on, so, in default of anything else to say, I asked, "Is it valuable?"

"Valuable? Heavens! lad, it is the one thing that lifts man above the beasts that perish and makes him heir to immortality!" (34)

The respectable attitude toward human life includes reverence for the moral sense, and it is from respectability in general as well as from the moral sense in particular that Theodor breaks. Satan in his own person dramatizes the logical necessity for the break by projecting in action the futility of a sense of moral responsibility against a background of determinism. The explicit statements are clear enough. Satan first clarifies for Theodor what exactly the moral sense is and explains that its effect is to degrade man " 'to the bottom layer' " of existence: " 'There shouldn't be any wrong; and without the Moral Sense there couldn't be any' " (51), says Satan. Then he shows Theodor the wrongs that shouldn't exist, social and personal: French factory conditions in the eighteenth century, and petty cruelty in Eseldorf. Surely these should not exist, but why are they blamed on the moral sense? Because the moral sense enables man " 'to distinguish between right and wrong . . . and in nine cases out of ten he prefers the wrong' " (51). It is, in other words, the perversity of his conscience that provokes man to do evil.

The moral sense is responsible for evil in a second way: it forces men to call evil those actions which offend them but which the actor was powerless not to commit. Thirty pages after his diatribe against the moral sense, Satan explains the deterministic nature of life:

"Among you boys you have a game: you stand a row of bricks on end a few inches apart; you push a brick, it knocks its neighbor over, the neighbor knocks over the next brick—and so on till all the row is prostrate. That is human life. A child's first act knocks over the initial brick, and the rest will follow inexorably." (81)

As Theodor realizes, man " 'is a prisoner for life . . . and cannot get free' " (83).

If man is trapped by the flow of events that is his life, he cannot be blamed for anything he does. The spectacle of Satan's righteous indignation before human culpability serves, then, to underline the futility of all respectable judgments. Satan's vivid condemnation of the race for what it cannot help may be interpreted as Twain's thrusts at the damned human race, but in *The Mysterious Stranger,* an organized, artistic creation, they serve to bring to the surface of Theodor's—and the reader's—mind the discrepancy between Theodor's own customary way of looking at experience and Satan's "new" way. Since Satan finally emerges as a part of Theodor's dream, it is not surprising that he should be a projection of Theodor's conscious respectability at the same time that he furnishes new insights from Theodor's nonconscious self.

That Satan is from the beginning a projection of something inside Theodor is plain. One notices that the three boys
have spent the night preceding their first encounter with
Satan in the company of old Felix Brandt, keeper of the
castle, and that Felix has, as usual, regaled them with stories
of ghosts and of war, and entertained them royally with
coffee, the astonishing new drink from Turkey. This time,
however, Felix has added yet another attraction to his list
of wonders:

The strangest thing was that he had seen angels—actual angels
out of heaven—and had talked with them. They had no wings,
and wore clothes, and talked and looked and acted just like any
natural person, and you would never know them for angels except
for the wonderful things they did which a mortal could not do,
and the way they suddenly disappeared while you were talking
with them, which was also a thing which no mortal could do.
And he said they were pleasant and cheerful, not gloomy and
melancholy, like ghosts. (10)

The day following "that kind of a talk," the boys are discuss-
ing Felix' revelations when "there came a youth strolling
toward us," and the youth is Satan, an angel. He does indeed
"talk and act" like any "natural person"; also, however, he
quickly performs acts beyond the capacity of mortal man
(11, 12, *passim*); he can disappear suddenly, and also in a
way that "was a strange and beautiful thing to see" (27).
As for being "pleasant and cheerful," not only is he himself a
pleasure to be with, but his mere presence infuses in other
people a joyous vitality and cheerfulness that contrasts with
the habitual leaden anxiety under which they labor (40,
passim). Satan, in other words, is everything that Theodor's
imagination has been prepared to accept an angel as being,
and Theodor's imagination—let us anticipate for the moment
Twain's final revelation of Satan's place of origin—never

hesitates in projecting more and more of Theodor's preconceptions, conscious and nonconscious, onto its creation, Satan.

Satan is, above all else, a supernatural being, and, as such,
he is given the attributes of Theodor's—and Eseldorf's—God.
The nature of this God is made clear to Theodor at the very
end of the story, when Satan demolishes the known world as
being " 'so frankly and hysterically insane—like all dreams' "
(139), and adduces as his prime example man's conception
of God:

A God who could make good children as easily as bad, yet pre-
ferred to make bad ones; who could have made every one of
them happy, yet never made a single happy one; who made them
prize their bitter life, yet stingily cut it short; who gave his angels
eternal happiness unearned, yet required his other children to
earn it; who gave his angels painless lives, yet cursed his other
children with biting miseries and maladies of mind and body;
who mouths justice and invented hell—mouths mercy and invented
hell—mouths Golden Rules, and forgiveness multiplied by seventy
times seven, and invented hell; who mouths morals to other
people and has none himself; who frowns upon crime, yet commits
them all; who created man without invitation, then tries to
shuffle the responsibility for man's acts upon man, instead of
honorably placing it where it belongs, upon himself; and finally,
with altogether divine obtuseness, invites this poor, abused slave
to worship him! (139)

That this "Jekyl and Hyde of sacred romance"[3] is indeed the
God of Eseldorf we have already seen in Theodor's initial
characterization of Father Peter as one who had been
maliciously accused of saying "that God was all goodness
and would find a way to save all his poor human children"
(5): this appraisal of God is directly counter to Satan's conclusion, and to Theodor's belief; Theodor had been quick to
affirm that "it was out of character for [Father Peter] to say
it." The credo of Eseldorf is clearly as Satan finally says it is,

and Theodor's projections of Satan into the supernatural are in keeping with Theodor's deepest beliefs about the nature of God. Satan creates a "crowd of little men and women the size of your finger" (13), who immediately go to work to build a "cunning little castle." The work goes on as Satan and the boys talk, and then two of the little workmen, in pathetically human fashion, disturb the conversation with "cursing and swearing" in "buzzing little bumblebee voices" (16). "Satan reached out his hand and crushed the life out of them with his fingers, threw them away, wiped the red from his fingers on his handkerchief, and went on talking." Satan finally butchers the whole group, in as lofty and detached a manner as any God's; his power is complete, and, as we see later in the story, his attitude toward these tiny figures of his own creation, an attitude which we can share because we are not they, is identical with his attitude toward all of humanity. Why, asks Satan, should an angel care about the fate of mere human beings when always "there were plenty more" (105)?

Satan is not only as callous as a God, but—more important for Twain's purposes—he is also explicitly punitive. The sins of the children of earth are noticed and the sinners punished, despite the inherent contradiction that Satan himself points out in the passage already quoted from the end of the book. One notices that Satan's self-righteous words prior to his expression of scorn for a God who would "shuffle off the responsibility for man's acts upon man"(139) underscore the discrepancy between his own behavior and his precepts. The visit to India, just before the end of the story, dramatizes not only Satan's inconsistency but also Theodor's notions of God. Disguised as a fakir, Satan causes a wondrous multi-fruited tree to arise and bids the assembled natives fill their baskets. A white man, owner of the land, kicks away the poor crowd and insults Satan, who, in turn, causes the fruits on the tree to wither away and advises the Sahib that the tree, henceforth to be fruitless, is now identified with the owner's life: if it dies, he dies. To preserve its life, the owner, and only the owner, must water it "once in each hour every night" (134). Theodor considers the man's fate for a while and draws his conclusion: "'Satan, you have given him a hard life, I think.'" "'Comparatively. It must not be mistaken for a holiday'" (136).

Now the Sahib's behavior to the poor Indians has been truly barbarous and unfeeling. Similarly, his gratuitous insults directed at Satan reveal how venially base the man is. Nevertheless, Satan himself has placed the fruit tree in the path of the poor fool, and the reader can only assume that he knew precisely what he was doing. Earlier, when Theodor accuses him of manipulating people's lives unthinkingly, "he only looked amused and surprised, and said: 'What? I do random things? Indeed, I never do. I stop and consider possible consequences? Where is the need? I know what the consequences are going to be—always'" (77). And if one tries to explain away the contradiction by observing that the white man is in any case a blackguard and deserves whatever comes to him, one is brought up short yet again: "How foolish people are when they blame themselves for anything they have done. Satan knows, and he said nothing happens that your first act hasn't arranged to happen and made inevitable; and so, of your own motion you can't ever alter the scheme or do a thing that will break a link" (100). It is shortly after this pronouncement that Satan speaks of several villagers and their eventual destination to heaven or hell (103, 104), yet later (140) reveals to Theodor that there is "no heaven, no hell." Not only do Satan's actions contradict the words he uses, but even his words in time manage to contradict themselves.

These problems are resolved when Satan is finally re-

vealed to be Theodor's projection. "'I am but a dream,'"
confesses Satan, who has taken the name "Philip Traum"
("Dream," 69) during his stay in the village; "'—your dream,
creature of your imagination. In a moment you will have
realized this, then you will banish me from your visions
and I shall dissolve into the nothingness out of which you
made me....'" (138). By page 103, Theodor has not yet been
able to consider the possibility of there being no heaven or
hell; the projection outward of his thoughts, his beliefs, still
retains some of the theological forms of village belief, although he has questioned within himself far enough for
Satan to tell him "privately that there was no purgatory"
(101). So far as human responsibility is concerned, Theodor
by page 100 has accepted intellectually the promptings of
his projected insights and can confidently assert that "Satan
knows," but the knowledge has not as yet become an accepted
part of Theodor's world view. He has himself been tortured
by remorse for the "little, shabby wrongs" (91) he has committed against his best friend. Hence, he projects into action
the conflict between his still-powerful beliefs and the idea of
determinism: Satan's punishment of the Sahib on the one
hand assumes that the victim is morally responsible for his
actions and on the other hand demonstrates through the
cruelty and irrelevance of the punishment how arbitrary and
nonlogical the delivery of cosmic justice is. Clearly, Satan is
"showing off" as much when he punishes the Portuguese
Imperialist as when he performs his fruit-tree magic for
the natives.

Satan, in actions and in words, is Theodor's projection,
and in so far as he is a projection of the same part of Theodor's, or man's, psyche that creates such an image of God as
the one Satan finally denounces, he is also a projection of the
human conscience, the accusing superego of the damned
human race. That Satan condemns the human race is clear

enough: " 'The first man was a hypocrite and a coward, qualities which have not yet failed in his line' " (112). The criticism of the "Moral Sense" is to be found throughout his running commentary on man: "Satan was accustomed to say that our race lived a life of continuous and uninterrupted self-deception" (131). This is Mark Twain talking, to be sure, but his words as they come from Satan take on a significance beyond the obvious attack against human moral corruption. Satan, in condemning the human species of insect, adduces example after example to convince the inexperienced boys of the validity of his evaluation, "although he knew that what he had been saying shamed us and wounded us" (110).

His behavior is precisely that of the human conscience as Twain described it in "The Facts Concerning the Recent Carnival of Crime in Connecticut" (1875; XIX). His condemnation of the race, the race of which Theodor is a representative, is no more irrational than is the ego-destroying condemnation of each man by his own conscience, as Twain sees it. Just as Satan knows perfectly well "how foolish people are when they blame themselves for anything they have done," and yet still metes out blame, so, too, does Mark Twain's conscience in the earlier piece joyfully make his victim suffer no matter what he does. " 'Is there *any* way of satisfying that malignant invention which is called a conscience?' " (XIX, 316) asks Twain. And the answer: " 'I don't care *what* act you may turn your hand to, I can straightway whisper a word in your ear and make you think you have committed a dreadful meanness. It is my *business*—and my joy—to make you repent *every*thing you do' " (316-17). It is perhaps not coincidental that Twain's conscience, appearing in human form, first astonishes the narrator (Twain) by reading his thoughts, as does the Stranger on his arrival into his story, and that, when asked who he thinks his visitor is,

Twain answers: " 'I think you are Satan himself.' " " 'Well,' "
comes the reply, " 'I am your *Conscience!*' " (310)—and one
quickly sees that between the devil and the conscience there
is little to choose. " 'You called for your most pitiless
enemy,' "* explains the conscience; " 'I was that person by a
very large majority' " (312).

A descriptive analysis of one part of what we may call
"conscience" presents it as "the unconscious adversary within
the human psyche, a force which attempts to bar the way to
happiness, success, enjoyment of life, and which has as its
purpose unhappiness, despair, and even self-destruction."[4]
Edmund Bergler's words on the superego are surely anticipated by Twain, who shows in his notebooks as well as in his
fiction a strikingly modern sense of what the conscience
is, how it is formed, and how it operates on a nonconscious or subconscious level. In 1906, Twain inserted in his
Autobiography an unpublished article written twenty-two
years previously in which he insists, against popular opinion,
that conscience is not "created by the Creator," that it is not
"put into man ready charged with the right and only true
and authentic correctives of conduct" (XXXVII, 8), and that
"the self-same correctives, unchanged, unmodified," are not
"distributed to all nations and all epochs" (9). Twenty-two
years before 1906 would be 1884, approximately the date of
Huck Finn's appearance and determination to "go to hell"
rather than betray Jim, a decision the terms of which point
directly to the same moral relativity Twain suggests in his
article. Conscience, then, is not a God-given absolute; it is
a purely human development that man acquires somewhere
and somehow. "It is merely a *thing;* the creature of *training;*

---

*This is precisely the term used by the narrator at the beginning of
the story: "I said to myself, 'I am thoroughly happy and content now. If my
most pitiless enemy could appear before me at this moment, I would freely
right any wrong I may have done him' " (303).

it is whatever one's mother and Bible and comrades and laws and system of government and habitat and heredities have made it. It is not a separate person, it has no originality, no independence."[5]

Twain wrote this last in his notebook on January 7, 1897, a year and some months before *The Mysterious Stranger* was written. On the same day, he discussed his old "Carnival of Crime in Connecticut" and Stevenson's *Dr. Jekyll and Mr. Hyde,* concluding that he had been wrong to make his conscience a separate character in the "Carnival." "Now I come to my *new* notion";[6] he goes on to infer a dual personality from the findings of the Nancy and Salpêtrière schools of hypnotic theory, the work of Liébault, Berheim, and Charcot —or so one might interpret his reference:

The French have lately shown (apparently) that that other person is in command during the somnambulic sleep; that it has a memory of its own and can recall its acts when hypnotized and thrown again into that sleep, but that *you* have no memory of its acts. You are not present at all.
Very good. That *is* distinct duality....

He then speculates about the existence of the "wholly independent personage who resides in me—and whom I will call Watson," but he encounters the same problem met by psychiatrists when they try to discuss the subconscious, for "the two persons in a man do not even *know* each other and are not aware of each other's existence." Just how seriously he meant this depiction of duality is an open question. The presence of twins in his recent fiction (*Pudd'nhead Wilson,* 1894; *Those Extraordinary Twins,* 1892; and *Tom Sawyer, Detective,* 1896), and his preoccupation with the confusion of reality with dream in many subsequent manuscripts, unfinished ones as well as *The Mysterious Stranger* and "The $30,000 Bequest," suggest in any case that either as metaphor or as fact the compartments of personality intrigued his imagination.

The really destructive part of the conscience as Dr. Bergler sees it is as unknown to the conscious self as is the "Watson" of Twain's ruminations. On the other hand, Twain thought, "I *am* acquainted (dimly) with my spiritualized self,"[7] just as our conscious conscience is something of which we are all aware. But Twain, writing years before Freud had even suggested the tripartite division of the psyche into id, ego, and superego, and therefore before the various phases of the superego had been formulated, has no way to distinguish between the purely destructive side of "conscience" and the milder, uplifting, or "ego-ideal" division, the part of us that is our own interpretation of what the outside world expects of us, distinguished from the part that punishes us when we fail to live up to the impossible ideals we have reared for ourselves. "The time that my dream self first appeared to me and explained itself (apparently I was for the moment dreaming) it was as insubstantial as a dim blue smoke, and I saw the furniture through it, but it was dressed in my customary clothes."[8] Satan, too, is conventionally dressed, and when he disappears gradually for the boys, "you could see the bushes through him" (XXVII, 27). So, too, the conscience in the "Carnival" "seemed to bear a sort of remote and ill-defined resemblance to me! It was dully perceptible in the mean form, the countenance, and even the clothes..." (XIX, 304).

When we remind ourselves that the *Notebook* entries were written just a few months prior to the commencement of work on *The Mysterious Stranger,* we begin to understand more clearly the precise way in which Satan is used in the story. As a projection of Theodor's destructive conscience, Satan satirizes the human race unmercifully. He wounds the sensibilities of Theodor and the boys again and again with his sneers at the race. But apart from purely destructive name-calling, Satan also has various ideals to present to Theodor. He explains the way of the world, and he encourages Theodor to think more accurately and to measure up to a kindlier view of human nature than the maliciously punitive part of Satan could ever admit exists. " 'The vast majority of the race, whether savage or civilized, are secretly kindhearted and shrink from inflicting pain' " (XXVII, 118), advises Satan after the stoning of a hanged lady. But this is the opposite of Satan's earlier distinction between man and brute, for an animal " 'does not inflict pain for the pleasure of inflicting it—only man does that' " (51). Satan is both destructive conscience and beneficial conscience, and the insights that he offers to Theodor are the projections of Theodor's unconscious better self as well as of his worse. Satan, in this other phase of his being, becomes synonymous with the creative imagination in its best sense. " 'My mind creates!' " he boasts. " 'I think a poem, music, the record of a game of chess—anything—and it is there' " (80). We see Satan create life from nothing; we see him spin goblets and fruit out of the air; but more significant is his statement to Theodor of the immense value of laughter, the " 'one really effective weapon' " of the human race (132).

Man is trapped in a net of social and economic forces just as surely as in the internal forces of psychological determinism. Man is " 'a prisoner for life,' " Theodor laments, " 'and cannot get free.' " " 'No, of himself he cannot get away from the consequence of his first childish act. But I can free him' " (83), says Satan. Through his creative powers Satan alters the threads of destiny for several of the townspeople. Through humor, he proclaims, humanity itself has the power to free itself from the grasp of institutions and confinements, from the "colossal humbug" that oppresses it. But only if it will courageously awaken to the potentialities of humor can the race win its battle, and even in the matter of humor we are lacking, says Satan, for we " 'have a mongrel perception of humor, nothing more.' "

And yet humor alone can save us, for so far as our other alleged good points are concerned, we regard ourselves "as gold" but are "only brass" (131). This allusion to the gold and brass of Plato's trio of the metals in man is significant in that it reminds one specifically of the kinds of human "engines"—gold, steel, leaden, copper, and so on (XXVI, 4)— that Twain's Old Man in *What Is Man?* evokes to explain his notion of determinism. Satan's evocation of the metals, however, is to distinguish between what man thinks he is and what he is "in truth," to make Theodor aware of what man might be if he would *"train [his] ideals upward and still upward"* (XXVI, 59). Satan can free man from the chains that hold him, but Satan can do this only in a world that doesn't exist. " 'God—man—the world . . . a dream, all a dream; they have no existence,' " says Satan (XXVII, 138). " 'I myself have no existence; I am but a dream—your dream, creature of your imagination.' " The world, then, is a gigantic hoax—it pretends to exist, but it doesn't. If man can bring himself to refrain from taking the world seriously, if, in other words, he can laugh at it and at its manifestations, then he is free.

III

To make of the world nothing at all is to defend oneself against experience through the same distance that humor imposes. Satan rallies mankind under the banner of humor to sweep away the oppression of humbug. So too the creative imagination of man uses humor as an attack not against the outside world, but against the enemy within, the destructive superego. *"The joke—every joke—is on the superego."*[9] Laughter is a *"necessary and healthy* INTERNAL *debunking process* and therefore a *fear-reducing* process, . . . not directed at *external* powers."[10] By laughing at what exists outside the self, one denies the power of the social controls that have been introjected, that is, internalized by the psyche. Since conscience is, in essence, the dictates of society (parents, teachers, and all other authority) as they have become a part of the individual's own personality, to laugh at society is to relax, for a moment, the anxieties that the conscience—society's emissary within—produces. The enemy within and the enemy without capitulate before the force of laughter, and if the whole universe can become a joke, then the victory can be permanent, and there will be nothing to fear, no matter how fearful the apparent terror may be. "Last night," wrote Twain in August of 1898, "dreamed of a whaling cruise in a drop of water."[11] The fictional development of this dream was to be terrifying indeed, and by the time Twain wrote it he was more given over to fear than could be compensated for by any sense of fun. Personality was no longer the servant of art, yet, as in *The Mysterious Stranger*, a suggestion is made of a possible escape from the horrors of the dream-hunt into a cosmos that is itself a hoax.

It is relevant to note that the setting for this unfinished story, suggested by a dream, and discussed in DeVoto's *Mark Twain at Work*, is that of a whaling voyage. Certainly, as Herman Melville makes clear, the whale is the most awesome creature of the deep, and direct confrontation of it might well drive anyone into fearful shock. Melville's Ishmael, unlike the narrator of Twain's very late attempted tale, can utilize the attitude taken for the last time by Twain in *The Mysterious Stranger*. After his first encounter with a whale, followed by a night in an open boat, and aware that he must eventually grapple with Moby-Dick, whose metaphysical implications he has already suggested, Ishmael deliberately adopts an attitude of disinvolvement as the alternative to blind fear:

There are certain queer times and occasions in this strange
mixed affair we call life when a man takes this whole universe
for a vast practical joke, though the wit thereof he but dimly
discerns, and more than suspects that the joke is at nobody's
expense but his own. However, nothing dispirits, and nothing
seems worth while disputing. He bolts down all events, all creeds,
and beliefs, and persuasions, all hard things visible and invisible,
never mind how knobby; as an ostrich of potent digestion gobbles
down bullets and gun flints. And as for small difficulties and
worryings, prospects of sudden disaster, peril of life and limb; all
these, and death itself, seem to him only sly, good-natured hits,
and jolly punches in the side bestowed by the unseen and unac-
countable old joker. That odd sort of wayward mood I am speaking of, comes over a man only in some time of extreme tribulation;
it comes in the very midst of his earnestness, so that what just
before might have seemed to him a thing most momentous, now
seems but a part of the general joke. There is nothing like the
perils of whaling to breed this free and easy sort of genial,
desperado philosophy; and with it I now regarded this whole
voyage of the Pequod, and the great White Whale its object.[12]

The preservation of equanimity at a "time of extreme
tribulation" is the attitude toward the universe that Satan
recommends to Theodor. Following *Moby-Dick,* Melville
himself lost the capacity to maintain this attitude with any
consistency, as the alternation of earnest disillusionment and
bitter humor in *Pierre* suggests, but in *The Confidence Man*
there are once more indications that this is a topsy-turvy
world, that things are seldom as they seem and had better
not be taken too seriously. Minimal as this position is, it is a
better defensive position—if one needs to be defensive—than
is Henry Adams' pose of seeing himself as lost and inadequate, as he so eloquently does in the *Education.* The point
here might well be that Adams had less need to protect himself from his "conscience" than did Melville or Twain: the
suicide of Melville's son and of Adams' wife and the deaths
of Susy and Livy Clemens obviously affected the three men

in far from identical ways—but the workings of dead men's subconsciouses are not our concern. We notice, though, that of the two who compel the universe to assume the shape of a hoax, only Twain follows up the implications of his strategy completely. In the last works, there are repeated escapes into the world-as-hoax, or dream, or nonexistence, with at least two principal results.

Most obviously, escape into dreams, into the uncontrolled imagination, can be disastrous. "The $30,000 Bequest" shows almost didactically how potent for misery the world-as-dream can be. But the culmination of Twain's hoaxes also holds out the one hope for the otherwise damned race that Twain saw, a hope not far removed from Ralph Waldo Emerson's view of Nature: the individual mind, turned loose in a chimerical existence, might well build its own world.

DeVoto reports in *Mark Twain at Work* that in many of the unfinished stories that tell their pathetic tale of Twain's last years, characters confront disasters similar to Twain's own: loss of fortune and loss of loved ones. Twain, as DeVoto points out, projects his own feelings of guilt and his own calamities into his fiction, involving his protagonists in horrors from which he is unable or unwilling to extricate them. Not the least terrifying of the uncompleted tales is the one DeVoto entitled "The Great Dark." He reprints enough of it so that one can sense the tone as well as the story. In it, as in many of these unpublished fragments, the bedeviled protagonist finds his escape in dreams, in convincing himself that what is real is a dream, or that what he dreams is real. The mind, in other words, out of fear creates its own world. In despair, in retreat, Twain allows the Great Dark of existence to press in on a haunted consciousness that can tolerate no more.

The story of the Edwards family is, in essence, a working

out in fiction of that dream "of a whaling cruise in a drop of water." After examining a drop of water under a microscope with his daughters and noticing the "bulky creatures," the "grotesque fishes" that inhabit the drop, Edwards nods off to sleep and makes arrangements with "the Superintendent of Dreams" to explore that "ocean in a drop of water." He asks for " 'a crew of whalers . . . in case we have trouble with these creatures.' " Then Edwards is at sea, lost in a storm, and the disasters commence: there is mutiny; Edwards' daughters and wife finally die after ten years of sailing; his sense of loneliness is intolerable. The importance of this for our purposes lies in Twain's notes for the completion of the story, of some of which DeVoto prints a photostatic copy. Here are the last few lines; what Twain crossed out appears in brackets. ("Cap" is the captain of the dream ship; George is Edwards' servant; Alice is Edwards' wife.)

Cap begins to grow violent when he finds his younger (young woman) daughter dying, comes furious with the dead one—says, "That is your work, with your cursed voyage" [& strikes me down with his fist] two days later when *all* are dead but George & [Alice & we] me, & we are sitting with our dead & I have finished writing this. [& reading this] [The blow wakes me.] It is midnight —Alice & the children come to say goodnight. I think them dreams. Think I am back home *in a dream*.[13]

The sense of blame projected into the captain's accusation is obvious, and Twain's sense of personal guilt has been discussed often enough to need no explication here. Of fresh interest is that one notices in these notes explicit reference to the confusion of dream and reality. So beset by disaster is Edwards that disaster alone has reality to him. Twain and the reader know that Edwards' losses are dream-losses only, that Edwards has merely to look around him to realize that his beloved family, wife and daughters both, are safely with him and that ten years of chartless wandering through the Great Dark are but a few minutes of nightmare, ghastly but insubstantial. So Twain, no doubt, longed to awake and find his own bereavements dreams.* In fear, the mind of Edwards has lost touch with life-as-it-is. Driven by fantasy, he has constructed his own world of horror from which he cannot escape, just as the Fosters were unable to escape from their dreamworld of speculation and debauchery in "The $30,000 Bequest."

If man is left to build his own new world, there is, then, no guarantee that his creation will be any improvement on what he has known. The architecture of fear is no pleasant product; it surely has little in common with Emerson's theory of that ideal which "presents the world in precisely that view which is most desirable to the mind."[14] Only a man driven by fear (or by guilt) would desire such a world as Edwards creates for himself.

There is, however, another way in which Twain's characters are led, or at least exhorted, to create their own worlds. At the very end of *The Mysterious Stranger*, after Satan has shown to Theodor the moral insufficiency and brutal misery of the world which Theodor had thought so fair, Satan, in effect, blames the present condition of things-as-they-are on Theodor himself by revealing to him that " 'there is no God, no universe, no human race, no earthly life, no heaven, no hell. It is all a dream .... *Nothing exists save empty space— and you!* ' " (XXVII, 140, 138). Theodor himself is, as he says, "appalled" by what Satan has told him; but that Theodor is to be permanently dismayed by this new gospel is, at the very least, doubtful. " 'I, your poor servant,' " says Satan,

---

*In Twain's *Notebook* (p. 395): "Sept. 24, '05. At 8 A.M. a beautiful dream and vividly real. Livy. Conversation of two or three minutes. I said several times 'Then it was only a dream, only a dream.' She did not seem to understand what I meant." Livy Clemens had died on June 5, 1904.

" 'have revealed you to yourself and set you free. Dream other
dreams, and better!' " (138). Not in fear, but in hope, does
Theodor Fischer contemplate the past and anticipate the
future. Without laboring the connection between what Satan
says and Emerson's notion that man is a God in chains, in
need of recognizing himself so that he can "build therefore
[his] own world,"[15] one can still sense in this conclusion
to Twain's last major work an integrated commitment to the
artist's autonomy as maker, as well as a symmetrical balance
between disgust at what man has made of man and hope for
what a self-aware humanity might make of itself and its
world. "There are many dream-worlds" ("My Platonic
Sweetheart," 1898; XXVII, 293).

Theodor, to be sure, has been shown enough of the world
that "exists" as the product of his present vision—of past,
present, and future—to make him want something different, a
sight that Emerson does not vouchsafe to his readers. Theodor experiences evil directly, whereas in Emerson's world
evil is merely the absence of positive good. Twain's response
to Emerson's death while Twain was in New Orleans—"So
glad I visited him two or three weeks before"[16]—does, however, suggest that the similarity is not simply coincidental
between the Old Man's admonition in *What Is Man?* to
"train your ideals upward and still upward" (XXVI, 59) and
Emerson's notice that "the voice of the Almighty saith, 'Up
and onward for evermore!' "[17] Helen Keller wrote Mark
Twain in 1906, "You once told me you were a pessimist, Mr.
Clemens, but great men are usually mistaken about themselves. You are an optimist" (XXXVII, 302-3). Even in the
nihilism of *The Mysterious Stranger* this seems to be true,
although one must remember that it is true artistically and
not personally. Satan reveals that the world is rotten, and
next reveals that the rottenness is worse than that—it is
nonexistent. But the note around which his revelation orga-

nizes itself is that of optimistic hope that Theodor will indeed "dream other dreams, and better." This is not the nihilism of despair.*

IV

To carry a reader with him through the successive stages of revelation in *The Mysterious Stranger*, Twain uses his narrator to advantage. Theodor's point of view, conditioned by dreams and by an old keeper's ghost stories as well as by sixteenth-century Eseldorf (Ass-ville), is that of a naïve young boy who has, over the years since the events he narrates transpired, determined for himself that what Satan tells him is true: life, the world, existence, are only dreams. The significance to the reader of this nihilistic cosmology lies in the nature of the change that its acceptance brings to Theodor. Forced from the superstition and the fearful worship of such false idols as the astrologer and Father Adolph, and freed from his slavish fear of public opinion, Theodor is able to contemplate his existence with a Brahma-like detachment. He is above and beyond the reach of the social pressures that make life a hell for so many of Twain's people.

---

*Considering Twain's interest in telepathy, another possible analogue to the Old Man's adjuration may well be found in various popular works on hypnotism that appeared toward the turn of the century. The renowned Santanelli (James H. Loryea) states that "Man does not choose . . . he must be led; and it is the duty of man . . . *to lead* his fellow man"(*Is Man a Free Agent? The Law of Suggestion including Hypnosis what and why it is, and how to induce it,* Lansing, Mich., 1902, p. 248). The very title of Charles Godfrey Leland's work (London, 1899) is suggestive of what Satan, at the very end of *The Mysterious Stranger*, is talking about: *Have you a strong will? or How to develop will-power, or any other faculty or attribute of the mind, and render it habitual by the easy process of self-hypnotism.* Thomas Jay Hudson's *The Law of Psychic Phenomena, a Working Hypothesis for the systematic study of hynotism, spiritism, mental therapeutics, etc.* (Chicago, 1902 [first printed in 1893]) is another book interesting to examine in this connection.

For Twain's sense of kinship with Emerson, see, for example, *Mark Twain—Howells Letters,* ed. Henry Nash Smith and William M. Gibson (2 vols.; Cambridge: Belknap Press of Harvard University Press, 1960), I, 185, 215, 412.

Through Satan—who "alone can free man"—Theodor has learned to use his imagination to escape from the wheel of things to the contemplation of essences. Through the use of a specific narrator who looks back upon the events of his past, Twain takes his reader through the maze of contradictory experience we call life and—like Emerson in "Illusions"—confronts one, finally, with the Gods, "they alone with him alone."[18] We needn't fear the external world if it isn't really there, and in *The Mysterious Stranger* Twain shows us, almost schizophrenically, that it isn't there.

This is all very far from the "realism" of frontier humor; Twain is seriously concerned with the problems of existence, with what it means to live. Through his protagonists and through his devices of humor, he shows with increasing vehemence that life is what one projects into it, rather than what one merely thinks it to be. Cosmological order, as existing outside of the human psyche, is a hoax that the psyche in its own weakness tries to play upon itself, with disastrous results, via the moral sense, or conscience.

Twain's humor is aimed squarely against the superego, as the latter is made manifest in the outside world. Huck Finn would light out for the territory, but, like most of us, he is tied to what cripples him. His respect for respectability and his commitment to Jim (to human affection) will bind him to civilization, as Twain shows in "Tom Sawyer Abroad." On the other hand, for Huck to cast off his chains would be for him to lose his newfound identity, as Twain also shows in an uncompleted fragment that sketches Huck's return from the "territory," late in life, "a broken, helplessly insane old man."[19] Only the artist can at times break loose in his imagination, remaining, "like the God of the creation, . . . within or behind or beyond or above his handiwork, invisible, refined out of existence, indifferent, paring his fingernails."[20] Or, to put it less optimistically, "Art is the terms of an

armistice signed with fate."[21] The materials and the techniques of Twain-the-humorist culminate in an image of the
universe that transcends any other presented in American
fiction. The realist, the social critic, and the visionary become
fused in the woven texture of Mark Twain's work.

> This crown of the laughter-loving, this rose-chaplet
> crown: to you, my fellows, do I fling this crown! Laughter
> I declare to be blessed; you who aspire to greatness, learn
> how to laugh![22]

Appendix

I. From *A Tramp Abroad*

The bracketed numerals inserted in the following selection from A Tramp Abroad *(IX, 130-33) refer to the elements and themes discussed in Chapter 4 (pp. 118-21) of this volume:*

1. Affection or love.

2. The seemingly puny, which will turn out to be mighty.

3. The use of slang, or of unheroic language, to degrade.

4. Understatement.

5. The use of modern expressions or of deliberate anachronisms.

6. An insistence that what usually passes as a component of romantic adventure is dully matter-of-fact rather than exciting.

7. Rational and materialistic motivation as opposed to heroic idealism.

8. Defeated expectation.

9. "The calm confidence of a Christian with four aces," and other parallels to the story of Christ.

10. Parallels to the story of David and Goliath.

11. The telling of a story to explain, however outlandishly, the existence of some phenomenon.

A mile or two above Eberbach we saw a peculiar ruin projecting above the foliage which clothed the peak of a high and very steep hill. This ruin consisted of merely a couple of crumbling masses of masonry which bore a rude resemblance to human faces; they leaned forward and touched foreheads, and had the look of being absorbed in conversation [1]. This ruin had nothing very imposing or picturesque about it, and there was no great deal of it [2], yet it was called the "Spectacular Ruin."

LEGEND OF THE "SPECTACULAR RUIN"

The captain of the raft, who was as full of history as he could stick [3], said that in the Middle Ages a most prodigious fire-breathing dragon used to live in that region, and make more trouble than a tax-collector [4]. He was as long as a rail-way train [5], and had the customary [6] impenetrable green scales all over him. His breath bred pestilence and conflagration, and his appetite bred famine. He ate men and cattle impartially [3], and was exceedingly unpopular [4]. The German emperor of that day made the usual [6] offer: he would grant to the destroyer of the dragon, any one solitary thing he might ask for; for he had a surplusage [3] of daughters, and it was customary [6] for dragon-killers to take a daughter for pay [1;7].

So the most renowned knights came from the four corners of the earth and retired down the dragon's throat one after the other [8]. A panic arose and spread. Heroes grew cautious. The procession [3] ceased. The dragon became more destructive than ever. The people lost all hope of succor, and fled to the mountains for refuge.

At last Sir Wissenschaft, a poor and obscure knight [2], out of a far country, arrived to do battle with the monster. A pitiable object he was [2], with his armor hanging in rags about him, and his strange-shaped knapsack [5] strapped upon his back. Everybody turned up their noses at him, and some openly jeered him [2;9]. But he was calm [9]. He simply inquired if the emperor's offer was still in force [7]. The emperor said it was—but charitably advised him to go and hunt hares and not endanger so precious a life as his in an attempt which had brought death to so many of the world's most illustrious heroes [2].

But this tramp [2;5] only asked—"Were any of these heroes men of science?" [5] This raised a laugh, of course, for science was despised [2] in those days. But the tramp was not in the least ruffled [9]. He said he might be a little in advance of his age [3], but no matter—science would come to be honored, some time or other [9]. He said he would march against the dragon in the morning. Out of compassion, then, a decent spear was offered him [10], but he declined [10], and said, "spears were useless to men of science." They allowed him to sup in the servants' hall, and gave him a bed in the stables [9].

When he started forth in the morning, thousands were gathered to see [9;10]. The emperor said:

"Do not be rash, take a spear [10], and leave off your knapsack"[5].

But the tramp [5] said:

"It is not a knapsack," and moved straight on.

The dragon was waiting and ready. He was breathing forth vast volumes of sulphurous smoke and lurid blasts of flame. The ragged knight [2] stole warily [7] to a good position, then he unslung his cylindrical knapsack—which was simply the common fire-extinguisher known to modern times [5]—and first chance he got [7] he turned on his hose and shot the dragon square in the center of his cavernous mouth. Out went the fires in an instant, and the dragon curled up and died [10;3].

This man had brought brains [5] to his aid. He had reared dragons from the egg, in his laboratory [3], he had watched over them like a mother [1], and patiently studied them and experimented upon them [5] while they grew. Thus he had found out that fire was the life principle of a dragon; put out the dragon's fires and it could make steam no longer, and must die. He could not put out a fire with a spear, therefore he invented the extinguisher [7]. The dragon being dead, the emperor fell on the hero's neck [1] and said:

"Deliverer, name your request," at the same time beckoning out behind with his heel [3] for a detachment [3] of his daughters to form and advance [3;1]. But the tramp gave no observance [7]. He simply said:

"My request is, that upon me be conferred the monopoly of the manufacture and sale of spectacles in Germany" [7;5;8].

The emperor sprang aside and exclaimed:

"This transcends all the impudence I ever heard! A modest demand, by my halidome! Why didn't you ask for the imperial revenues at once, and be done with it?"

But the monarch had given his word, and he kept it. To

everybody's surprise, the unselfish monopolist [1;7] immediately reduced the price of spectacles [7] to such a degree that a great and crushing burden was removed from the nation [7:1]. The emperor, to commemorate this generous act, and to testify his appreciation of it, issued a decree commanding everybody to buy this benefactor's spectacles and wear them, whether they needed them or not [11].

So originated the wide-spread custom of wearing spectacles in Germany [11]; and as a custom once established in these old lands is imperishable, this one remains universal in the empire to this day. Such is the legend of the monopolist's [7] once stately and sumptuous castle, now called the "Spectacular Ruin."

II. From *Life on the Mississippi*

This selection appears at pages 535-46 in the manuscript of Life on the Mississippi *in the Pierpont Morgan Library, New York (Mark Twain's original pagination was 440-51). The passage is also printed in* Life on the Mississippi, *edited by Willis Wager (New York: Heritage Press, 1944), pp. 396-98. See this volume, Chapter 5, page 152.*

This mournful episode reminded Mr. Harvey of an experience of his own which did not resemble it. It was when he was in the balloon business. He said he had always been aware of the existence, high away among the upper levels of the atmosphere, of a belt or stratum of dead air, where, once in, you remain—going neither up nor down, for weeks, months, years—indefinitely. "And of course I had always hoped to steer clear of that belt. But at last I got into it. Got into it, & presently realized the fact; realized it, & gave up hope. Might drift sideways, maybe, to all eternity; but never up nor down—*that* was settled. Time dragged along—land alive, how lonesome it was! No birds, no breeze, world a mere ten-pin ball, away down there; nothing to do, nor look at, & no way to amuse one's-self. Well, after I had been drifting around & around, about two years—"

"What did you live on?"

"I am coming to that, presently—woke up one morning & saw another balloon coming towards me. I almost fainted for joy.

I swung my hat, I waved my handkerchief, I shouted & hurrahed. Nobody answered. Yet as she drifted nearer & nearer, I began to see people in her. I waved & shouted again, but they wouldn't take any notice. She came closer & closer, & ranged up right alongside of me. And what a spectacle! two men, a young woman, & a dog, all dried, mummified, green, mildewed; skinny lips drawn back, teeth exposed, grinning horribly! And there they staid—days, weeks—& always bobbing around & bobbing around, to-day on one side of me, to-morrow on the other, & staring at me with their fishy eyes. One day I reached in & got their log-book—& right away it accounted for the obsolete fashion of their clothes: they were from France—been out sixty years! And—"

"Why, how had the balloon & gas managed to last all th—"

"Coming to that, presently. I read their log, for it was in quite good French, though a little shackly as to style, & this amusement was a great relief to me while it lasted. It appeared that it was a bridal party: Young man of twenty-six, young girl of seventeen, the third person the priest—ah, poor devils, a sorrowful sequel to their gay adventure, a pathetic ending to a pretty dream! But what the dog was along for, was not stated; & so sort of disordered had I become by my trouble & lonesomeness, that for days & days together I worried & fretted over that triviality to the exclusion of every other interest in life—if you can call it life to be bob-bobbing in the remoteness of hollow space in the company of mildewed dead people. Well, by & by, I got to fretting over the everlasting staring & grinning of these corpses; I got so I couldn't sleep, except by cat-naps; you see, the priest was sort of hanging over the edge of the basket, with his arm & skeleton fingers stretched out & wagging with the balloon's motion, & often these fingers would rake my cheek & wake me up. So at last I determined to get those shadows overboard—better no company than such. I reached for the priest, & pulled him out with a boat-hook. It actually made matters a hundred times worse—for we were right on the very top of the atmosphere—I might have thought of that, before—& the priest didn't descend an inch!—merely bobbed around,—as if in water—in a bent & drunken way, that same old arm stretched out & claw hanging down, & leering from under his hood! Well, after that, he was forever hanging around & looking in—first on one side, then on the other—day & night the same. I hit him a crack with the boat hook every time I got a first rate chance; but I stopped that, presently, because I saw that the more I battered him the more disagreeable he looked & the more unpleasant it was to have to live with him. Up there, matter attracts matter—& powerfully. As the years rolled on, one ragged balloon after another came along & bunched up with us—and all of them full of dead people in all possible stages of greenness & mildew, & all of them grinning & staring; sixteen balloons in all, fifty-four corpses & a lot of dried animals of one sort & another —hailed from various countries—all strangers; & also came other corpses that had got joggled out by balloons colliding; & these joined the drunken priest—eleven of them, there were, & all fluttering with rags,—& week in & week out, & night & day, they noiselessly & drunkenly balanced & sasshayed to each other, there in the empty air, & wagged their skinny arms, & grinned & leered, & the balloon-audience looked on, as if from opera boxes; & they, too, grinned & leered, and—excuse me just a moment, I will be back right away."

So saying, Mr. Harvey ran below, & left us waiting & panting. And he did not return, because he found that the boat was stopping at a landing where he wished to see a man on business. The man was up town, & he had to go up there & look for him. The captain waited a while for him, but gave him up at last, & backed out & went ahead. So Mr. Harvey got left; & in a sense, so did we; for we never found out how he got down out of the sky, unless he lied himself out, which is a thing anybody could do but a steamboat mate. But if he ever turns up again & fails to qualify, he is not unlikely to get shot.

Reference Notes

BIBLIOGRAPHICAL NOTE: Because so many bibliographies of Twain's works and of secondary material relating to Twain are available, it has seemed sufficient simply to mention here sources of specific insight and information rather than to provide a formal bibliography.

CHAPTER 1

1. See *Mark Twain and Southwestern Humor* (Boston: Atlantic-Little, Brown, 1959), pp. 61 ff.

2. Quoted from Augustus B. Longstreet by Donald Day, "The Humorous Works of George W. Harris," *American Literature*, XIV (January, 1943), 393.

3. George Washington Harris, *Sut Lovingood: Yarns Spun by a 'Nat'ral Born Durn'd Fool'* (New York, 1867), p. 111.

4. Johnson J. Hooper, *Simon Suggs' Adventures* (1845, reprinted Philadelphia, 1881), p. 26.

5. *Major Jones's Chronicles of Pineville* (Philadelphia, 1843), pp. 99-135.

6. Hooper, *op. cit.*, p. 132.

7. *Ibid.*, p. 138.

8. *Ibid.*, pp. 142, 143-44.

9. Reprinted from the Nashville *Union and American*, February 28, March 2, and March 5, 1861, in *Sut Lovingood*, ed. Brom Weber (New York: Grove Press, 1954), pp. 219-37.

10. *Ibid.*, pp. 221-22.

11. *Mark Twain at Work* (Cambridge: Harvard University Press, 1942), p. 69.

12. All volume and page references, unless otherwise indicated, are to *The Writings of Mark Twain*, "Definitive Edition" (37 vols.; New York: Harper & Bros., 1922-25).

13. Dixon Wecter, *Sam Clemens of Hannibal* (Boston: Houghton Mifflin, 1952), pp. 107-8.

14. In *Major Jones's Chronicles of Pineville*. Twain, says DeVoto, "was thoroughly familiar with Thompson's work" (*Mark Twain at Work*, p. 68n).

15. *Major Jones's Chronicles of Pineville*, p. 18.
16. Hooper, *op. cit.*, p. 141.
17. *Ibid.*, pp. 141-42.
18. *Ibid.*, pp. 144-45.
19. In Edgar M. Branch, *The Literary Apprenticeship of Mark Twain* (Urbana: University of Illinois Press, 1950), p. 227.
20. Hooper, *op. cit.*, p. 136.
21. In Mody C. Boatright, *Folk Laughter on the American Frontier* (New York: Macmillan, 1949), p. 22.
22. Quoted in F. O. Matthiessen, *American Renaissance* (New York: Oxford University Press, 1941), p. 639.
23. Reprinted in Branch, *op. cit.*, p. 218.
24. Quoted from the Mark Twain Papers by Henry Nash Smith in "Mark Twain's Images of Hannibal," *Texas Studies in English*, XXXVII (1958), 3.
25. *Moby-Dick*, chap. xlix, "The Hyena."
26. *Dodsworth* (New York: Modern Library ed., 1929), p. 231.
27. *Ibid.*, p. 121.
28. *Ibid.*, p. 76.
29. *Ibid.*, p. 112.
30. *Ibid.*, p. 119.
31. *Ibid.*, p. 11.
32. *Ibid.*, pp. 139, 140, 188, 190.
33. *The American* (Rinehart ed.; New York: Rinehart, 1949), p. 332. See Cooper's *The Prairie* for Natty's silent laugh (Rinehart ed.; New York: Rinehart, 1950), pp. 437 and *passim*.
34. *The American*, p. 98.
35. *Ibid.*, p. 212.
36. *Dodsworth*, p. 23.
37. *The American*, p. 2.
38. *Ibid.*, p. 3.
39. *Ibid.*, p. 21.

CHAPTER 2

1. Keokuk *Post*, April 10, 1857; reprinted in *The Adventures of Thomas Jefferson Snodgrass*, ed. Charles Honce (Chicago: Pascal Covici, 1928), p. 37.
2. Printed, along with the Snodgrass passage, in Walter Blair, *Native American Humor, 1800-1900* (New York: American Book Co., 1937), p. 150.
3. See Branch, *The Literary Apprenticeship of Mark Twain*, pp. 217-18.
4. See *The Adventures of Thomas Jefferson Snodgrass*, pp. 224 ff.
5. *Major Jones's Travels* (Philadelphia, 1845), pp. 128, 130.
6. *Mark Twain in Eruption*, ed. Bernard DeVoto (New York: Harper & Bros., 1940), p. 217.
7. *Ibid.*, pp. 223-24.
8. *Ibid.*, pp. 217-18.
9. *Mark Twain's America* (Boston: Little, Brown, 1932), p. 255.

CHAPTER 3

1. *The Education of Henry Adams* (New York: Modern Library ed., 1931), p. 445.

2. George Washington Harris, *Sut Lovingood: Yarns*, p. 114.

3. *Ibid.*, pp. 115-16.

4. *Ibid.*, p. 121.

5. Letter to J. H. Burrough, November 1, 1876, in *The Portable Mark Twain*, ed. Bernard DeVoto (New York: Viking Press, 1946), p. 751.

6. *Mark Twain at Work*, p. 9.

7. "Man and His Imagination," in *The Intent of the Artist*, ed. Augusto Centeno (Princeton: Princeton University Press, 1941), pp. 67, 70.

8. *The Liberal Imagination* (New York: Viking Press, 1950), pp. 112-13.

9. *Mark Twain in Eruption*, pp. 211-12.

10. *The Autobiography of Mark Twain*, ed. Charles Neider (New York: Harper & Bros., 1959), pp. 346-47.

11. See Herbert Marcuse, *Eros and Civilization* (Boston: Beacon Press, 1955), for a full and illuminating discussion of the terms *productive* and *receptive*.

CHAPTER 4

1. *The Liberal Imagination*, p. 110.

2. *The Spy* (New York, 1821), chap. iv.

3. *Studies in Classic American Literature* (New York: Doubleday Anchor Books, 1953), p. 92.

4. See S. B. Liljegren, "The Revolt Against Romanticism in American Literature as Evidenced in the Works of S. L. Clemens," in *Essays and Studies on American Language and Literature* (Uppsala: A-B Lundequist-ska Bokhandeln, 1945).

5. *Hawthorne* (London, 1879), chap. v.

6. "The Pilot and the Passenger: Landscape Conventions and the Style of *Huckleberry Finn*," *American Literature*, XXVIII (May, 1956), 129-46.

7. *The Education of Henry Adams*, p. 289.

8. *Ibid.*, p. 57.

9. *Ibid.*, p. 100.

10. *Ibid.*, p. 292.

11. *Ibid.*, p. 319.

12. *Ibid.*, p. 337.

CHAPTER 5

1. F. Scott Fitzgerald, *The Last Tycoon*, ed. Edmund Wilson (New York: Charles Scribner's Sons, 1953), p. 137.

2. Edgar Allan Poe, *Works* (New York: Funk & Wagnalls, 1904), X, 120, 121.

3. *Ibid.*, VI, 46.

4. *Ibid.*, III, 76.

5. *Ibid.*, I, 124.

6. "A Curious Experience," in *The Curious Republic of Gondour and Other Whimsical Sketches* (New York: Boni & Liveright, 1919), p. 33.

CHAPTER 6

1. *Art and Social Responsibility* (London: Falcon Press, 1946), p. 30.

2. *Mark Twain's America*, p. 255.

3. *Mark Twain in Eruption*, p. 233.

CHAPTER 7

1. In *Tid-Bits,* New York, Saturday, December 20, 1884 (Vol. I, No. 18). See Merle Johnson, *A Bibliography of the Works of Mark Twain*... (rev. ed.; New York: Harper & Bros., 1935), p. 140.
2. Henry James, *The Portrait of a Lady* (New York: Modern Library ed., 1936), II, 36.
3. Edmund Bergler, M.D., *The Battle of the Conscience* (Washington, D.C.: Washington Institute of Medicine, 1948), p. 274.

CHAPTER 8

1. *The Curious Republic of Gondour,* pp. 130-31.

CHAPTER 9

1. Friedrich Nietzsche, *Zarathustra,* Part IV, "Of Greater Men," in *The Birth of Tragedy* and *The Genealogy of Morals,* trans. Francis Golffing (New York: Doubleday Anchor Books, 1956), p. 15.
2. *The Ordeal of Mark Twain* (New York: Meridian Books, 1955), pp. 213, 215.
3. *Mark Twain's Notebook,* ed. Albert Bigelow Paine (New York: Harper & Bros., 1935), p. 392 (Fall of 1904).
4. Edmund Bergler, M.D., in *Laughter and the Sense of Humor* (New York: Intercontinental Medical Book Corp., in co-operation with Grune & Stratton, 1956), p. 44.
5. *Mark Twain's Notebook,* pp. 348-49.
6. *Ibid.,* p. 349.
7. *Ibid.,* p. 350.
8. *Ibid.,* p. 352.
9. Bergler, *op. cit.,* p. 59.
10. *Ibid.,* p. viii.
11. *Mark Twain's Notebook,* p. 365.
12. *Moby-Dick,* chap. xlix.
13. *Mark Twain at Work,* opposite p. 122. See p. 136 for preceding quotations.
14. "Nature" (1836), in *The Heart of Emerson's Essays,* ed. Bliss Perry (Boston: Houghton Mifflin, 1933), p. 45.
15. *Ibid.,* p. 54.
16. *Mark Twain's Notebook,* p. 165.
17. *The Heart of Emerson's Essays,* "Compensation," p. 142.
18. *Ibid.,* p. 358.
19. Lynn, *Mark Twain and Southwestern Humor,* p. 245.
20. James Joyce, *A Portrait of the Artist as a Young Man,* in *The Portable James Joyce* (New York: Viking Press, 1947), pp. 481-82.
21. *Mark Twain at Work,* p. 109.
22. Nietzsche, *op. cit.,* p. 15.

Index

"The McWilliamses and the Burglar Alarm," "Mrs. McWilliams and the Lightning"
Marx, Leo, 72n, 130
Mayflower, the, 164-65
Meine, Franklin, 3
Meiosis, 12; *see also* Exaggeration
Melodrama, 90, 123-24, 127, 132, 171; *see also* Sensation-seeking
Melville, Herman, 3, 15, 19, 243; *The Confidence Man,* 243; *Moby-Dick,* 15, 31, 206, 227, 242-43; *Pierre,* 15, 19, 132, 133-34, 243
Mencken, H. L., 35
Milton, John, 190; *Paradise Lost,* 198-99
Moore, Thomas, "Those Evening Bells," 139
Moffett, Samuel E., 198
Morgan, Hank, 25-26, 27, 36, 63-64, 97-98, 113, 212; *see also* Narrators; *see also* Twain, Mark, works: *A Connecticut Yankee in King Arthur's Court*

Naïveté, 85-86, 89-90, 174, 182; *see also* Irony through narrative point of view
Narrators, 39-109 *passim*
Blaine, Jim *(Roughing It),* 52, 56-59, 60-61, 63, 65
Brown, Mr. *(Life on the Mississippi),* 59-60, 61-62
Carraway, Nick *(The Great Gatsby)* 65-66
Dunham, Mr. *(Life on the Mississippi,* balloon hoax), 152-53
Edwards ("The Great Dark"), 245, 246
Finn, Huckleberry, 40, 63-64, 65-70, 75-78, 83-84, 87-89, 91, 161-62, 173, 174-75, 209-10
Fischer, Theodor *(The Mysterious Stranger),* 221, 228-29, 230, 248-49
Harris, George Washington, 73-76
Harvey, Mr. *(Life on the Mississippi,* balloon hoax), 152-55
Ishmael *(Moby-Dick),* 31, 242-43
Jones, Major *(Major Jones's Travels,* by William Tappan Thompson), 44-45

Lovingood, Sut ("Eaves-Dropping a Lodge of Masons," by George Washington Harris), 73-76, 77
McWilliams, Mortimer (the three "McWilliams" stories), 45-47
Morgan, Hank *(A Connecticut Yankee in King Arthur's Court),* 25-26, 63-64, 92, 93-96, 99, 101-9
Sawyer, Tom, 78-80
"Self-controlled Gentleman," 39-40
Snodgrass, Thomas Jefferson *(The Adventures of Thomas Jefferson Snodgrass),* 42-43, 45, 63
Twain, Mark; *see* Twain, Mark, Twain-the-narrator
Wheeler, Simon ("The Celebrated Jumping Frog of Calaveras County"), 48-51, 63, 173

Owsley, William, 17

Parkville camp meeting; *see* Twain, Mark, works: *Adventures of Huckleberry Finn*
Parody, 113-39 *passim,* 143-44, 148, 160, 167, 175, 181, 182, 185, 216; defined, 118, 122
Plato, 241
Poe, Edgar Allan, 3, 148-52, 153-54, 155-56; "The Balloon Hoax," 150-51, 153; "How to Write a *Blackwood* Article," 148; "Ligeia," 151; "Mellonta Tauta," 153; *Narrative of A. Gordon Pym,* 150, 151, 154; "The Pit and the Pendulum," 148; "A Predicament," 148; "The Premature Burial," 149; "The Unparalleled Adventures of One Hans Pfaall," 150-51, 153-54
Poker face, 26-27, 28, 29-31, 33-34, 36, 40, 48-51, 56-57, 75, 85, 145, 173, 213
Poker talk, 20-27, 36, 39, 189
Pokeville camp meeting; *see* Twain, Mark, works: *Adventures of Huckleberry Finn*
Pretension, 8-9, 18-19; *see also* Affectation